Coming Up Short

Coming Up Short

WORKING-CLASS ADULTHOOD IN AN AGE OF UNCERTAINTY

JENNIFER M. SILVA

OXFORD
UNIVERSITY PRESS

OXFORD
UNIVERSITY PRESS

Oxford University Press is a department of the University of Oxford.
It furthers the University's objective of excellence in research,
scholarship, and education by publishing worldwide.

Oxford   New York
Auckland   Cape Town   Dar es Salaam   Hong Kong   Karachi
Kuala Lumpur   Madrid   Melbourne   Mexico City   Nairobi
New Delhi   Shanghai   Taipei   Toronto

With offices in
Argentina   Austria   Brazil   Chile   Czech Republic   France   Greece
Guatemala   Hungary   Italy   Japan   Poland   Portugal   Singapore
South Korea   Switzerland   Thailand   Turkey   Ukraine   Vietnam

Oxford is a registered trademark of Oxford University Press
in the UK and certain other countries.

Published in the United States of America by
Oxford University Press
198 Madison Avenue, New York, NY 10016

© Oxford University Press 2013

First issued as an Oxford University Press paperback, 2015.

Library of Congress Cataloging-in-Publication Data
Silva, Jennifer M.
Coming up short: working-class adulthood in an age of uncertainty / Jennifer M. Silva.
pages   cm
Includes bibliographical references and index.
ISBN 978-0-19-993146-0 (hardcover); 978-0-19-023189-7 (paperback)
1. Working class—United States—History—21st century.
2. Working class—United States—Economic conditions—21st century.
3. Working class—United States—Social life and customs. I. Title.
HD8072.5.S575   2013
305.5′620973—dc23   2012047890

9 8 7 6 5 4 3 2 1

Printed in the United States of America
on acid-free paper

To my grandmothers, Jean and Mary, for teaching me to draw
wisdom, laughter, and strength from our family past.
To my parents, Michael and Paula, and my brother, Mikey,
for believing in and nurturing me in the present.
And to Ahrum, for our future.

CONTENTS

PREFACE

My desire to document the lives of working-class young adults is animated both by personal history and intellectual curiosity. My paternal grandparents were born in Lowell, Massachusetts, one of my two research sites. My grandfather Joe started work in a textile mill on Market Street at age nine, where he ran the empty spools of thread upstairs to be re-spun with cotton. One of eight children, his wife, Mary, was born in 1929, just a few months after the stock market crash and the start of the Great Depression. She still fondly recalls her bustling Irish Catholic family home on Orleans Street. Eighty years later, I often drove by it on my way to an interview. After they married in their early twenties, they moved to the suburb of West Concord, Massachusetts, where my grandfather worked as a state prison guard. The six children they raised were part of the postwar generation who realized the American Dream of upward mobility through hard work and stable, unionized jobs. Joe and Mary hoped that their grandchildren would achieve even more; my parents promised each other on the day I was born that I would be the first in my family to graduate from college.

But my generation is slowly losing the stability hard-won by their grandparents and parents. Over the years I have watched my cousins and my brother face many of the same obstacles as my informants—joining the military because they couldn't find a job; moving back in with their parents; or struggling to get through college, pay back their loans, and make their monthly car payments. Two years ago, my younger brother moved back to Lowell and is currently waiting to be placed on the civil service hiring list. Once a thriving industrial site, the street where he works is now lined by billboards promising "Car Loans! Bad Credit OK! We approve everyone!" This book tells the story of a family and a country that has run full circle, from my grandparents' birth at the start of the Great Depression, to middle-class suburban dreams, and back to economic insecurity, riskiness, and recession. It is a story of institutions—not individuals or their families—coming up short.

From college to graduate school to postdoctoral studies, I have been extraordinarily blessed to have been surrounded by people and organizations that have nurtured and inspired me, both professionally and personally. First and foremost, I am deeply indebted to the young men and women who graciously welcomed me into their lives, shared their personal experiences, kept in touch with me over Facebook, and believed from the beginning in my work. The desire to be true to their stories motivated me to keep coming back to this book until I got it right.

I completed this manuscript as a National Science Foundation (NSF) and American Sociological Association (ASA) Postdoctoral Fellow at Harvard University. The financial and intellectual support of the NSF and the ASA allowed me to focus on writing while embedded in a first-rate community of scholars. James Cook took an immediate interest in the project, generously providing detailed and incisive feedback and guiding me through the revision process with assurance. The final manuscript reflects his encouragement, attention to detail, and tireless commitment. I am also grateful for the dedicated mentoring I received from Bruce Western and Michèle Lamont, who willingly read drafts, provided perceptive comments, and offered encouragement and helpful career guidance. While at Harvard, I was fortunate to meet Robert Putnam and join his talented and lively research team. The Saguaro Seminar's focus on social connectedness and inequality inspired me to look closely at narratives of trust and betrayal among my informants.

From my first week at Harvard, Nicole Deterding pulled me into department life, read my work more closely than I could have asked for, forced me to go to the gym when I needed a break, and generously and thoughtfully grappled with ideas with me on Thirsty Thursdays. The members of the Harvard Culture and Social Analysis Workshop helped me to sharpen my focus and clarify my ideas over two fruitful years. My fellow NSF-ASA postdoc Jeremy Schulz was always willing to brainstorm ideas, offer insightful feedback, and exchange career advice. Finally, my students in my Coming of Age in the 21st Century junior tutorial reinvigorated my interest in coming of age and reminded me weekly of the real-world importance of studying the transition to adulthood.

At the University of Virginia, my dissertation committee—Sarah Corse, Allison Pugh, Milton Vickerman, and Paul Freedman—provided invaluable support and assistance. Sarah, my chair and mentor whom I now feel lucky to call my close friend, spent countless hours talking about ideas, reading and commenting on drafts, and helping me to navigate my academic future. Sarah (and Bill and Robbie) welcomed me into her family and continues to show daily that she cares about both my professional and personal success. I look forward to many years of scholarship and friendship. Allison, who fortuitously came to the University of Virginia as I was formulating my research questions, taught me to think critically about issues of care, intimacy, and inequality. I am grateful for her creative approach, warmth, and ongoing intellectual camaraderie. Milton Vickerman gave me numerous helpful suggestions throughout the research process. Paul Freedman proved incredibly flexible and supportive as an outside reader. My research was generously funded by the Woodrow Wilson Women's Studies Dissertation Fellowship, the University of Virginia's Graduate School of Arts and Sciences Dissertation Year Fellowship, and the University of Virginia Department of Sociology.

I am very grateful to have had the intellectual guidance and support of many outstanding teachers. During my first semester at the University of Virginia, Sharon Hays captivated me with social theory and taught me the importance of seeing power and inequality in all aspects of social life. Over the years, as she willingly read my drafts and offered incredibly sharp feedback, knowing that Sharon saw promise in my work was deeply meaningful and inspiring. Jeffrey Olick's contemporary theory class gave me an extraordinarily strong foundation for thinking about culture. Over just a few brief email exchanges, the generous and brilliant Eva Illouz was able to get right at the heart of what I was trying to do in this book, crystallizing my analysis of culture, power, and emotion. Rosanna Hertz and Jonathan Imber, my undergraduate mentors at Wellesley College, fueled my passion for studying social inequality and continue to inspire my academic career. At Concord Carlisle High School, Andrei Joseph introduced me to the study of sociology, challenging me to examine the social world through a critical lens.

I am equally thankful for an amazing group of colleagues and friends. Matthew Morrison painstakingly read every draft of every chapter, patiently fixing my numerous formatting errors and offering flashes of insight along the way. He is both a loyal friend and a constant source of comic relief. Janice Morrison diligently and thoughtfully helped with transcribing and editing the recorded interviews. My incredibly close and devoted circle of sisters and friends—Ali Parramore, Bethany Blalock, Kate

Sanger, Heather Price, KimMi Whitehead, Emily Seekins Peter, Lauren Woodward, Sara Danielson, Karishma Patel—cheered me on at every step.

While finishing this manuscript, I achieved a marker of adulthood of my own, getting engaged to my fellow sociologist Ahrum Lee. Ahrum and his wonderful parents supported me in countless ways while I was researching and writing. I am especially grateful for his creative insight, commitment, sense of humor, and unfailingly encouraging and calming presence. Finally, this work is a testament to the generosity and love of all my family, who have believed in me unconditionally. Mom, Dad, and Mikey: without your daily nurturance, guidance, and love, this book would not have been possible.

Coming Up Short

1 | Coming of Age in the Risk Society

WHEN I ASKED BRANDON,[1] A thirty-four-year-old black man, to share his coming of age story, he promptly labeled himself "a cautionary tale." Growing up in the shadow of a small southern college where both his parents worked in maintenance, he was told from an early age that education was the path to "the land of milk and honey." An eager and hard-working student, Brandon tested into the college preparatory track at his high school and graduated in the top 9 percent of his class. He was elated when he earned a spot at a private university in the Southeast: finally, his childhood dream of building spaceships was coming true. He was even unconcerned about the $80,000 in loans he accrued, joking, "Hey, if I owe you $5, that's *my* problem, but if I owe you $50,000, that's *your* problem!"

Yet, as Brandon explained with a mixture of bitterness and regret, college proved to be the start of a long series of disappointments. Unable to pass calculus or physics, he switched his major from engineering to criminal justice. Still optimistic, he applied to several police departments upon graduation, excited about a future of "catching crooks." The first department used a bewildering lottery system for hiring, and he didn't make the cut. The second informed him that he had failed a mandatory spelling test ("*I had a degree!*") and refused to consider his application. Finally, he became "completely turned off to this idea" when the third department disqualified him because of a minor incident in college in which he and his roommate "borrowed" a school-owned buffing machine as a harmless prank. Because he "could have been charged with a felony," the department informed him, he was ineligible for police duty. Regrettably, his college had no record of the incident. Brandon had volunteered the information out of a desire to illustrate his honest and upstanding character and improve his odds of getting the job.

With "two dreams deferred,"[2] Brandon took a job as the nightshift manager of a clothing chain, hoping it would be temporary. Eleven years later, he describes his typical day, which consists of unloading shipments, steaming and pricing garments, and restocking the floor, as "not challenging at all. I don't get to solve problems or be creative. I don't get to work with numbers, and I am a numbers guy. I basically babysit a team and deal with personnel." When his loans came out of deferment, he couldn't afford the monthly payments and decided to get a master's degree—partly to increase his earning potential and partly to put his loans back into deferment. After all, it had been "hammered into his head" that higher education was the key to success. He put on twenty-five pounds while working and going to school full-time for three years. He finally earned a master's degree in government, paid for with more loans from "that mean lady Sallie Mae."[3] So far, Brandon has still not found a job that will pay him enough to cover his monthly loan and living expenses. He has managed to keep the loans in deferment by continually consolidating—a strategy that costs him $5,000 a year in interest.

Taking stock of his life, Brandon is torn between feelings of betrayal and hope. On the one hand, he sees himself as a "rare and unique commodity— a black man with a college degree and no prison record."[4] Yet despite these accomplishments, he has achieved less than his own parents, who were married with children and owned a home by his age. He pondered:

> I feel like I was sold fake goods. I did everything I was told to do and I stayed out of trouble and went to college. Where is the land of milk and honey? I feel like they lied. I thought I would have choices. That sheet of paper [his degree] cost so much and does me *no good*. Sure, schools can't guarantee success, but come on; they could do better to help kids out. You have to give Uncle Sam your first born to get a degree and it doesn't pan out!

Barely able to support himself, he has avoided committed relationships, resigned to the fact that "no woman wants to sit on the couch all the time and watch TV and eat at Burger King." He reflected, "I can only take care of myself now. Money isn't love, but you need to be stable to be in a relationship. And once you start with kids you can't go back. I am missing out on life but making do with what I have." But on the other hand, he still holds tight to the American Dream of buying his "own piece of land" and landing "a nine-to-five with a salary," insisting that opportunities do exist for the taking. He ruefully explained, "My biggest risk is myself. I don't want to leave or just take another job even though I could. I limit my opportunities too much. I hold on too much to what I have. I don't want to uproot my life for a job because pulling up the stakes is too much to handle." In the end, he sees *himself*—his unwillingness to uproot everything he has to get ahead—as his greatest barrier to success.

Six hundred miles away, in a working-class neighborhood in Lowell, Massachusetts, I sit across the kitchen table from a twenty-four-year-old white woman named Diana. Dressed in a neon pink tank top that shows off just a hint of the shamrock tattoo on her lower back, Diana lends a brightness to the peeling white paint and murky linoleum floors of the duplex she lives in with her mother and two brothers. The daughter of a dry-cleaner and a cashier, Diana graduated from high school with a partial scholarship to a private university in Boston. She embarked on a criminal justice degree while working part-time at a local Dunkin' Donuts. While she enjoyed learning about the criminal justice system—her eyes lit up as she explained the nuances of due process to me—Diana began to doubt whether the benefits of college would ever outweigh the costs; after two years of wavering back and forth, she dropped out of school to be a full-time cashier. She explained, "When I work, I get paid at the end of the week. But college, I would have had to wait five years to get a degree, and once I got that, who knows if I would be working or find something I wanted to be." Now, close to $100,000 in debt, Diana has forged new dreams of getting married, buying a home with a pool in a wealthy suburb of Boston, and having five children, a cat, and a dog by the time she is thirty: "That is all I can think about. I am old-fashioned like that."

Just a few minutes later, however, Diana frankly admitted that she would never find a man with a stable, well-paying job to marry and that she would regret her decision to leave school: "Everyone says you can't really go anywhere unless you have a degree. I don't think I am going to make it anywhere past Dunkin' when I am older and that scares me to say. Like it's not enough to support me now." Living at home and bringing home under $275 a week, Diana feels stuck in an extended adolescence with no end in sight. Her yardsticks for adulthood—owning her own home, getting married, having children, and finding a job that pays her bills—remain spectacularly out of reach. She reflected: "Like your grandparents would get married out of high school, first go steady, then get married, like, they had a house . . . since I was sixteen I have asked my mother when I would be an adult, and she recently started saying I'm an adult now that I'm working and paying rent, but I don't *feel* any different." Mainly, she feels stuck, unable to figure out how to change the direction that her life has taken: "I just wish someone like a fifty-year-old would tell me what to do, and make it easier, because I can't make up my mind!"[5]

How would you tell your coming of age story without the milestones—graduations, weddings, promotions, births—that propel it forward? How might you make sense of the broken promises—unused degrees, unexpected layoffs, or failed relationships—that disconnect the pieces of yourself that you spent a lifetime carefully assembling? This is a book about what happens when taken-for-granted models for organizing one's life—whether in terms of relationships, work, time, or commitment—become obsolete, unattainable, or undesirable. Both Brandon and Diana, like many working-class young adults, are growing up in a world where taken-for-granted pathways to adulthood are quickly disappearing; they do not feel "grown up."

What, then, does it mean to "grow up" today? Even just a few decades ago, the transition to adulthood would not have been experienced as a time of confusion, anxiety, or uncertainty.[6] In 1960, the vast majority of women married before they turned twenty-one and had their first child before twenty-three. By thirty, most men and women had moved out of their parents' homes, completed school, gotten married, and begun having children. Completing these steps was understood as normal and natural, the only path to a complete and respectable adult life: indeed, half of American women at this time believed that people who did not get married were "selfish and peculiar," and a full 85 percent agreed that women and men *should* get married and have children (Furstenberg et al. 2004).

But amid the economic and social turmoil of the 1960s and 70s, the triumph of global capitalism in the 80s, the technology boom of the 90s, and the grinding recession of the 2000s, something strange happened: American youth stopped "growing up." As over a decade of scholarship has revealed, traditional markers of adulthood—leaving home, completing school, establishing financial independence, marrying, and having children—have become increasingly delayed, disorderly, reversible, or even forgone in the latter half of the twentieth century.[7] By 2009, almost 50 percent of people ages eighteen to twenty-four and 10 percent of those twenty-five to thirty-four were living with their parents, compared to 35 percent and 7 percent, respectively, in 1960.[8] While the median age at first marriage remained at twenty years old for women and twenty-two for men from 1890 to the early 1960s, it had soared to almost twenty-six for women and twenty-eight for men by 2010.[9] In 2008, a greater percentage of births were to women ages thirty-five and older than to teenagers (Livingston and Cohn 2010). And in 2007, nearly 40 percent of births were to unmarried mothers, up from less than 5 percent in 1960 (Pew Research Social & Demographic Trends 2010). Unlike their 1950s counterparts who followed a well-worn path from courtship to marriage to childbearing, men and women today are more likely to remain unmarried; to live at home and stay in school for longer periods of time; to have children out of wedlock; to divorce; or not to have children at all (Berlin, Furstenberg, and Waters 2010; Cherlin 2009; Livingston and Cohn 2010).[10]

The growing numbers of men and women in their twenties and even thirties who are living (or moving back in) with their parents, jumping from job to job, and postponing marriage and child rearing have been met with disdain and mockery from the popular media, where articles proclaiming "Here Come the Millenials!," "20-Somethings: No, I Won't Grow Up," "The Peter Pan Generation," and "College Grads, 30 Isn't the New 20" depict a youth culture that shuns conformity, structure, and responsibility, frolicking away the decade or so after high school before settling down to responsible adult life. Perhaps most tellingly, a 2007 *60 Minutes* episode warning "The Millenials Are Coming!" summed up popular attitudes toward this generation with the following snide dismissal: "They're living and breathing themselves and that keeps them very busy."

As these examples suggest, both popular and scholarly depictions of the Millenials often portray the transition to adulthood as a process of self-exploration in which young people try out different identities and lifestyles—perhaps backpacking through Southeast Asia, adopting a skinny-jeaned hipster existence in Brooklyn, or taking an unpaid internship with a congressman in Washington, DC—between graduating from college and choosing a future career path. In this vein, the prominent psychologist Jeffrey Arnett labels the years between adolescence and adulthood the "self-focused age" (2004: 12) equating twenty-first-century adulthood with learning to "stand alone" and make choices and decisions independently from among a wide range of options (1998). An emerging genre of self-help literature on the "quarter-life crisis" reinforces this conception of adulthood as an exploration-filled adventure. In *Quarterlife Crisis: The Unique Challenges of Life in Your Twenties*, for instance, Alexandra Robbins and Abby Wilner (2001: 3) presume a wide range of choices and possibilities for today's youth: "The sheer number of possibilities can certainly inspire hope—that is why people say that twenty-somethings have their whole lives ahead of them. But the endless array of decisions can also make a recent graduate feel utterly lost." Implicit in these characterizations of young adulthood are the resources and privileges of the middle and upper class—a college education, a secure foothold in the labor market, a safety net to fall back on—where anxiety is rooted only in the need to create the best possible life out of a vast array of options.

But what about the growing numbers of young men and women who lack the knowledge and resources that render such choices possible? In emphasizing the sense of entitlement and freedom available to today's middle-class young adults, much of the existing literature obscures the *absence of choice* that defines coming of age for working-class youth like Brandon and Diana. In this book, I tell the stories of working-class men and women for whom coming of age is not just being delayed, but fundamentally dismantled by drastic economic restructuring, profound cultural transformations, and deepening social inequality. I explore how paths to adulthood are being reshaped by the powerful forces of race, class, and gender—and how, in turn, young working-class men and women are putting the pieces of adulthood back together amid the chaos, uncertainty, and insecurity of twenty-first century life.

The Remaking of Working-Class Adulthood

In order to tell this story, I examine the transition to adulthood through the voices of 100 working-class young people in their mid-twenties to early thirties (see the Appendix for my research design and interview questions). From service sector workplaces like casual-dining restaurants and clothing chains, to community colleges and temp agencies, fire stations and army bases, and bowling alleys and movie theaters, I sought out the younger members of the working class in Lowell, Massachusetts; Richmond, Virginia; and a handful of other cities that embody the rise and fall of the American industrial working class. I spoke with blacks and whites, men and women, investigating the changing meanings, practices, and consequences of working-class adulthood through the accounts of those who are living it.

For the young men and women I spoke with, adulthood is not simply delayed, as much of the existing literature on the transition to adulthood would suggest. Instead, adulthood is being dramatically *reimagined* along lines of work, family, relationships, intimacy, gender, trust, and dignity. The majority of the young people I spoke with bounce from one unstable service job to the next, racking up credit card debt to make ends meet and fearing the day when economic shocks—an illness, a school loan coming out of deferment—will erode what little stability they have. This economic insecurity seeps into their homes, where experiences of family dissolution (through divorce and premature parental death), illness and work-related disabilities, domestic violence, and constant financial stress leave them uncertain and anxious about the viability of marriage and child rearing. Douglas, a twenty-five-year-old black man who lives with his godmother, said wistfully: "People used to get married at twenty-one. You don't see that anymore. *Trust is gone. The way people used to love is gone.*" As Brandon and Diana underscore, experiences of powerlessness, confusion, and betrayal within the labor market, institutions such as education and the government, and the family teach young working-class men and women that they are completely alone, responsible for their own fates and dependent on outside help only at their peril. They are learning the hard way that being an adult means trusting no one but yourself.

In our collective imagination, and in earlier sociological studies of the iconic industrial working class (Halle 1984; Lamont 2000; Rubin 1976; Willis 1977), dwells a working-class adult who is stoic, taciturn, and down-to-earth. He wears denim, drinks American beer, and actively participates in his community, whether the Catholic Church, the local union, the Irish-American society, or simply his neighborhood (Putnam 2000). He has calluses on his hands from working "forty hour week for a livin', just to send it on down the line," as the country singer Alan Jackson famously describes in his tribute to the steel mill workers of America. He believes in hard work, family, God, and the promise of the American dream. Dignity and integrity for this man are born of providing for his wife, raising decent kids who will have a better life than he did, being part of his community, and "keeping it together" in the face of adversity (Lamont 2000).

Over the last thirty years, however, the daily rhythm of work, family, and community that gave this man's life purpose and structure has been replaced by a fast-paced and flexible service economy, declining union membership and civic engagement, and a post-traditional, secular world (Cherlin 2009; Beck and Beck-Gernsheim 1995; Giddens 1991; Putnam 2000; Putnam et al. 2012; Western 1997). Simultaneously, the less visible and measurable aspects of industrial working-class life—the very sources of dignity and meaning that are believed to make an adult life worthy of living—have also become unworkable. Indeed, when I set out to find the sons and daughters of the American industrial working class, they looked almost nothing like the iconic steel mill worker. Instead, the young men and women I spoke with were reworking the definition of the ideal adult self along new cultural logics and under new structural constraints (see Bettie 2003; Illouz 2007; Lamont 2000; Weis 2004). As I will underscore throughout the book, tracing out the emerging working-class adult self—how he or she now conceives of loyalty, dignity, obligation, community, and trust—is central to understanding both contemporary American politics and new forms of social inequality.

At its core, this emerging working-class adult self is characterized by low expectations of work, wariness toward romantic commitment, widespread distrust of social institutions, profound isolation from others, and an overriding focus on their emotions and psychic health. Rather than turn to politics to address the obstacles standing in the way of a secure adult life, the majority of the men and women I interviewed crafted deeply *personal* coming of age stories, grounding their adult identities in recovering from their painful pasts—whether addictions, childhood abuse, family trauma, or abandonment—and forging an emancipated, transformed, and adult self (see Illouz 2007, 2008; Smith et al. 2011). As the sources of dignity and meaning of adulthood of their parents' and grandparents' generations—the daily toil of the shop floor, the making of a home and family—slip through their fingers, the young men and women I spoke with are working hard to remake dignity and meaning out of emotional self-management and willful psychic transformation. Stuck in an unpromising present and wary of the future, working-class men and women are launching into adulthood from the *past*, using the pain and betrayal in their relationships with family members and partners and their interactions with institutions as a platform for self-transformation.

Wanda, a twenty-five-year-old black woman who works as a server at a casual dining chain restaurant in central Virginia, provides an example of psychic transformation and self-growth. Wanda's dad is a tow-truck driver and her mom is an administrative assistant at a nonprofit organization. They have been separated, but legally married, for the past nine years. When I asked Wanda to describe the years following high school graduation, she laughed, but then quickly turned somber: "It's not funny, actually." After four years of working in the shipping and receiving department at a warehouse, sometimes from five in the morning until five in the evening, Wanda decided that her ticket out was to become an engineer: "Building roads for poverty-stricken people, that is what I would do." Wanda took out loans so that she could attend community college, which she has been juggling with her waitressing job ever since.

Like Brandon and Diana, Wanda also avoids romantic commitments as her vision of an ideal partner is fundamentally incompatible with the structural realities of her life:

I want someone who is successful, to be honest, and is a man. I like a man, anything about a man that isn't a man I don't like. Like that crying stuff or . . . you know what I'm saying, all that weakness, I don't really like that because I'm not a weak person. Like, I'm one of those people, you know how some people don't mind if their husband doesn't make more than you? I would. I don't settle for nothing less.

Unwilling to marry a man with fewer resources than herself—and nostalgic for a traditional masculinity of stoicism and strength—Wanda is part of a growing trend of working and lower-middle-class women who are now less likely than middle-class women to marry (Edin and Kefalas 2005; Goldstein and Kenney 2001; Martin 2004).[11] She would rather be alone than "settle" for something that might ultimately fall short.

When I asked Wanda to identify the hardest part about growing up, she did not mention the long hours she worked as a server, the difficulty of taking a full course load in community college, the scariness of taking out loans to finance her education, the monthly struggle to pay the rent on her studio apartment, or even the seeming impossibility of finding a (black) man who makes more money than she does. Instead, Wanda turned to her past, measuring her progress toward adulthood in terms of her ability to set herself free from the "pathological" family patterns of her childhood and create a healthy, strong adult self. She reflected:

I would have to say just where I grew up and, like, how I grew up. And the fact that, like, my parents, they've been addicted to so many things. I don't hold that against them, whatever. Like, my brother having to grow up by himself when he was thirteen, you know. And then my sister was raising us, my older sister. And so it's like not growing up with some kind of foundation. It's like you can get definitely, if you're a weak-minded person, you can get stuck thinking this is the only thing that you're capable of doing. Like you're not capable of doing more.

Wanda struggles to prove that she is not a "weak-minded" person like her parents. She confided, "There's a lot of comparisons. For example, when I was younger my mom and my dad were on crack. . . . So I mean I compare that to me smoking weed, do you know what I'm saying? And then when I was younger, like probably, like, seven or eight my mom, she used to always go out to the club all the time. I go out to the club all the time." Her thinly veiled anger toward her parents for not being able to beat their addictions—or get on their feet financially—comes out when she talks about having to take out loans for college: "*I feel like it's their fault that they don't have nothing.*" Wanda steels herself against becoming her own parents by policing her own potentially destructive behavior—smoking marijuana, going out to clubs—and psychically willing herself to overcome the family legacies that she views as pathological: "If my *mentality* were different, then most definitely I would just be stuck."

Over and over again, the working-class men and women whom I spoke with told coming of age stories like Wanda's—stories of anger and betrayal, of forging an adult self out of the emotional turmoil of the past, of breaking free from "pathological" family ties and learning that being an adult means trusting no one but yourself. Simply put, they are redefining adulthood in terms of willful self-change at the level of the psyche, as Wanda's emphasis on her "mentality" underlines. Just as the market economy compels them to continually monitor and transform themselves in order to stay employed throughout the life course (through investing in new degrees or moving to new cities in search of employment, as in Brandon's case), the *mood economy* requires vigilant self-monitoring and transformation in the emotional sphere in order to achieve happiness and well-being (Hochschild 2003; Illouz 2008; Martin 2007). In turn, the mood economy generates a particular sense of dignity, well-being, and progress that shores up the culture of competition, self-reliance, and self-blame that they are growing up in, as evidenced by Wanda's disdain for her parents who cannot control their addictions and "have nothing" as a result (Illouz 2008; Martin 2007).[12] The dignity and legitimacy due adults are purchased not through working in a job for life, serving one's community, or staying married until death but through actively and strategically transforming one's emotional flaws into an ongoing story of *willful self-change* (Illouz 2008; Martin 2007). Those who cannot "fix themselves" emotionally are met with disdain and disgust; they are the very opposite of worthy adults.

This emerging working-class adult—bewildered in the labor market, betrayed by institutions, distrustful of love, disconnected from others, and committed to emotional growth—turns taken-for-granted notions of stable adulthood on their head. To make sense of this dramatic shift in the meanings and practices of adulthood, one needs to understand the changing landscape of adulthood—the economic and political changes that have destabilized work and the cultural transformations that have disrupted traditional gender and family arrangements. To begin, I situate the stories of the men and women in this book within four key changes that have disrupted the transition to adulthood: the rise and fall of risk-pooling and social safety nets; the ascendance of neoliberal ideology and policy; the decline of the industrial working class; and the cultural transformations across gender and race of the 1960s and onward.

From Stable Endings to the Risk Society

Nearly seventy years ago, the United States emerged from the devastating poverty of the Great Depression and the traumas and triumphs of the Second World War with an unprecedented prosperity and sense of common purpose. The risks of modern capitalism that proved so devastating during the Depression—namely, lack of income as a result of old age, unemployment, sickness, or disability—were reconceived as collective social problems from which it was the duty of a nation to protect its citizens (Taylor-Gooby 2004). In turn, the United States government embarked on a political project of *pooling* the risks of millions of citizens, thereby providing a basic floor of protection even for those with limited abilities and resources (Hacker 2006b).

Within the postwar era of secure wages, low unemployment, and stable nuclear family structures, coming of age was a journey with stable, predictable, and clearly gendered endings.[13] Since the 1970s, however, the American economic, political, and social landscape has changed dramatically. As mounting stagnation, inflation, and fear of communism in the 1970s called into question the feasibility and desirability of government intervention in the coming global economy, drastic economic and political restructuring seemed urgent, opening the door for neoliberal ideology and policy (Harvey 2005). In his famous disavowal of social safety nets, Milton Friedman, who later became the economic adviser to Ronald Reagan, advocated a free market system with little intervention by government in the belief that only by allowing capitalism to function unhindered could economic health and political freedom be achieved. Friedman (1962) argued that the government should exist only to protect private property, calling for the *privatization of risk*—an end to all currency controls and trade barriers, labor laws, and social welfare programs that were put in place to protect citizens from the market. In the 1980s, neoliberalism gained widespread support, solidifying "America's sweeping ideological transformation away from an all-in-the-same-boat philosophy of shared risk toward a go-it-alone vision of personal responsibility" (Hacker 2006a: 34) and privatized risk.

The Culture of Neoliberalism

The rise of neoliberalism in the economic sphere has prompted a radical re-envisioning of social relationships at the deepest level of the self. As an ideology, neoliberalism has promoted self-reliance, rugged individualism, untrammeled self-interest, and privatization, equating lack of state interference and labor market efficiency with human freedom (Beck 2000; Sewell 2009; Slater 1997). Its cultural logic is perhaps best articulated by Margaret Thatcher's 1987 declaration: "Who is society? There is no such thing! There are individual men and women and there are families and no government can do anything except through people and people look to themselves first." As a policy paradigm, neoliberalism has spurred the deregulation of labor, the loss of institutional protections from the market, the decline of risk-pooling, and the relentless pursuit of profit (Calhoun 2010; Hacker and Pierson 2010; Sewell 2009). In its wake, the social contracts forged in the decades following the Second World War have been severed. Freedom has been reduced to freedom *from* government intervention; lower taxes, less regulation, and more labor market flexibility are its new rallying cry (Beck 2000). US congressman Ron Paul epitomized the spirit of privatization in 2011 when he passionately argued in a televised debate that individual risk management—such as the decision to forgo health insurance—is a fundamental freedom of Americans. When the moderator of the debate asked him if this would mean that someone without health insurance who was critically injured should die rather than receive government help, the audience could be heard shouting, "Yeah!"[14]

The Decline of the Industrial Working Class

The neoliberal turn has had grave consequences for the American working class. Since 1973, the real wages of working-class jobs have declined by 12 percent for those with a high school diploma, and by 26 percent for those without one (Johnson 2002: 33). Fifty years ago, a third of US employees worked in factories, "making everything from clothing to lipstick to cars" (Hagenbaugh 2002). But as the economy stagnated in the 1970s, businesses sought to move their industries to the American South—or outside the United States altogether—in search of union-less workers, subsidies, and tax cuts. Today, millions of these jobs have been shipped overseas, leaving only about one-tenth of the nation's 131 million workers employed by manufacturing firms. The American working-class man (the steelworker or the coal miner) of the postwar generation has experienced a steep decline in employment, job security, compensation, access to pensions, and employer-subsidized health insurance (Cowie 2010; Danziger and Ratner 2010; Wilson 1997).[15] His twenty-first century counterparts have been displaced to the service economy—as cashiers, office clerks, cooks, retail workers, or customer service representatives—where they are poorly paid, vulnerable to layoffs, and much more likely to be female (Barich and Bielby 1996; US Bureau of Labor Statistics, 2010; Weis 2004).

In the wake of these economic and social shifts, the broadly distributed prosperity of the postwar generation has given way to soaring levels of income and wealth inequality, crippling economic insecurity, and declining social mobility. Since 1979, for example, the top 20 percent of earners have captured 75 percent of overall income gain, while the bottom 20 percent gained only.4 percent (The Stanford Center on Poverty and Inequality).[16] As a result, by 2007, over a quarter of low-income families were making debt payments of at least 40 percent of their incomes, as opposed to only 3.8 percent of the highest-income families.

These economic and cultural transformations have destabilized traditional pathways to adulthood, leaving working-class youth like Diana, Brandon, and Wanda struggling to finish school, move out, get a job, or create a stable relationship (Danziger and Ratner 2010).[17] Caught in the teeth of a merciless job market and lacking the community support, skills, and knowledge necessary for success, working-class young adults are relinquishing the hope for a better future that is at the core of the American Dream. Cory, a thirty-four-year-old bartender who has been living paycheck to paycheck since he was sixteen, shrugged, "If I had, like, goals, like real live goals, then there could be a lot to let that down. So I am floating. Whatever happens next, happens, and I will deal with it when it happens."

Race, Class, and Gender in the Neoliberal Era

These statistics on rising insecurity and inequality can certainly spark a longing to return to the 1950s and 60s and their promise of job security, high wages, lasting families, home ownership, and affordable higher education. But our nostalgia threatens to obscure that these were also years of coercion, restriction, and discrimination, when African Americans were prevented from voting by bogus literacy tests and outlawed from drinking at the same water fountain as whites; when political dissent was silenced; when women couldn't serve on juries or own property or take out lines of credit in their own name; when alcoholism and physical and sexual abuse within families went ignored; and when factory workers, despite their rising wages and generous social benefits, reported feeling imprisoned by grueling, monotonous work and merciless supervision (Coontz 2000; Katznelson 2005; Milkman 1997).

Without a doubt, the 1960s onward brought forth struggles for rights and recognition that politicized many of these previously accepted sites of inequality. Civil rights groups, unions, activists, and the court system fought to make the "all-white textile mills, strictly gendered office spaces, lily-white construction sites, and segregated hiring practices at steel mills" a remnant of the past (Cowie 2010: 240).

Ironically, this fight for gender- and race-based rights came to the workforce just as stable manufacturing jobs were leaving it, breeding competition and resentment among those fighting for a slice of the rapidly diminishing pie.[18] Inequality persists along gender and racial lines, where women remain dramatically underrepresented in politics and business and continue to earn less than their male counterparts for the same work, and African Americans face lower weekly earnings, lower rates of high school and college completion, higher rates of incarceration, lower life expectancies, and severely unequal amounts of wealth.[19]

Growing into Neoliberal Adults

As the previous sections reveal, working-class men and women born in the wake of neoliberalism are growing up in a very different economic and social climate from that of their grandparents or even their parents. In this book, I seek to understand these vast transformations "from the inside out" (Hall and Lamont 2013)—to trace how the larger context of economic insecurity and cultural uncertainty in which young working-class men and women come of age is restructuring the kinds of adults they are growing *into*. Indeed, whether in the classroom, the home, the workplace, or in the voting booth, they are renegotiating their community boundaries, their sense of connectedness and obligations to others, their definitions of a worthy life, and their understanding of where they fit and whom they can trust.

As they come of age, they must sift through the complicated legacy of rights, resentments, freedoms, and betrayals that they have inherited from their grandparents and parents. In doing so, they are remaking *social class*—and the potential for and limits of class solidarity—in a society where "working class" no longer simply means white and masculine manual labor (see Bettie 2003; Walkerdine et al. 2001; Weis 2004). I find that without a broad, shared vision of economic justice, race, class, and gender have become sites of resentment and division rather than a coalition among the working class (see Cowie 2010; Stacey 1998). As they grow up, they learn to see their struggles to survive on their own as morally right, making a virtue out of not asking for help; if they could do it, then everyone else should too. This sense of distrust and rugged individualism permeates intimate relationships and perpetuates gender and racial division. For women who have grown up with extreme economic and family instability, the need to hold onto hard-won independence makes them wary of commitment; they do not want to squander the selves they have painstakingly constructed on a partner who will be unfaithful, directionless, or needy. As Kelly, a twenty-eight-year-old line cook, explained, "I'd rather be alone and fierce than be in a relationship and be milquetoast." Both men and women intensely fear pouring time, emotion, and energy into a relationship that could ultimately fail. The traditional marriage at the heart of the industrial working-class family appears to young men and women as both impossible and undesirable in an insecure world where they must put themselves first to survive. Forced to be flexible in the labor market, these men and women become hardened outside it.

In a world of scarce resources, race emerges as a source of resentment and fear. For the white people I spoke with, the idea that racial minorities get more government help and hiring preferences sparks bitterness as they grapple with their own loss of privilege. Eileen, a white mother who grew up in poverty and who is currently unemployed, explained:

> Like I said I do have issues with black people that don't want to work and we have to pay for stuff. I tried to get welfare or child health when my daughter was born. They wouldn't give it to me because I owned a house [which she inherited from her grandmother]. So I have big issue with that. I was, like, you got people over here on [a predominantly black street] and they're out playing basketball, my tax dollars are paying for it and you know . . . it sucks, it bites that you've got people out there, like, that are able bodies that can get out there and work and you know.

For blacks, this foundational belief in self-reliance ultimately renders group solidarities repugnant and in turn undercuts the potential for collective action. Julian, an unemployed twenty-seven-year-old black man, rejects the idea that racism, rather than his own efforts, could shape his future: "Ethnicity plays in people, but I don't look at it as a part of my shortcomings, if that makes sense. Every day I look in the mirror, and I could bullshit you right now and tell you anything I wanted to tell you. But at the end of the day looking in the mirror, I know where all my shortcomings come from. *From the things that I either did not do or I did and I just happen to fail at them.*" This hardening against oneself and others has profound personal and political consequences for the future of the American working class, as the youngest of its members like Wanda, Brandon, Kelly, Eileen, and Julian embrace self-sufficiency over solidarity and blame those who are unsuccessful in the labor market. As potential communities of solidarity across race, class, and gender remain hostile and divided, levels of community engagement and social trust, at their highest in the postwar decades, are plummeting among the working class (Putnam 2000; Putnam et al. 2012; Smith 2007). They are left with a worldview that conceives of rights in terms of "I's" rather than "we's," with economic justice dropped out of their collective vocabulary. Rooted in everyday instances of disappointment and betrayal within the family and institutions, the cultural logic of neoliberalism resonates at the deepest level of the self.

Coming of Age in the Mood Economy

As these examples so powerfully demonstrate, working-class young men and women are growing up in a world without solidarities and without safety nets, leaving them wary and distrustful in their interactions with others. I now turn to examine how economic insecurity and social uncertainty are reshaping the ways in which working-class young people conceptualize the *self*, particularly as it relates to their definitions of legitimate and worthy adulthood.

Insecure and alone, working-class men and women cannot point to a blue-collared uniform, a diploma on the wall, or a wedding band on their finger to mark their progress through life. Instead, it is up to them to redefine the contours of a meaningful life. In this book, I argue that working-class young men and women inhabit a *mood economy* in which legitimacy and self-worth are purchased not with traditional currencies such as work or marriage or class solidarity but instead through the ability to organize their emotions into a narrative of self-transformation (Hochschild 2003; Illouz 2008). Rather than live and work within institutions that call for a stoic, taciturn, deeply gendered self, this generation is learning that the self—like their jobs and relationships—must be continually remade.

The need to continuously recreate one's identity—whether after a failed attempt at college or an unanticipated divorce or a sudden career change—can be an anxiety-producing endeavor. In a world of rapid change and tenuous loyalties, the language and institution of *therapy*—and the self-transformation it promises—has exploded in American culture (see, for example, Bellah et al. 1985; Cushman 1996; Davis 2005; Foucault 1979; Furedi 2004; Giddens 1991; Illouz 2003, 2008; Martin 2007; Moskowitz 2001; Rieff 1987), with one in four American adults reporting a mental health disorder in a given year ("NIMH: The Numbers Count: Mental Disorders in America"). In place of traditional modes of selfhood, structured by the external religious, moral, employment, and gender mores of a time past, the therapeutic model posits an inner-directed self preoccupied with its own emotional and psychic development. This self is individually negotiated and continually reinvented (Bellah et al. 1985; Illouz 2008; Rieff 1987; Smith et al. 2011). The "therapeutic narrative"—whether instantiated through best-selling self-help books like *Emotional Chaos to Clarity: How to Live More Skillfully, Make Better Decisions, and Find Purpose in Life* or on the Oprah Winfrey Network—provides a blueprint for bringing a reconstructed, healthy self into being.

It works like this: first, it compels one to identify pathological thoughts and behaviors; second, to locate the hidden source of these pathologies within one's past; third, to give voice to one's story of suffering in communication with others; and finally, to triumph over one's past by bringing into being an emancipated and independent self (Illouz 2003).[20] Inwardly directed and preoccupied with its own psychic and emotional growth, the therapeutic self has become a crucial cultural resource for ascribing meaning and order to one's life amid the flux and uncertainty of a flexible economy and a post-traditional social world (Bellah et al. 1985; Giddens 1991; Illouz 2008; Silva 2012).

One particularly illustrative example from American popular culture, *Eat, Pray, Love: One Woman's Search for Everything across Italy, India and Indonesia*, is a 2006 memoir by Elizabeth Gilbert that captures the process of psychic healing and self-transformation.[21] In this memoir, the thirty-two-year-old protagonist, unhappy in her marriage and feeling stunted in her job, initiates a divorce and travels around the world in a quest for self-discovery. Riding her bike "freely in the sunset through Bali," Gilbert (2006: 260) proclaims: "Happiness is the consequence of personal effort. You fight for it, strive for it, insist upon it, and sometimes even travel around the world looking for it. You have to participate relentlessly in the manifestations of your own blessings. And once you have achieved a state of happiness, you must never become lax about maintaining it. You must make a mighty effort to keep swimming upward into that happiness forever, to stay afloat on top of it." In this impassioned appeal, Gilbert articulates and advocates a self that is fluid, committed to psychic and emotional growth, and completely responsible for its own happiness. In this telling, her ability to create a meaningful and coherent adult life depends not on sustaining her marriage or developing her career, but on her ability to overcome her past unhappiness and transform her *self*.

The freedom made possible through therapeutic language to define the terms of one's life cannot be overstated, especially for a woman like Elizabeth, who uses it to leave an unfulfilling job, end an unhappy marriage, and achieve emotional and psychic satisfaction as she defines it (Illouz 1997, 2008; Stein 2011). But just as the new freedoms in the labor market only benefit those with the skills and knowledge to meet its demands, the freedoms made possible by therapy are also distributed unequally. Existing literature suggests that successfully creating a therapeutic narrative of self may require a class-based "tool kit" (Swidler 1986) of language skills, emotional expression, and material resources unavailable to the working class (Giddens 1991; Illouz 2008).[22] In her groundbreaking work on social inequality, culture, and emotion, Eva Illouz (2008: 235) explains: "Therapeutic emotional and linguistic skills and habitus are absent from working-class lives because they have less currency in the working-class man's workplace . . . blue-collar work mobilizes an ethos of bravery, strength, and distrust of words." In other words, one's place within social structures—and the everyday linguistic skills, embodied practices, and interactions that sustain it—shape the very capacity to feel and express emotion that is then experienced as natural (Collins 2004; Goffman 1959; Hochschild 1995; Illouz 2007; Williams 1977). Emotions may live within us, but we also live within a particular range of emotions and act within situations colored by particular moods.[23] The working-class men in Illouz's study worked and lived within an economy that made therapeutic language and expression irrelevant, inconceivable, and *un-feelable*; there was nothing to be gained and much to be lost by expressing emotion on the assembly line. In today's world, however, emotional expression and psychic growth have become central to achieving well-being (as it is socially and culturally defined). If working-class people are structurally disadvantaged in their ability to achieve it (Illouz 2008: 235), then *emotions*, in addition to material resources, are profoundly implicated in the reproduction of social inequality.

When I set out to discover how working-class men and women experienced adulthood at the level of the self, then, I was incredibly surprised to find that my working-class informants were absolutely fluent in the language of therapeutic needs, desires, emotional suffering, and self-growth. They used it without self-consciousness or skepticism, discovering through it the hidden roots of their past failures and their central purpose going forward. Whether poring over self-help books to develop strategies to manage their attention deficit disorder, religiously attending Narcotics Anonymous meetings and learning to express themselves through art, attending obsessive compulsive disorder conventions at the suggestion of Oprah, or coming to terms with a pornography addiction, the men—and women—of the post-industrial class could not sound more dissimilar from the working class of a generation or two ago if they tried to. The sources of meaning and dignity—hard work, social solidarity, family—found in previous studies of the industrial working class (Lamont 2000) had been nearly eclipsed by an all-encompassing culture of emotional self-management.

For the post-industrial generation of working-class men and women, it is not blue-collar work but rather the flux and flexibility left behind by its disappearance that defines their coming of age experiences. Young working-class men and women employ emotional suffering as the new currency of adulthood; it is through managing this suffering within the self that they access the dignity and sense of forward-moving progress due adults. This model is ubiquitous in their everyday interactions, propagated through school psychologists, family services, the service economy, self-help literature, online support groups, addiction recovery groups, medical trials, or even talk shows such as *Oprah* (Black 2009; Hochschild 2003; Illouz 2003; Imber 2004; Nolan 1998).[24]

The mood economy underlines a drastic transformation in the relationship among selfhood, inequality, and emotion. As working-class young people come to understand emotional self-management as the key to happiness, the predominance of the family past obscures the shaping power of the market present. Like Wanda, many draw unforgiving boundaries against their family members and friends who cannot transform their selves—overcome addictions, save money, heal troubled relationships—through sheer determination alone. Just as neoliberalism teaches young people that they are solely responsible for their economic fortunes, the mood economy renders them responsible for their *emotional* fates. Weaving together the therapeutic ethos with timeless American cultural tropes of pulling oneself up by one's bootstraps, and religious narratives of redemption, the mood economy transposes self-reliance, progress, and success from one's character or one's soul to one's psyche (Illouz 2007). To put it succinctly, the mood economy dovetails with neoliberalism by privatizing happiness.

Exploitation of the Self

But does the mood economy deliver on its promise of happiness—of new, individualistic, emotionally based, stable endings of dignity and self-worth? One tragedy of this book is that it often does not; indeed, as Ewick and Silbey (1995: 212) explain, "We are as likely to be shackled by the stories we tell (or that are culturally available for our telling) as we are by the form of oppression they might seek to reveal." Rob, a twenty-six-year-old white man who serves in the National Guard, brings to life the false promise of the mood economy. Rob's father is currently in prison, serving eight years for assaulting an elderly woman while intoxicated, a source of deep shame and anger for Rob. His mother lost custody of Rob and his sister when they were younger, leaving the responsibility of raising the children to his grandmother. In examining the interview transcript, it is striking to note that while Rob answered each of my questions about work, education, and money in a few sentences, his accounts of his family often take up more than a single-spaced page. Indeed, Rob raised the themes of family turmoil and anguish unprompted, illustrating how important these issues are to his sense of self-understanding.

Rob's central goal in life is to be a man different from his father in every way: he has never had a drink or taken drugs, and I was told by several men in his unit that he would risk his life, without a second thought, to protect any woman whom he perceived to be in danger. As he explained, "My father and I have similar temperaments; we like doing the same things, but so do my mother and I. Like I said, I have the same temperament as my father, which is one of the reasons I don't drink. I just saw him get drunk and beat people up and I was, like, I am not having any part of that." Here, he constructs his story as one of suffering and self-realization: he has used the painful experiences of his past as building blocks for his own narrative of self. Rob feels redeemed because he has managed to successfully defeat the "temperament" he inherited from his father and to grow into a morally worthy person, despite his inability to find a full-time job or keep a relationship going. However, as his story reveals, his adult self remains incomplete: his stepfather, the one person who mattered most to him, cannot witness and affirm his personal triumph:

JS (AT THE END OF THE INTERVIEW SCHEDULE): Do you think I missed anything from your life? Like, in terms of what made you who you are as an adult?

R: I think we pretty much covered it . . . we already talked about my dad being alcoholic and abusive. And my mom putting up for it for a while. And then she separated from him and I was just living with my mother. After she got out of jail, she had a boyfriend who was more my father than my real father was. He was a big part of my life until I was eighteen. He passed away. It was pretty upsetting. It never really occurred to me how much he was more my dad than my dad until he was gone. And actually, it happened when I was sixteen, before I joined the military. Even now I wish he could see how I actually turned out. I'm an atheist and I don't believe he's in heaven looking at me. Death is the end of it. I mean I would like to believe that there is something else, I just don't. I wish he could see how I turned out. My father can see how I turned out, but he doesn't want to be part of my life, so it makes it kind of rough.

To make matters worse, he continues to be haunted by his relationship to his sister, yet another family member who did not take seriously the markers of progress he so carefully staked out on his coming of age journey:

We made a pact when we were younger, that we weren't gonna be anything like our parents, and as soon as my father turned his back, she was just like our parents, smoking, drinking, doing drugs, at fifteen years old, having sex with multiple partners. What are you doing, you idiot? But when you give me your word, I expect you to keep it, I don't care if you were eighteen years old when you said it, I mean it's not like I believe I am asking too much. It is exactly what I am doing. I am not asking her to do something that I am not keeping. So we really, a long time ago, we were very close. I was a small boy, so a lot of people thought we were twins . . . and I got in a lot of fights protecting my sister. We were very close, and then she started changing. She broke this sacred oath we took when we were kids. It was sacred to me; she was, like, whatever, I don't care, and went on about her way, which really, really made me angry.

Rob believed that he could depend on his sister to share his journey of self-realization and transformation and held the bond they forged as sacred. Her decision to follow an alternate path—one not in accord with his own—fills his mind with constant anguish and bewilderment. In the end, he realizes that he is alone in his quest for redemption, with no one to validate the worthiness of his life but himself. Rob, like many working-class youth, is trapped in the mood economy, longing for a *witness* in a world in which he has only himself to rely on. The exploitation of the labor market is thus reproduced in the mood economy, where Rob puts his emotions "to work" in service of self-management and self-transformation but gets nothing but frustration and betrayal in return.

Outline of the Book

This is a book about the very real suffering that young men and women like Brandon, Diana, Wanda, and Rob endure as they come of age. While these four young adults are separated by race, gender, family background, and even region of the country, they are struggling to remake adulthood—and the sense of dignity and progress at its core—in a world without stable endings. In order to make sense of the transformation of working-class adulthood, I begin Chapter 2 by delving into the various social and cultural forces that frame, and in many ways work against, their attempts to create stable and predictable adult lives. Whether bouncing from one temporary job to the next, dropping out of college because they can't figure out how to fill out financial aid forms, relying on their credit card to survive, or joining the military out of desperation for a steady paycheck and a daily routine, I reveal how and why working-class men and women come to feel bewildered, disoriented, and powerless as they come of age. In particular, I illuminate their fragile hold on the American Dream, particularly for women, African Americans, and young parents trying to balance the competing demands of work and family.

Moving from the public to the private sphere, Chapter 3 explores how the disappearance of stable unionized jobs with benefits and the attendant rise of unstable, poorly paid, service jobs have made lasting marriages less attainable, exacerbating feelings of distrust or even fear about intimate relationships. Commitment, rather than a hedge against external risks of the market, becomes one demand too many on top of the already excessive demands of the post-industrial labor force. I explore how working-class intimate life is further threatened by the emergence of a therapeutic model of relationships that prioritizes self-fulfillment and communication, the achievement of which requires material and cultural resources that are in short supply. Children symbolize the last bastion of hope and commitment, but the institutions that frame young parents' lives work against their efforts to provide stable lives for their children. Taken together, Chapters 2 and 3 illuminate the impossibility and even undesirability of traditional markers of adulthood such as employment, living on one's own, getting married, finishing school, and raising children.

In Chapter 4, I move beyond the transitions to adulthood literature, asking, What does it mean to be working class in the post-industrial economy? What kinds of symbolic boundaries do young people construct to distinguish between worthy and unworthy adults? In particular, I investigate why young people who would seemingly benefit most from social safety nets and solidarity with others cling so fiercely to neoliberal ideals of untrammeled individualism and self-reliance. I demonstrate how, over and over again, working-class youth experience bewilderment and betrayal in institutions, learning that they can depend on others only at great cost. The more "flexible" they must become in the labor market—that is, the more they learn to manage short-term commitment and disillusionment— the more "hardened" they become toward the world around them. This "hardening" is particularly acute across lines of gender and race, as they see others as competition in the fight for stable jobs and secure futures.

In Chapter 5, I explore the emerging ways in which young people ascribe meaning, order, and progress onto their chaotic experiences of coming of age. In contrast to previous studies of working-class identity, I find that the majority of respondents embrace a model of therapeutic selfhood—that of an inwardly directed self preoccupied with its own psychic development (see Silva 2012). In their interactions with the state (rehabilitation homes, support groups, social workers and psychologists, foster care), the media (talk shows, Internet blogs, self-help books), or the medical field (hospitals, free drug trials), young people learn over and over again that happiness is theirs only if they work hard enough to control their negative thoughts, feelings, and behaviors on their own. Through my concept of the mood economy, I demonstrate that the therapeutic narrative allows working-class men and women to redefine competent adulthood in terms of overcoming a painful family past. However, it also transforms the *self* into one's greatest obstacle to success, happiness, and well-being and leads young people to draw harsh boundaries against those who cannot will themselves to succeed.

Finally, in the Conclusion, I reflect on what I call the "hidden injuries" of risk. As it stands, the economic, political, and cultural systems that frame these men's and women's coming of age stories are coming up short, leaving them powerless, distrustful, and hostile toward human interdependence. Only by understanding the sources, consequences, and meanings of twenty-first-century adulthood can we hope to rewrite the futures of working-class youth.

2 | Prisoners of the Present
I OBSTACLES ON THE ROAD TO ADULTHOOD

JALEN IS A TWENTY-FOUR-YEAR-OLD BLACK man whose dry wit and easy laugh conceal the pervasive disquiet of his daily life. He was raised up and down the East Coast, accompanying his mother as she searched for work in Virginia, North Carolina, Vermont, and Maine—"I don't know exactly where I was raised for sure." Jalen has recently moved into his aunt and uncle's basement in an urban, mostly black neighborhood in Massachusetts so that he can work the baseball season as a nighttime security guard at a local stadium. He has never met his father, but he has been told he works for a tractor company in the Midwest. His older brother is in prison, but Jalen shrugged off my look of concern: "It's okay, he's alive now, so I guess he's doing good."

Sitting at the picnic table in the shady backyard—his nonchalant "my aunt doesn't let me have white girls in the house" ringing in my ears—Jalen recounted his coming of age story with a weariness that belied his twenty-four years. With my own ideas of adulthood as a journey with stable endings unconsciously informing my questions, I asked Jalen, "When you were younger, did you have an idea of what you wanted to do when you grew up?," trying to gauge whether he was disappointed in how his life has turned out so far. He replied, "No, I don't know, I still don't." Pressing him further, I questioned, "So when you were in high school you were trying to figure it out? Or were you not thinking about it?" "I didn't think about it," he laughed. Undaunted, I continued, "Did you think about going to college, or did you think about getting a job out of high school?" He shrugged and shook his head. "I knew college was out of the question for me. I couldn't afford it, wasn't smart enough, didn't have the discipline to go, still don't (*laughs*). Yeah, that was that, college wasn't an option."

Instead, Jalen joined the Marine Corps after high school, explaining:

Actually I was going to a party, a graduation party, I think I had just graduated myself. A real friend of mine that I have in North Carolina called me and he asked me what the hell was I doing. I said I don't know. I'll figure it out as I go. I'll get a job first, right. He was, like, well I'm joining the Marine Corps. I didn't even know the Marine Corps. I didn't know what it was. So I was, like, I'll do it. I joined and, I don't know, went from there. I really didn't know anything about anything. I just kind of just joined. I didn't even know a war was going on. That's how oblivious I was to everything going on around me.

Jalen proceeded to serve three tours of duty in Afghanistan as a radio operator with the infantry patrol. After five years of service, which he described as initially frightening but then surprisingly comforting in its routines—"I had some sort of sense of security in everything I did"—he was honorably discharged.

Jalen swears by a code of meritocracy, self-reliance, and determination, insisting that opportunities to become a "real adult"—"an established person, like somebody [who] has a job, a home, a car, all paid on time"—are his for the taking. "Like, when I see people out on the street even still nowadays, I think it's just lack of effort," he explained. "There's so many different things you can do to try to help yourself out or get the skills and whatnot that you need to do other things that you wouldn't ever have to be on the streets."

Yet since his honorable discharge a year ago, Jalen's attempts to go to college and find a stable job have been stymied at every turn. Following the advice of his first sergeant, he took the civil service firefighting exam shortly after returning from his third tour of duty. With his veteran, minority, and resident status, he made the city's hiring list and enrolled at the fire academy. A career in firefighting—one of the few remaining stable, unionized, and well-paid jobs with benefits and a pension left for blue-collar workers—beckoned on the horizon, just three short weeks of training away.[1] On the second day of training, however, Jalen tested positive for marijuana and failed his mandatory drug test. He was promptly expelled from the fire academy and thrown back into minimum-wage service work. When I asked Jalen if he was considering taking the civil service exam again, his normally succinct speech turned incoherent as he struggled to find the words to express his feelings: "It's like the odd part right now where I'm at odds with myself I guess you know. I haven't been back over there to really see what's up, the next class picking up, or what I might have to do in order to . . . I'm getting pushed in the back, but you know I'll see what I want to do, I don't know yet."

Wrestling with self-doubt, he enrolled in a local community college. He would rather work, he says, but the GI Bill will pay for his schooling and he knows he needs a college degree to get a good job. "But it's going to be challenging just because I still don't have the grammar, damn writing skills and all sort of craziness. I just don't have it. I'm not book smart." A few minutes later, he reveals that while the semester started over two weeks ago, he still doesn't have his books. With more resignation than anger, he sighed:

> I'm waiting for these fools right now. They got a message man, I call them up. I'm, like, it's been like six or more weeks. I'm trying to get my money. They're paying the school, but they ain't paying me. So it's, like, okay. So I ain't got no books or nothing. I'm going to these damn classes and they're, like, break out your books. That's great. I'm just going to sit back here and listen. I called them and they got this automatic message, please wait for six weeks for your checks to come. It's, like, okay, so six weeks, a month and some change go by and I have all these assignments due and I'm just now getting checks to get books and whatnot. It's crazy.

With the knowledge that his security guard position will be eliminated at the end of baseball season and little faith in his ability to pass his classes at school, Jalen is tentatively considering "jump[ing] right back over into that dangerous whole country to try to make some money." The "hot $18,000" in debt he accrued in his early twenties—"I was running credit cards up, stuff like that. Not paying my stuff on time, and not paying stuff at all"—ironically makes the Marine Corps, and even "the thought that you might die or come back with, you know, some missing body parts and whatnot," feel like a safety net.

Elusive Adulthood

In the contemporary United States, legal conventions identify age-based criteria as markers of adulthood (Blatterer 2007). In most states, individuals are considered adults at eighteen, granting them access to a wide array of rights (voting, making a will or end of life decisions, signing a contract or applying for credit in their own names) and obligations (jury duty or Selective Service for men). However, age is certainly not the only or most salient criterion of adulthood; on the contrary, the full achievement of adult status requires "sets of practical accomplishments and repertoires of behavior" that are commonly recognized as *social* markers of adulthood: nest-leaving, stable employment, marriage, parenthood, and financial independence (Pilcher 1995: 86, cited in Blatterer 2007).

Jalen, at twenty-four years old, has not been able to maintain a grip on *any* of these markers: he lives with his aunt and uncle, moves in and out of temporary and low-paid work, can't afford the books for his college classes, and dismisses marriage and parenthood as "out of the question." While the word adulthood connotes forward progress and stable, knowable endings, Jalen's experiences of family disruption, labor market insecurity, and confusion and discomfort within powerful institutions have left him feeling stunted in the present and wary of the future. Indeed, his description of being "at odds" with himself points to a profound disconnect between the paths that feel comfortable and available to him on one hand, and the paths that lead toward "adulthood" on the other.

Jalen's story is far from unique: of the 100 working-class young people in this sample, only fourteen are married, live with a spouse, and have children, and not even all of these hold stable jobs. In contrast, a third lives with a parent or older family member. While twenty-seven respondents have children, less than half of them are married. Five are already divorced. As these numbers suggest, the transition to adulthood, and adulthood itself, has become delayed, unstable, reversible, and sometimes even impossible (see Berlin, Furstenberg, and Waters 2010). Traditional markers of adulthood have been swept away by a rising tide of economic insecurity and social uncertainty that have transformed coming of age into a precarious journey with no clear destination in sight.

In this chapter, I focus on how young men and women encounter the changing world of adulthood. Through the accounts of young people themselves, I delineate the various social and cultural forces that frame, and in many ways work against, their attempts to create stable and predictable adult lives. Labor market flux, tensions between work and family, discrimination across race and gender, and the constant strain of risk-bearing solidify into a nearly impenetrable wall that blocks forward momentum, often rendering the military the only (seeming) vehicle for upward mobility. Young working-class men and women find themselves trapped as *"prisoner[s] of the present,"* unable to push their lives forward in any measurable way (Sennett 1998: 91, italics added). While organizations such as higher education are expected to offer the possibility of social integration and upward mobility, unsuccessful interaction after interaction teach working-class youth to be distrustful and wary of the very institutions that shape their futures. In a time when work is unpredictable, families are fragile, social safety nets are shrinking, and the future is uncertain, coming of age means coming to terms with the absence of choice.

Crippled by the Market

The quest to find and keep a "job for life"—stable, predictable work that pays enough to live on, is reachable by available transportation, and lends a sense of meaning to their daily lives—runs through every interview transcript, from those who are unemployed to those who have "made it" to steady jobs like firefighting or nursing. Traditional blue-collar work—whether as a factory worker or a police officer—has become increasingly scarce and competitive, destroyed by a technologically advanced and global capitalism that prioritizes labor market "flexibility" above all (Beck 2000). Consequently, the post-industrial generation is forced to continuously grapple with flux and contingency, bending and adapting to the demands of the labor market until they feel that they are about to break.

Rob, for example, is a twenty-six-year-old white man whom I met while conducting research at a National Guard training weekend in Massachusetts. Rob's first job was in the paper goods factory where his mother worked, which has since closed, shipping its labor overseas in exchange for lower production costs. When he graduated from vocational high school, he planned to use his training in metals to build a career as a machinist: "I really liked working with wood and metal, carpentry. Manufacturing technology, working with metal, I loved that stuff." However, as he attempted to enter the labor market after high school, he soon learned that his newly forged skills were obsolete:

> I was the last class at my school to learn to manufacture tools by hand. Now they use CNC [computer numerical controlled] machine programs, so they just draw the part in the computer and plug it into the machine, and the machine cuts it. . . . I haven't learned to do that, because I was the last class before they implemented that in the program at school, and now if you want to get a job as a machinist without CNC, they want five years experience. My skills are useless.

Over the last five years, Rob has stacked lumber, installed hardwood floors, landscaped, and poured steel at a motorcycle factory. His only steady source of income since high school graduation has been his National

Guard pay, and he recently returned from his second eighteen-month deployment in Afghanistan. Currently unemployed, he has pursued several "promising leads" in the want ads, but always seems to be one step behind the competition: "Just yesterday, I called on a job offer that was offering $14 an hour for four and a half days of work a week as a driver, transporting car parts and stuff. I missed it by a day. It filled the day before." Reflecting on his current situation, Rob expresses a sense of profound hopelessness toward the future that was shared by over half of the sample:

> I am looking for a new place. I don't have a job. My car is broken. It's, like, what exactly can you do when your car is broken and you have no job, no real source of income, and you are making $400 or $500 a month in [military] drills. Where are you going to live, get your car fixed, on $500 a month? I can't save making 500 bucks a month. That just covers my bills. I have no savings to put down first and last on an apartment, no car to get a job. I find myself being, like, oh what the hell? Can't it just be over? Can't I just go to Iraq right now? Send me two weeks ago so I got a paycheck already!

When I asked him to identify the "hardest part of growing up," he replied, "I can't quite seem to keep my feet under me. I get them under me, and then I slide off to the next thing." In an economy devoted to the short-term and flexible, Rob desperately seeks solid ground from which to launch his adult life. Indeed, like Jalen, he is anxious to spend a year driving convoys in Iraq to lend stability and predictability to his life.

Besieged Families

For the men and women I interviewed, the only way to survive in such a competitive and bewildering labor market is to become highly elastic and unencumbered by other obligations—including their own families. This was made abundantly clear by Sandy and Cody, a white couple in their late twenties who invited me to their low-income condominium in a suburb of Massachusetts one evening, squeezing the interview into the everyday chaos of making dinner, overseeing their children's homework, washing clothes for school the next day, and helping Sandy's father convert a storage closet into a laundry room (unbeknownst to the zoning board, as Sandy recounted with a sly smile). As we ate homemade chicken soup from the crock-pot out of coffee mugs at the kitchen table, Sandy and Cody explained that they had gotten married in their late teens after Sandy became accidentally pregnant during her first semester of college. Nine years later, they have three children: a daughter, Riley, who is ten, and two sons, Timothy and Aiden, who are six and three. Lively and outgoing, the boys jumped from one couch to the other and watched cartoons and Riley ostensibly did her homework in the living room, artfully holding a book open while she watched the television screen out of the corner of her eyes. When her laughter finally gave her away, Cody threatened to write a note to her teacher that "Mommy and Daddy had to remind you to do your homework," but both he and Sandy were smiling, clearly charmed by their daughter's cleverness. In a moment that was both endearing and heartbreaking, Sandy confided: "The teachers all say she is awesome to teach, she has an awesome personality. But she just doesn't want to do her homework when she doesn't want to do it. She has to take special ed. reading. She loves school but can't keep up with the reading."

A few minutes later, their light-hearted tone disappeared as they confessed in hushed tones that they are struggling on Cody's income as a car mechanic and Sandy's tips from the lunch-time shift at a diner forty-five minutes away. Cody worried:

> The mortgage is three months behind and Verizon says we owe them $800. The heat bill is $1100. We are definitely in a crisis. Every three months, I get a bonus, and we are putting some aside for the mortgage. When it comes, it's $900 but we have to pay the mortgage for $1000, we also have the light bill and the phone bill.

While it may seem obvious to suggest that Sandy should be working more hours, or that perhaps they should move to a city with a lower cost of living, it turns out that Sandy and Cody have already tried these tactics. In order to save money on rent when their daughter was born, they moved into a one-bedroom trailer in a rural part of the state and asked Sandy's sister Lacey to move in with them and contribute to the monthly rent. Meanwhile, Sandy enrolled in a biomedical certificate program in Boston that was free to low-income mothers, hoping to increase her earning potential in the labor market. Yet they soon found that there were no jobs in close proximity to their home, and with only one car among three adults, their efforts to save backfired:

> s: It saved us a lot of money, staying there. But it cost us a couple of jobs, not being able to get to jobs on time because you are living out in the middle of nowhere. That cost us the job at Toyota.

c: That and my big mouth cost us Toyota. And we lost Sears.

s: He was always late no matter what we did. We had my sister at the time living with us and had to drive her . . . first thing in the morning we would get up at six with the baby. We were in the car, on the road, and that was forty-five minutes, to take Lacey to work. And then we would go another forty-five minutes to take Cody to work.

c: And then Sandy would go home. Then Lacey would get out of work at two and Sandy would drive forty-five minutes to get her. Come back until what, five, and then go to pick me up and drop me off with the baby. And then she would go to school in Boston.

s: I was doing a bio-tech certificate. I finished. But the question is now, daycare, cost of daycare and cost of driving into Boston and parking in Boston. By the time I get to work there, I am going to make $9 an hour. Why am I going to drive all that way to make that little? I have the certificate, and it was free school, a scholarship program, and I did it because I liked school.

Traditional conduits of adulthood are deeply gendered, dependent upon a division of labor that codes work as masculine and family as feminine. However, Cody cannot earn enough to support the family alone, and Sandy is torn between her role as a mother and her role as a worker (Hays 1996). Having abandoned her hope for a career in biotechnology—along with her hope for a fulfilling job and her pride in earning a certificate—Sandy squeezes in the lunch shift at the diner during school hours, sometimes bringing home only $40 a week in tips.[2] In today's increasingly individualized and competitive world, family-centered and career-centered markers of adulthood confront working-class young people as mutually exclusive, despite their best efforts to balance the two (Beck and Beck-Gernsheim 1995). Sandy and Cody are fighting to keep their family together despite the centrifugal forces that threaten to tear them apart—and this commitment incurs a heavy cost, especially for Sandy, who struggles to juggle poorly paid part-time work with mothering.[3]

The Heavy Burden of Racism

The ongoing struggle to find stable, living-wage work illustrated by Sandy, Cody, and Rob was magnified for black informants, who carried the additional burden of racism into the low-wage labor market.[4] For black men in particular, "not being called back" from job interviews was a particularly common and pervasive burden in the labor market, leading to reliance on contingent work and long, frustrating bouts of unemployment. Isaac, an earnest twenty-four-year-old black man who now works as a stocker and "full team member" at one of the largest discount retail companies in the United States, spent over a year after graduating from high school living with his mother, a prison guard at the nearby women's prison, and searching for a full-time job. Sitting in the cafeteria while he waited for his girlfriend's community college class to get out, he recalled: "I was going on interviews. I was calling people on the phone talking to people. And they were telling me they would give me calls back, never heard from anybody. And for a year and a half straight I was without a job. I was without money." Isaac's job search took on a desperate quality, as his need to ground his identity in paid work, self-sufficiency, and productivity only grew over the long, desolate months:

> I cleaned the house, I straightened up our basement. I would go outside three or four times, maybe walk up and down the highway. I would take care of the dogs. When it was time, like, you know in the summertime and the grass needed to be cut I'd cut that. I cut other people's yards. Something to keep my mind occupied until . . . You know there was a point where I said I need to get something. I would take anything. It doesn't matter if I worked at the Department of Sanitation. I just needed a job to do something with my time.

In this jarring recollection, Isaac sheds light on the emotional distress— and even desperation, as evidenced by his pacing up and down the highway and willingness to cut strangers' lawns just to be doing *something*—that is so often ignored in popular conceptions of the unemployed.

In a similar way, Grace, a twenty-five-year-old black woman, has looked all over Richmond and its surrounding areas for a job—she was aiming to make $8 an hour—since graduating from a state college two years ago. She eventually extended her search up through New Jersey, hoping to face less racial discrimination in the Northeast. "Richmond is, like, one of the most racist places in the world so I kind of grew up that way. I grew up that way and I carried it in my brain," she confided, then quickly shot me a look of alarm as if to assess whether I was offended: "I mean, I'm not saying like all white people are bad or anything like that, but it's like white people rule the world in a sense." As I nodded vigorously at her apt description, she continued, "They control whether or not you get a house or a line of credit from the bank, or a loan or a job."[5]

When Grace was finally offered a white-collar job in New Jersey, she faced a new dilemma: she could not afford to put first and last month's rent and a security deposit down on an apartment in her prospective new city. Currently, she is working a temporary job at a real estate office, living with her parents and feeling desperate to "get on [her] own and get out." When I asked her if she ever felt like giving up, she replied:

> G: Yeah. There's been plenty of jobs and I'm, like, no this is the last job I'm interviewing for. Because I've been on a lot of interviews. Out of state, in state, wasting gas. Buying suits, spending money I didn't have. You know, to make sure I look appropriate and all this etiquette, and all this other stuff and I just felt like it was a waste. You know, preparing for it mentally, I'm, like, okay they're going to ask me these crazy-ass questions. So sometimes I do feel like . . .
>
> JS: You just want to give up?
>
> G: Right.
>
> JS: What would you say is, like, the hardest part about growing up?
>
> G: Growing up. Like I think the realization that you're growing up or that the world is real.

Grace told me at the end of the interview that her dream was to open a sneaker store: "I got everything written up. I've been researching it for about a year now. I can't get the capital to open it up. That's my downfall. But if I could find a job to save the money . . ." About a year later, the last Facebook update I received from her read: "I'm staying busy with trying to open this sneaker store . . . as hard as it was [for you] finding 100 ppl to interview, I'm pretty sure it's gonna be even more difficult for me to find an investor." She closed with a smiley face.

The psychologist Jeffrey Arnett (2004: 16) labels the years between adolescence and adulthood as "the age of possibilities." The data tell the opposite story: in a competitive, bewildering, and precarious labor market, where racial inequality is perpetuated through hiring decisions and housing costs and families are subordinated to work, growing up means coming to terms with an impending sense of constraint toward their adult identities and futures (see Lareau 2003, 2008).

Privatization and the Burden of Risk

Working-class young men and women also report being crippled by the heavy burden of risk (Hacker 2006a). Unexpected economic and social shocks such as illness, family dissolution, disability, or injury leave them reeling, and they must rely on individual solutions—mainly their credit cards—to survive. At the same time, most believe that a stable and upwardly mobile life is possible if they only take the "right" risks, whether by borrowing money to pay their college tuition or even investing in a home. However, lack of accurate information, combined with pernicious financial practices such as subprime lending, circumscribe their attempts and often set them back, even further away from traditional milestones of adulthood. Within a context of privatization, managing flux and uncertainty in the present, rather than progressing toward a clear and knowable destination, defines the coming of age experience of the post-industrial working class.

Rebecca, a soft-spoken twenty-seven-year-old white woman from eastern Kentucky, told me her coming of age story over several hours and countless cups of jasmine tea. Rebecca's parents met in a coal mine, where her father worked his way up from carrying sticks of dynamite as a teenager to bolting the roofs when Rebecca was born. Her mother monitored the beltline, picking out the rocks and fossils as the coal passed by. When her father suffered a fall and was permanently disabled in the mines, he moved the family to central Virginia, where it was rumored to be easier to draw disability checks: "In Kentucky, there are a lot of people trying to get disability, and there really isn't much there because there are a lot of people, and my dad didn't want to be associated with that." After graduating from high school, she enrolled at a state university, hoping to fulfill her mother's dream of having a daughter who became a teacher. But Rebecca was put on academic probation after only a year because her Kentucky high school had not adequately prepared her for college coursework. "I struggled. I was all freaked out about writing," she said in a strained voice, reliving the panic and humiliation of her first semester of college.

During Rebecca's sophomore year, her college dreams continued to unravel:

> During that time I ended up plagiarizing my paper, so I can't go back to [college]. And it wasn't even intentional. I had a disk with notes and pieces from the Internet, you know, all on there to write my paper. And I plugged

in a paragraph of somebody else's words that I didn't mean to, at all. So the counselor I was seeing at the time had me start seeing another counselor there . . . and he was, like, you can probably get out of this if they know all the circumstances, but it was an emotional mess, so I didn't even go back to see him.

Feeling too emotionally distraught and overwhelmed to fight her way through the university bureaucracy, Rebecca dropped out of college and moved back in with her parents. Unhappy with her mother's eleven o'clock curfew, she moved into her car with a stray cat she found on the side of the road. "It was absurd," she laughed. "Just me and a cat that wasn't even mine, living in my car." Painfully putting her dreams of a college degree on hold, she found restaurant work, which she has been doing, in a variety of restaurants, ever since.

Rebecca's ideal job would be teaching at an alternative school for troubled youth, but her plans to pursue this path have been put on hold indefinitely:

R: Um . . . I have lots of debts. Right now, I have just been making enough to get by. I have my school loans, and then last year I blacked out and didn't have insurance, and I fell in my kitchen and got stitches.

JS: What happened?

R: They said it could be a mix of all sorts of things, like a little dehydration, but I never knew. I was making French toast and unloading the dishwasher, and I fell. I was very stressed, I was working at the diner, and then I was also working at a wine bar, which had just opened. And my plan was to leave the diner and work full time at the bar, but I couldn't make enough to do that. So I was just going at both ends. It was scary for a while.

JS: And you didn't have insurance?

R: Right, I went two years without insurance, like, "I don't need it until I am thirty!" It was the worst idea. [The stitches] cost over $2,000. That was one bill, and then there was a surgeon who was, like, another $3,000 to $4,000 and then there was another bill.

Rebecca put the medical bills on her credit card, and is still paying them off—at 24 percent interest.[6]

Rebecca's story illustrates the extreme vulnerability of the post-industrial working class to the lack of social protections from the market and the corresponding rise of ideology that constructs the self as solely responsible for one's fate. Creating a good life for oneself requires escaping the market through institutional protections, including tenure, subsidies for housing or education, wage regulation, labor laws, or health insurance (Sorensen 2000). Yet neoliberal policies have chipped away at these institutional protections, leaving Rebecca's generation on their own without a net—except, perhaps, for one made of plastic.

The men and women in this sample embrace the logic of individualism and self-reliance, gambling hard-earned money, stability, and self-worth in their quests to make it on their own. Most argued that economic stability and success could be theirs if they could only take the right risks, but their coming of age stories reveal that the odds are stacked against them. That is, taking risks in a context of neoliberalism means that they are betting against powerful corporations whose sole purpose is to make a profit (Hacker and Pierson 2010). They find themselves caught in a cycle of risk-bearing and risk-taking that drives them further and further into poverty and debt.

To provide an example, Alexandra is a striking twenty-eight-year-old black woman who grew up in a poor urban neighborhood with dreams of being a "model, a music producer with a glamorous life, or a school psychologist with a nice big office." While her mother struggled with a drug addiction, Alex was raised by her father, who had a GED and worked for a telephone company for thirty-one years. When she was five, her father enrolled her in a competitive state-funded program that bused urban students to prosperous suburbs for schooling. Upon graduating from her nearly all-white high school, Alexandra chose to attend a historically black college in the South in the belief that having a wide range of experiences and meeting a diverse array of people would make her a better person. Funding her education with a Pell Grant and a high school scholarship, she majored in criminal justice and graduated in four years, now envisioning a successful career as a lawyer.

Unable to find a full-time job upon graduation, however, she started out as a cashier at a jewelry store, and then found a job through a temporary agency at a law firm where the head lawyer was launching a real estate division. Highly motivated and eager to learn, Alex threw herself into every aspect of the new division, determined to make it a success. As she recalled, she researched real estate law, ordered titles, notarized forms, completed pre- and post-closing paper work, answered the phone, and even, she admitted while rolling her eyes, acted friendly and smiled a lot. Despite her efforts, the firm downsized a few months later, and she was laid off. Returning to contingent work, she temped at a bank, then another real estate law firm, and finally a phone company, taking reductions in pay and benefits as she went.

In her quest to get ahead, Alexandra bought an investment property with the goal of renting to tenants on the other side of town. When she signed the papers, she was slightly wary of the 13.75 percent interest rate, but her agent assured her that she could refinance in six months; later, she learned that she could actually not refinance for four years.[7] At the same time, she developed fibroid tumors, and accumulated $5,000 in debt when she underwent surgery without health insurance. Unable to pay her mortgage, she watched her house auctioned off, and while she later found out that she was part of a class-action suit for predatory lending, her credit score will remain dismal for the next seven years, which she worries will affect her ability to get a loan for law school. Reflecting on her coming of age journey, she forced a laugh: "I never thought I'd be working at the phone company like my dad."

As Alexandra's story reveals, extreme vulnerability to economic and social shocks like job loss and illness are exacerbated by unregulated and predatory lending, whether in the form of credit cards, car loans, or sub-prime mortgages. Together these forces make projecting their biographies into the future a perilous and often futile endeavor. Seven informants attested to watching their cars get repossessed or their family homes put up for short sale.[8] Craig, a twenty-five-year-old white server who grew up with dreams of singing on Broadway, complained of the tension that often arose when he borrowed his boyfriend's car to work the late-night shift. When I asked if buying his own car was a possibility for him, his face turned a deep shade of pink. He stammered:

> Um . . . I probably should have mentioned this before. The bank took all my savings because the car my mother had bought with me as the co-signer, in her name and mine, she stopped making payments on and they tried to re-possess. They charged me for the whole car, and my bank account was wiped out, and the credit counselor said that with $10,000 in debt the best idea was to declare bankruptcy. So I did. For seven years it will show that I declared bankruptcy. [The debt] was all taken off in the bankruptcy. It was so stressful and involved. I had to go to court and they read off my debts in front of a room full of people, which stressed me out.

In this passage, Craig recounts his experience of publicly declaring bankruptcy with shame and humiliation. The car dealership was eager to give him a loan—even though neither he nor his mother had steady jobs. The pervasiveness of this practice was thrown into relief for me one day when I drove down Middlesex Street in Lowell, where used car dealerships and fast food chains are interspersed with neon signs that boldly promise: "If we don't approve you for a loan, we'll give you $100!" When they could not make the monthly payments, Craig was left with the heavy burden of debt—one that limits his options as he strives to create a better life for himself by going to college. Taking full responsibility for his actions, Craig declared: "I am glad I did it, because I started over and I am a little bit smarter now."

Others reported running from creditors because they knew they could not repay the credit card debt they acquired in their late teens and early twenties.[9] Mindy, a willowy, blond twenty-four-year-old woman who moved out of her mother's house at eighteen to escape her controlling and derisive stepfather, explained:

M: I have a lot of expenses. I have a lot of credit card debt. I racked up a ton of credit cards when I was, like, eighteen to nineteen years old.
JS: When you were just trying to move out and make it on your own?
M: Exactly. It was so much, so, like, it's not enough because I have so many bills, but it's enough so that I can live off of.
JS: Are you making the minimum payments now?
M: Some of them, no, I'm not paying at all. I'm probably going to get a lawsuit from them. But I pay some of them.
JS: How much money do you have in debt, would you say?
M: I don't know at this point. I stopped opening my mail because I didn't want to know. Like I know probably it's not the right thing to do, but . . . I pay some, so say if I have an emergency, I still have one credit card that works.

As a teenager, credit cards seemed like a way out, like the safety net she never had. The deregulated credit card industry capitalized on her desperation, naiveté, and youthful desire to establish an independent life; when the low introductory rate exploded into hidden fees, endless penalties, and soaring interest, Mindy was saddled with a debt that she has no hope of ever paying back (see Draut 2005; Kamenetz 2006; Sullivan et al. 1999). Indeed, Mindy reports not knowing how much money she owes because she is too overwhelmed—or perhaps ashamed—to open her mail. As Mindy explains, she keeps one credit card up to date only because she knows she will likely need it in an emergency: what if she gets laid off or needs to go to the doctor? It is quite possible that she, like Craig, will come to consider declaring bankruptcy in a positive light, as her only chance at a fresh start. *But even bankruptcy is out of reach for some young adults.* Vanessa, who is currently unemployed, informed me, "My plan is to go bankrupt soon, and I had an appointment Friday with a lawyer. But I had to cancel it because the $100 I was gonna use, we need, so it's a vicious cycle."

The Military: Safety Net or Broken Promise?

As the stories in this chapter have revealed, young working-class men and women are struggling to maintain the most tenuous of grips on the American Dream. Whether plunged into debt from unpaid medical bills, held back by racism in their job searches, or realizing the impossibility of having both a fulfilling career and a family, their futures look bleak. I now turn to examine one possible on-ramp to upward mobility that many young adults reached for in their interviews: joining the military. By promising a steady paycheck, medical benefits, a daily routine, free college tuition, and even drill sergeants who would talk to them about their futures, the military appealed to young men and women as a beacon of security and choice in a storm of risk.

Scholars have pointed to the military as a vehicle for upward social mobility, especially among black youth (Kleykamp 2006; Moskos and Butler 1996; Segal 1989). As Kleykamp (2006: 276) explains, "The military is an especially important institution for minorities, particularly African Americans . . . the military may provide a source of social mobility for disadvantaged minorities during service because of the less discriminatory environment, steady employment that provides numerous benefits and compensation over civilian-equivalent jobs and especially because of the GI Bill benefits which can fund post-service college education." Of course, the military also entails a different sort of risk—of physical injury, trauma, and death, especially during times of war.

Through conversations with military recruiters at their high schools or even the local mall, older friends, and family members in the armed services, the military came to symbolize a rare opportunity to find direction, meaning, and economic security. For example, Ariel, a twenty-six-year-old white woman, desperately wanted to escape her job at Verizon:

> Out of high school, I worked at another stupid high school job, for like a
> year, and then I got a job at Verizon. I worked at 411, horrible job, don't ever

work there. . . . Oh my God, it was horrible, horrible! You would not believe the things that come out of old ladies' mouths. When they don't get the number to CVS, I am not kidding, like evil people—you wouldn't believe the way that people speak to the operator. It's just bad. I hated that job, honest to God, you would seriously commit suicide or at least think about it twice a day, it was that bad.

Additionally, "the pay sucked," so when her sister—who had joined the army several years earlier—suggested the National Guard, she jumped at the chance: "I needed something to do, I needed direction. I was uneducated, like, I didn't go to college, like an idiot. I was a big procrastinator in high school, partying and acting like a jerk, oh let's do drugs and drink pretty much. I needed something to do, and I thought that it looked better, it looked fun, and my sister had a great time at drill weekends." For other respondents, the military was an escape from even direr situations—bankruptcy or prison (Wilson 1987). When John, a twenty-seven-year-old black man who now works in clothing sales at a department store, witnessed his cousin (and fellow dealer) go to jail for selling drugs—"Times was so hard, the hood was gonna start taxing drugs"—he quickly enlisted to avoid a similar fate.

Respondents found comfort in the military's routines and rigidity. As Janisa, a thirty-three-year-old black woman explained, "My life is just one big mess. I think the best time so far was in the army. Everyone else dreads coming to drill, but I like to get away. Basic training, I thought was a vacation: you're telling me all I gotta do is keep my bunk cleaned and my shoes shined and you'll lay off of me? I can do that." Sennett (1998: 43) points out how "routine can demean, but it can also protect; routine can decompose labor, but it can also compose a life." The predictability and stability of military life—even in combat—allowed informants to gain a sense of control over their lives, often for the first time. The military was also a place where they felt safe to make youthful mistakes without paying the heavy emotional and financial costs they were accustomed to in the civilian world (mostly because the military needed their labor, but occasionally because a superior office took an interest in their well-being). Jalen, for example, admitted: "I did get in numerous amounts of trouble while I was in. . . . But I still got an honorable discharge because of the fact that they kept deploying me. It was like, the kid is going over here without question, so they gave me an honorable discharge."

The military created the perception of opportunities for respondents through the GI Bill and their new veteran status, which, as they learned from conversations with their superior officers as well as their fellow soldiers, dramatically increased their chances of making the hiring list for public service jobs such as police and firefighting.[10] A handful of informants were able to capitalize on these opportunities by earning coveted public sector jobs with good pay and benefits, which allowed them to buy homes and start families, or by finding civilian jobs that drew upon the skills they honed in the military, such as transportation or auto repair.

Benjy, a twenty-seven-year-old white man who admittedly had "no clue" what he wanted to be when he grew up, used his veteran status to bump up his position on the hiring list at the city fire department. Among working-class young people, firefighting represents one of the few remaining working-class jobs in the post-industrial economy that is stable; pays a living wage; provides benefits and a pension; and feels respectable, enjoyable, and meaningful (even more so than police work, which was off-putting because many young men had had negative run-ins with the law). Benjy is now married and plans to buy a house, and feels hopeful about and in control of his future for the first time: "Because I know this is my career. I don't have to search around or try to get certain jobs or whatever. I know this is where I'm going to be for thirty years."

Importantly, the five participants who attained firefighting jobs through their veteran status were male. Much of the stability of careers like firefighting or police work was hard-won by white, male unions struggling "heroically for a socially recognized male breadwinner wage that would allow the working-class to participate in the modern gender order" (Stacey 1998: 11). While affirmative action has to some degree opened up the ranks to men of color—in Lowell, for instance, I learned unofficially that one out of every three candidates for hire must be a minority[11]—firefighting remains a deeply gendered institution, as evidenced by the fact that fewer than 4 percent of the nation's firefighters are women.[12] Firefighting was inextricably intertwined with masculinity: as Benjy described the *one* woman in his firehouse: "She's more man than I am." The risks—of injury or even death—inherent in jobs like firefighting or police work were mitigated by the desire to prove oneself as a man (Silva 2008).

The military was not, however, a guarantee of upward mobility or even economic security, despite the heavy emotional and physical toll it took on soldiers who returned from Iraq with post-traumatic stress disorder, lingering injuries, and guilt over having survived when many of their peers did not. While twenty participants have some kind of present or former military experience, only five have been able to exchange their skills and veteran status for secure civilian careers. Why does the military's promise of upward mobility so frequently go unfulfilled? In particular, navigating the GI Bill bureaucracy upon returning to civilian life proves frustrating and fruitless. "I would have to get the paperwork to those guys, to those other guys, those guys over there, so it is kind of a run around. I hate paper work," sighed Rob, his lack of faith in bureaucracy, and a better future, overriding the potential for advancement. At the same time, fear—of taking risks, of being disappointed, of failure—also undermined young people's few chances at upward mobility through military service. For example, when I asked Rob if he would consider taking a full-time position in the army, he replied:

> I have been turning down promotions since my second year. I am an E4. I see some of the hassles that the higher ranks deal with, and I don't think I am leadership material. I work on my own, and I can help people work, but I am not really the guy to say, you and you, do that. Instead of delegating, I would put myself in the job. As a higher ranking NCO, you have other responsibilities to take care of and it wouldn't work out well for me. I really don't want them. If I had to yell at somebody, I would feel ridiculous, like who am I to yell at this person. It doesn't work out for me.

Lack of confidence in his abilities, combined with long-standing discomfort within and distrust of positions of authority, led Rob to undercut his potential for advancement.

For women, gender interacts with class position, structuring women's notions of what is possible and ultimately reproducing gender division and inequality. The women who became soldiers generally found these jobs meaningful and challenging, relishing the opportunity to prove themselves. Janisa stated defiantly:

> I see a lot of discrimination against women. Not in the National Guard, but on active duty. Well they think because you are a woman, you can't do the work, and I didn't like that. A couple of times I had to prove myself, um, I remember I used to get bored when we had nothing to do, and I would go down in maintenance and bust tires, you know, tires are, like, they're huge, just huge. So I would go and bust tires with the maintenance guys. . . . They would say, oh you can't do that, and I would say, oh yes I can, I can do anything I want to (Janisa, black female, thirty-three).

Despite the prevalence of this attitude, only two of the seven military women in my sample used the social capital (Putnam 2000) derived from their military experiences to attain stable jobs: both Ariel and Janisa work full-time in uniform, Ariel as a supply monitor and Janisa as a transportation specialist. The remaining five, however, treat the National Guard as a secondary weekend job despite having deployed several times, and work full-time in feminized professions such as customer service or retail. Other women in the sample mentioned that they had thought about joining the military but had encountered resistance from their families when they considered these careers. Kathleen, a white twenty-five-year-old, for instance, wanted to join the army and eventually become a police officer, but decided to work with troubled children instead: "My dad kind of made me promise that that's the one thing I wouldn't do. I'm daddy's girl, so he doesn't want to see me in harm's way." Two years later, however—and still without a stable job—Kathleen is once again considering the military.

Indeed, the dreaded alternative of dead-end, precarious service jobs prompts continual reenlistment because informants were convinced that just one more term would allow them to save up enough to pay off their debt or finally find the time to go to college.[13] As Rachel, who works at Best Buy and has deployed to Iraq three times with the National Guard, explained, "It's always something, one thing after another. That is one reason I reenlisted: I had to go to school. It's always something. I put in for an application, and then there is something else, and I have to wait. I keep reenlisting so that I will find time to get to school." Young men and women get trapped in a vicious cycle, embracing the risks of military service— whether driving convoys through Baghdad or patrolling in Afghanistan— as an escape from the insecurity and desperation of the civilian labor market.[14]

Learning Powerlessness on the Path to Adulthood

Experiences of confusion and frustration were not limited to the military setting; on the contrary, young adults striving for a better future—one in which they earned a college degree, wore "a suit every day," and "even owned things"[15]—encountered obstacles in a wide range of institutions that determined their futures. Whether unable to pay bills on time, fill out paperwork, or argue effectively within bureaucracies, informants could not figure out the logic of institutions and were left feeling overwhelmed, vulnerable, and inadequate. While the children of the middle class inherit the skills, resources, social networks, and knowledge required to succeed in the today's competitive, individualistic economy (Lareau 2003), working-class young adults like Jalen, Rebecca, Alexandra, or Mindy feel a sense of powerlessness and mystification toward the institutions that order their lives. Over and over again, they learn that choice is simply an illusion.

The most common site where this phenomenon occurred was education—the very place where they thought they could acquire the tools to change the direction of their futures. In our conversations, these men and women explained that they felt uncomfortable and unprepared in school, from elementary school and even into college. Daniel, a twenty-four-year-old white man who works at a video store outside of Richmond (at least until it is put out of business by online movie companies), was home-schooled by his mother after a fellow high school student held a pair of pruning shears to his throat. Distracted by the excitement of his part-time job at the movie theater, Daniel recalls floating through his schoolwork:

> We had this thing where you get this little book, there are twelve books per grade and you fill out the workbook. And I was sitting there and I was supposed to be working and I just held the pencil and looked like I was doing something, and every ten minutes I would turn the page. Then my mom caught on and yelled at me and I would bring out my books, I was just doodling and scribbling, and she would look at it and get upset and I would have to erase everything and do it all over again.

Daniel's parents believed in education as the key to success and tried to prepare him for college, but without college degrees themselves, they struggled to provide the necessary structure and skills for success. When Daniel enrolled at a private Christian college in the South, his "grades were horrible because [he] didn't do any work in high school." After paying for two semesters fully with loans, he failed out. To make matters worse, Daniel was blamed for property damage to his dormitory and continues to be hunted by debt collectors:

> It was damage to the dorm room and the main hall. Which I don't know how they blamed me for that, I think just because I was there and they said I did it. So I got it back to $20 and sent it to them, and now they are giving me a new bill for the whole amount again. And I don't know what happened but it really . . . I try to call them, and they say, call your Hire One account. So I call that office, and they say, You have an outstanding balance online, so I go online and they say to call the office. Back and forth. Then they say my account has been deleted. So I can't do anything. I don't know what to do with them. All I can do is look to the future and hope for the best.

The knowledge and skills required for successfully navigating bureaucratic systems continue to elude Daniel, leaving him feeling resigned to his powerlessness in the face of institutions, to say nothing of destroying his credit. He reflected, "I can't even get a bank account or a credit card. I can't even get one to store money in and put away and save. I bought a safe so I could keep my money in it but it's easy to pick that lock and I put money in and the next time I go in it, it's gone, probably someone [in his family] took it for gas or for a house payment." Daniel has not, however, abandoned his dreams of higher education; like Rebecca, he wants to be a teacher so that he can help children like himself. Indeed, I met Daniel in the courtyard of a community college, and our interview ended abruptly when he realized he was late for class.

Despite their belief in education as the path to upward mobility, pupils from working-class backgrounds who lack familiarity with the rules of the system enter with a structured disadvantage. Tracked into special education classes and suspended frequently for fights, some could not wait to leave the field of education, labeling themselves "idiots" who "sucked in school," and judging themselves unworthy of higher education. Others, however, could simply not afford to go (Leonhardt 2005). Alyssa, a twenty-four-year-old parking lot attendant, was admitted to a state college but left before completing her first semester because her family could not pay her tuition. She did not know how to apply for financial aid (or that the Free Application for Federal Student Aid, or FAFSA, existed). She recalled: "It was my mistake; I didn't really look for it as much as I should have. It was hard finding the time for everyone to sit down. I don't know much of our financial situation and I never had the time to sit down with my parents and sort it out. All that stuff."

In line with recent studies which have found that the majority of eighteen- to twenty-five-year-olds believe in the value of higher education, these young people buy into "an educational ideology that emphasizes 'college for all'" (Reynolds and Baird 2010: 168), about half of the young people I spoke with have pursued some kind of higher education. Yet the promise of college enrollment to lead to professional jobs and higher salaries most often went unfulfilled: sixteen dropped out or were expelled from community colleges or universities, while ten linger in a sort of educational limbo, mainly in community college, for much longer than the normative four years.

Aside from financial concerns, the other most common reason for leaving college before attaining a degree was fear that the cost of college would exceed the benefits; in these cases, the risk of debt, shouldered solely by respondents, felt too overwhelming.[16] Like many others, Ian, a twenty-eight-year-old white man who works in customer service at a grocery store, dropped out of community college because he could not decide on a major:

> I started with art, but I couldn't do the assignments the way I wanted to do them, or express them in ways I wanted to express because the ways I wanted to express them apparently were wrong. So I just gave it up. I switched my major to computers. I liked where it was going, but I didn't like the whole programming aspect. Unfortunately, this community college didn't offer a . . . they only offered, like, a computer programmer kind of SYS admin sort of thing. They didn't offer anything in the way of PC repair. So I was stuck taking that kind of course, and I really didn't see where it was going.

Working-class young people overwhelmingly believe that picking the "right" major is vital to future success. Rather than understand the college degree as a credential, they see their choice of major as determining their future trajectories. Describing her sister, who is now a nurse, Mindy explained, "I don't want to go to college for something I don't want to do, you know. My sister did that, she had to go again, so . . . Yeah, she found out she wanted to do something else and had to go again. I don't want to go to school twice." In these instances, the logic of higher education—that is, the knowledge that what you learn in college is often not explicitly connected to the requirements of middle-class, professional jobs—eludes them, leading to high financial and emotional costs.

For those who attained two- or four-year degrees, transitioning into professional middle-class jobs proved complicated.[17] Three women have associate degrees: one in nursing, one in business administration, and one in arts. The former two have used their qualifications to attain better jobs, Ellie as a registered nurse at a hospital, and Allie as a personal secretary. Both of these women earn enough money for rent and car payments, and feel secure in the labor market. Carley, however, holds an associate degree in arts that she paid for herself. Community college was appealing to her because of the small class size and flexible schedules: "If I went to a major university those big classes would be too much for me." Clearly uncomfortable in the field of higher education, Carley nonetheless earned a degree after several years of taking classes on and off. However, she cannot decipher how to exchange this form of institutional capital for economic capital in the labor market and continues to work retail at a local amusement park, earning enough money for her monthly car payments but not enough to move out of her parents' house. Now, she has decided to become a radiology technician after her neighbor told her about the good pay and benefits, but cannot afford to go back to school.

For Carley, as well as the seven other people in my sample who have attained or are in the process of attaining two-year degrees, it is clear that knowing how to use their education in the labor market is just as important as the degree itself. When young people cannot figure out how to use their degrees, community college simply acts as a holding pen for working-class youth slated to eventually enter the service economy—but with loan debt to pay off.[18]

This unpredictable relationship between higher education and improved labor market position holds true for young adults who hold bachelor's (n = 20) or master's degrees (n = 4). Fully half of these are currently in jobs that require only on-the-job training, including office work, medical billing, food services, and temporary labor. After seven years of attending various state and community colleges, Jay, a twenty-eight-year-old black man, finally earned a bachelor's degree. Yet his experience of college has left him angry, bitter, and disillusioned to such an extent that he now works in a coffee shop, unable to decipher how to use his communications degree to his advantage. He seethed:

> They tell everyone, to be something you have to go to college. So here I am, finishing high school, trying to go to college, and I get there and I don't know what I want to do. So I change majors every year. Sometimes I would be a major for one semester, I was dicking around, not knowing what I wanted. It was this thing where you don't know what you want until you have it and see if you like it. So I would try something out and it wouldn't work out and I would realize it was not for me. The problem is that it was taking up time and money, money I didn't have, my family didn't have. And financial aid, they are not there for people who dick around, they give you only so many chances, so it is, like, a really hard time, you know. . . . I graduated with a communications degree. Which ultimately I'm not even sure if that was what I wanted, but there was a point where I was, like, I have to pick some bullshit I can fly through and just get through. I didn't find it at all worthwhile.

Jay has abandoned his dreams of a professional career in politics. He feels lost when it comes to creating a narrative of self, unable to pin down the meaning of adulthood or to measure his progress going toward it. When I asked him if he "felt like an adult," he pondered:

I think about it all the time, I mean, Am I an adult? One of the things that really irks me about society . . . have you ever seen *Fight Club*? Well one of the things is like wanting to go back to a tribal way of living and the guy blames society for all of our problems, and one of the things I agree with is that we have no coming of age rituals that dictate when we are a man. Like, look at the Jews and Bar Mitzvah. There is some indication that you are now a man doing a ritual, or maybe a tribe back in the day would take you on a hunt and you might have ritual combat, but there was some sort of thing to elevate you into manhood, and we just don't have that. We're like . . . I mean does college really mean anything? These other things, rituals that make you a man, are usually functional, like you learn to hunt because you need to hunt to survive, but for instance college doesn't necessarily prepare you for anything. Are you a man afterwards? Adolescence seems to keep going on and on. Now our entire generation is lost. We're coasting and cruising and not sure about what we should be doing.

For the working-class young people in this study, social institutions confront them as obfuscated and difficult to navigate, leaving them grappling to define what it means to be an adult on their own. Unable to rely on traditional sources of social integration and identity, they feel profoundly lost, "coasting and cruising" on the long and winding road to nowhere.

The Remnants of the American Dream

But what about those who *do* have choices—who are able to achieve stable, economically secure adult lives? Upward class mobility does occur in the United States, although clearly less than our ideologies of meritocracy and individualism imply (Sawhill and Morton 2007). In this study, a small but not insignificant number of respondents were able to surpass their parents' standard of living by following the ideal-typical path from high school to college to a professional career such as teaching or nursing.[19] I close this chapter with an exploration of the skills and resources needed to achieve upward mobility—and traditional markers of adulthood—for the post-industrial working class. My data reveal that the often accidental transmission of middle-class social and cultural capital—rather than inherent talent or even hard work—provide a bridge to adulthood, allowing a few informants to move up the social ladder.

Will, a twenty-five-year-old white man, has not had an easy life. As a child, he watched his father turn to drugs and alcohol after an accident at work left him disabled. When his father overdosed on painkillers—"It was a lot of emptiness there, was it an accidental overdose? Was it suicide?"— Will's mom joined a hospice support group, where she met her current husband, the chief financial planner for the city. As a teenager, Will became close with his stepfather, who not only brought financial security to the household but also took an interest in his future. After spending weeks by his grandmother's bedside, Will was inspired by the deep level of care and support, and decided to become a nurse, paying for college through a combination of parental support and loans. After six months of work, he makes more money than his mother (an insurance agent). He also feels closer to his stepfather than to either of his biological parents: "I think I'm more in line with my stepfather, he has lived a lot, he's been places. I relate more to him and have more understanding for him that I do my mother. My stepdad understands me more than my mom does, she grew up in a southern Baptist church. I go to a Unity church, and she doesn't understand that. My stepfather is intrigued and asks questions."

When I asked Will if he believed he would continue to climb the social ladder, he answered affirmatively: "Through further work, through further education. The jobs I'll have, actually believing in myself. That's the main basis at the end of the day, actually believing I can do it." Will's narrative of self constructs his successes as solely personal, glossing over the ways in which the economic and cultural capital of his stepfather made possible his transition into the middle class. Indeed, his laudatory descriptions of his stepfather as having "been places," and "intrigued and ask[ing] questions" suggest that a middle-class tool kit (Swidler 1986) was transmitted at least partially to Will, who now feels more comfortable with his stepdad than with his mother. In drawing these connections, I do not mean to imply that Will did not overcome tragedy and hardship to make it to where he is today, or that he did not earn his success, but to point to the ways in which cultural and economic resources enable hard work to pay off.

In a similar way, Tom, an electrical engineer, described himself as "never really good at school," opting to attend a vocational high school where he could get practical experience in electronics. Tom's grandfather was an elevator operator, and his father continued the family tradition by becoming an electrician at a time when the field was open to high school graduates. When Tom graduated from high school, he assumed he would follow in his grandfather's and father's footsteps, but was told by his father and grandfather that he would need a college degree to do so, especially in light of his father's struggles to advance without one. After six years of attending college part-time (and partying a great deal), Tom finally earned a degree in electrical engineering and embarked on his career making $50,000 a year. He "absolutely love[s] the job" and has no trouble paying his bills. What separates Tom from, for example, Alexandra (who works for the phone company like her dad), is not motivation or talent, but instead the presence of opportunity—and the visibility of a well-worn path—to translate a college degree into a professional job. For Tom, the social and cultural capital accrued within his family made engineering a clear and natural career path. Similarly, respondents whose parents or family friends had knowledge of or experience within trade or government professions experienced entry into the labor market as less obfuscated. For most, however, parents could not transmit this kind of knowledge or connections; on the contrary, they were experiencing the same lack of choice—factory closings, insecure service work—in the labor market as their children. Accordingly, I now turn to life inside the family for working-class young adults.

3 | Insecure Intimacies

LOVE, MARRIAGE, AND FAMILY IN THE
RISK SOCIETY

N HER CLASSIC STUDY, *Worlds of Pain: Life in the Working-Class Family*, Lillian Rubin (1976) chronicles the lives of young working-class white men and women as they grow up, get married, and start families of their own in the early 1970s. Examining the paths that they took to marriage, Rubin reveals that getting married was often seen as an escape from repressive parental authority, symbolizing "a major route to independent adult status and the privileges that accompany it" (56). When Rubin asked her respondents why they got married, both men and women displayed a "seeming lack of awareness" (52), framing marriage—whether the result of accidental pregnancy or simply the desire to move out of one's parents' home—as the only logical choice. Their difficulty in explaining why they got married underscores that, just forty years ago, marriage was understood as a taken-for-granted, unexamined component of adult identity; as one man put it, "What do you mean, how did we decide?" (53).

The men and women in Rubin's study entered marriage with deeply gendered but unspoken dreams of the future: "For her, the realization of her womanhood—a home and family of her own. For him, the fulfillment of his manhood—a wife to care for him, sons to emulate him, and daughters to adore him. For both, an end to separateness, to loneliness" (Rubin 1976: 70). But economic hardship forced these young people to grow up quickly, and soon their dreams gave way to the hard reality of married life, where expectations of a "good life" shrank to signify one in which unemployment, violence, and alcoholism were rare. The women in *Worlds of Pain* were discontented by the lack of emotional connection in their relationships and the burden of balancing paid labor and child rearing. The men felt overburdened by the strain of providing for a growing family and angry at their inability to fulfill their wives' emotional needs. Still, they stayed married, anchoring their commitments in distinctive gender roles, mutual dependence, and, sometimes, a lack of alternative options.

Nearly forty years after the publication of *Worlds of Pain*, I sat across from Allie, a thirty-year-old white secretary, at a small Irish pub on the outskirts of Lowell. Allie launched breathlessly into her coming of age narrative before I could even open my menu. "In your early twenties you think you have it all mapped out already, and then life throws you a curveball, and you start at square one. And it is like, oh no, what do I really want out of life? Where do I want to go, what do I want to do?" I met Allie through her father, a white-haired police officer who eagerly wrote down her phone number on a paper napkin for me. "She's young, pretty, but just hasn't met the right guy yet," he beamed. What he left out of his description, I would soon come to find out, was that Allie was recently divorced. This omission proved to be an important clue in understanding the generational cleavages that divide Allie's visions of successful intimacy—and adulthood—from that of her parents.

Allie grew up in what Rubin (1976) would have termed a "settled" working-class family: her parents were high school sweethearts who married in their late teens, had Allie and her brother in their early twenties, and had weathered the ups and downs of marriage for over three decades. Brought up with "old school traditions and values," Allie lived with her parents while earning a two-year administrative degree and then began work as a secretary. At church with her family one Sunday, she ran into Jake, the son of her parents' old friends, and the two quickly became inseparable, marrying soon after she turned twenty-three. In hindsight, Allie explains that she was trying hard to follow the well-trodden path of her parents—even though something about it didn't quite feel *right*. Recalling the day Jake proposed, she confided:

We were at my parents' house and he came downstairs and said, "Close your eyes, I have a surprise for you." I was thinking he had candy or something. I probably would have been more excited about that. I could feel him in my face, like, "why are you so close to me?," and when I opened my eyes he was down on one knee with the ring. And I kind of, my heart sank, like this wasn't special. . . . I'm in my pajamas and I look like hell. So you know I acted surprised but I was so disappointed and I felt horrible that I felt disappointed. It just wasn't special and I think I knew then that it wasn't . . . that chemistry was missing. But hey, you live and learn. And I did not go through all that stuff to make that mistake again. Oh, no.

As Allie acknowledges hesitantly and even guiltily, what she wanted was *chemistry*—psychic satisfaction, a sense of uniqueness, of self-fulfillment. What she got instead was a relationship full of tension over housework, gender obligations, and money, culminating in the painful realization that they could not cope with the "pressures and expectations" of married life. Allie and I discussed:

A: We just grew apart. He . . . I don't want to say he was responsible, I am responsible for 50 percent of why it didn't work, even though I didn't realize that fully at the time. You know I went through a lot of counseling to get my head on straight again and figure out where I wanted to go and what I wanted to do and accept my part of responsibility for it not working. So, we had gone through counseling together as a couple too, separation counseling. Just to get us on the same track because I was the one that asked for the divorce. I was very unhappy and I knew that I couldn't make him happy. He really wanted a family and was pressuring me for it. At that point I didn't know if I ever wanted kids.

JS: What was holding you back?

A: Money. Money and, um, he was never home. And I felt like I was a single parent taking after him anyway because he is messy and I am like, there is no way I can have a baby and do this full-time and have the baby and him never home. We were barely scraping by as it was money-wise. I didn't think it was good timing, and there was a little missing maternal piece to me for a very long time. Until I had my nephews, I had never been around babies and I had no interest in them. And when we got married, we said next year we will think about it. Next year came, and neither one of us were ready, and the next year, he was like, I am ready, and I was still not ready. So we said okay, another year, and by that time, I was like, I don't know if I ever really want kids. I mean, you see how your parents' relationship went—they got married and had kids and bought the house at a young age, and my brother followed that too. . . . It's a lot of pressure being the black sheep of the family, divorced with no kids.

While Allie idealized her parents' smooth transition from marriage to children to home ownership in their early twenties, this path felt neither authentic nor viable to her. She undertook a central ritual of adulthood—marriage—but her performance felt empty: she could not convince herself of its legitimacy (Alexander 2004). Reflecting on their divorce, Allie sighed: "I feel like I am eighteen playing in the adult world."

In comparing Rubin's respondents to Allie, it becomes strikingly clear that the structure and expectations of intimate relationships in American society have shifted dramatically in the span of just one generation (see Gerson 2009). In this light, this chapter explores the meanings and experiences of intimacy among young working-class men and women, asking, How do working-class men and women imagine the ideal romantic relationship? And, can they put their ideals of love into practice in their everyday lives? Approaching love as socially and historically shaped, I begin by delving into the shifting cultural blueprints of love that shape—or constrain—the feelings, expectations, and practices of modern intimacy (Giddens 1991; Illouz 1997; Lamont 1992; Swidler 2001). I put inequality at the center of my analysis of intimacy, exploring how economic insecurity and lack of financial and cultural resources can make attempting—let alone achieving—committed relationships feel too risky.

The Intimacy Trap

Since the courtships and marriages of Allie's parents and grandparents, men's labor power has diminished, prompting women's mass entrance into the workforce.[1] The gendered division of labor at the core of industrial society has become unworkable, thereby releasing men and women from the traditional roles and expectations that once anchored partners, for better or worse, in the institution of marriage (Beck and Beck-Gernsheim 1995). Simultaneously, through its efforts to combat gender discrimination in the workplace; legalize no-fault divorce, contraception, and abortion; and promote educational equality, the Second Wave feminist movement also sparked a decline in the legitimacy of gendered marriage, empowering women to leave marriages that were unequal, abusive, or emotionally unfulfilling (Stacey 1998).

In the wake of these momentous social transformations, young people like Allie are finding that their relationships are less and less determined by external moral, religious, and legal codes. Consequently, intimacy must be increasingly negotiated "from individual biographies, from discussing and questioning each step, finding new arrangements, meeting new demands, justifying one's decisions" (Beck and Beck-Gernsheim 1995: 4). While Allie's parents' relationship was based on distinct social obligations, a gendered division of labor, a lack of choices, and a shared history that bound them together (Rubin 1976), Allie felt a strong pull to be true to her authentic feelings and protect her own interests (Bellah et al. 1985; Cherlin 2009). Enabled by her earning power in the labor market as well as the availability of birth control, she rejected the traditional role performed by her own mother: she became angry at her husband's refusal to share equally in domestic tasks and chose to postpone childbearing because she wanted, and needed, to continue to work full-time. Her husband, in response, felt betrayed by her rejection of traditional marital roles: like Rubin's male respondents, he yearned for "a wife to care for him, sons to emulate him, and daughters to adore him" even though he in turn could not fulfill the traditional, masculine provider role (Rubin 1976: 70).

Allie and Jake were thus trapped, haunted by the meanings of traditional adulthood but unable to make them work within the constraints of their daily lives. Ultimately, Allie prioritized equality and emotional satisfaction over marriage: she could not be happy in a relationship that forced her to pull a "second shift" of housework and sacrificed her interests, opinions, and desires (Hochschild 2003). In doing so, Allie illustrates the power of the modern cultural ideal of love and marriage as *therapeutic:*

> This therapeutic attitude . . . begins with the self rather than with the set of external obligations. The individual must find and assert his or her true self because this self is the only source of genuine relationships to other people. External obligations, whether they come from religion, parents, or social conventions, can only interfere with the capacity for love and relatedness. Only by knowing and ultimately accepting one's self can one enter into valid relationships with other people. (Bellah et al. 1985: 98)

As scholars of intimacy and modernity have documented, in place of traditional marriage, a new cultural ideal of romance and love has developed: a "pure relationship" of "sexual and emotional equality, which is explosive in its connotations for preexisting forms of gender power" (Giddens 1992: 2). The ethos of modern love is predicated on the autonomy, rather than the mutual dependence, of partners: "The principle of autonomy entails open discussion about the respective rights and obligations of the partners, and the contract may be renegotiated or voided if the relationship is perceived as unfair or oppressive" (Illouz 1997: 206). Marriage has been rendered more equitable, but also much more fragile.

Giddens (1992) celebrates the emancipatory features of modern intimacy, and he is certainly right to do so in the sense that the pure relationship empowers people—and women (like Allie) in particular—to hold greater control over their romantic destinies. However, as Illouz (1997) has demonstrated, making this new kind of relationship "work" in everyday life may require a particular set of emotional, linguistic, and material resources that are more accessible to the professional middle classes than to the working class. For Allie and her ex-husband, concerns about money, and the affordability and desirability of children in particular, drove a wedge in their relationship that ultimately led to their divorce.

The Changing Landscape of Sex, Love, and Marriage

Marriage and child rearing once represented core milestones of adulthood, yet their relevance to adulthood may be fading: while 95 percent of Americans consider education, employment, financial independence, and the ability to support a family to be important steps on the path to adulthood, only half believe that it is necessary to marry or to have children to be considered an adult (Furstenberg et al. 2004). Today's young men and women are waiting longer to get married, as evidenced by the fact that at age thirty, only 46 percent of women and 31 percent of men are married, compared to 77 percent of women and 65 percent of men in 1960 (Furstenberg et al. 2004). They are also less likely than their Baby Boomer counterparts to *stay* married—23 percent of marriages end in divorce in the first five years, while half of marriages end in divorce within fifteen years—or to have children all together (Cherlin 2009).[2]

While these statistics may be read as a commentary on the declining value of marriage and family, a closer look reveals that they are more accurately a story of inequality—not only of the economic benefits of married such as pooled material resources, but also of symbolic and emotional goods such as lasting ties, trust, and love itself (Illouz 1997). That is, national data reveal a growing "divorce divide" in the United States: since the 1970s, marital dissolution rates have fallen dramatically among highly educated men and women but remained steady among those with lower education such that women with a four-year college degree are half as likely as other women to experience marital dissolution in the first ten years of a marriage (Cherlin 2009; Martin 2004).[3] While nine out of ten college-educated women wait to have children until after they get married, only six out of ten with a high school degree postpone childbearing until after marriage, which means that the material and symbolic benefits of marriage (e.g., pooled income and assets, less financial risk in making large purchases) accrue to those already born in the top of the income distribution (Cherlin 2009). These patterns are particularly pronounced for black couples, whose divorce rate is even higher (Cherlin 2009).

Among the 100 working-class young people in my sample, only eighteen are married, while fifty-six identify as single, twenty-one as dating or cohabiting, and five as divorced. I find that most are trapped between the rigidity of the past and the flexibility of the present. On one hand, young people express anxiety over the fragility of commitment, yearning nostalgically for the lifelong marriages of the past. They long for enduring relationships, based not solely on personal happiness but also on transcendent roles and obligations that ensure stability over time. Indeed, many single men and women avoid entering relationships precisely because they would rather be alone than loosely and tentatively attached. On the other hand, respondents speak of a desire to form therapeutic or "pure" relationships that nurture their deepest selves, meet their personal needs, and, most important, do not weigh them down with emotional or financial obligations.

Economic and social vulnerability only exacerbate this tension: indeed, both models are rendered fragile by the strain of job insecurity and the privatization of risk. Among informants who were single (56), dating (21), or divorced (5), *fear*—of being deemed unworthy, of losing their selves, of betrayal, of failing and losing what little they have—dominated their experiences in the romantic sphere. For those who were married, the family became a constant battleground where they wrestled with these fears and their longing for solid, lasting ties. In an era when economic and social shocks such as job loss, illness, or disability are the responsibility of the individual alone, intimacy becomes yet another risk to bear, especially for black men and women who carry the additional burden of racism in both the labor and the dating market. The unpredictability, insecurity, and risks of everyday life come to haunt young people *within* their most intimate relationships, not only by shrinking their already limited pool of available social resources but also by disrupting their sense of security, destabilizing their life trajectories, and transforming commitment into yet another risky venture. Children remain the last bastion of commitment and stability—yet the social institutions in which young parents create families often work against their desire to anchor their lives in connection with others (Edin and Kefalas 2005; Silva and Pugh 2010).

The Impossibility of Forever

Despite the rise of egalitarian relationship ideals, men in unstable, low-paying service jobs feared that they could not adequately fulfill the traditional provider role and thus avoided entering into relationships despite their longing for intimacy. Kevin, a white customer service representative at a grocery store, told me that relationships were "way in the back burner" because of his unpredictable and demanding work schedule at the twenty-four-hour grocery store:

> Oh man, I mean, yeah, I would have a girlfriend, but I don't know if I would really have a lot of time. I just would want to make sure I had time to spend with her, especially working here, since I never know what hours I am going to be working. It would be hard because I couldn't say, I can be there, or we could go out this time . . . and you know, women have needs.

The fear that he could not meet his partner's needs because of his long and irregular hours prevents Kevin from even trying to have a girlfriend. Instead, he takes refuge in daydreams of the stability and commitment of a time past that seemed more nostalgic than realistic given the fragility of the post-industrial working-class family:

> Mainly I'd like stability out of life. It sounds kind of corny but I just want to be one of those pops who sits in the armchair with my wife, watching the *Dick Van Dyke Show* and stuff like that. Growing up, like I said, I moved around a lot and I never really had a solid family structure so that is something I have always wanted. Quiet, secure household, where everything is fine. And, I mean, everybody would like to have a lot of money, though whether or not you need it is a different story. I would just like to feel comfortable, stable.[4]

Andrew, a twenty-seven-year-old car mechanic, also described his vision of successful adulthood in terms of lasting commitment and trust:

> Like I have always pictured growing up as not so much having a set career, not even so much a picture perfect life, but I want, you know, a wife, you know, somebody that you can trust 110 percent. Because if you don't have that, you don't have anything. I want two kids, maybe three, and I just want to live my life so that my wife doesn't have to work if she doesn't want to. I mean if she does, then she does, but if she doesn't . . . my kids will be

taken care of. All the things I had to work for when I was a kid . . . I want to be able to give my kids all the stuff my parents couldn't give me. It's the big picture. It's not, "I want to be a firefighter when I grow up." It's the big picture, just being able to get old with somebody and know that you did the best you could.

On one level, these men mourn the loss of (white) male labor power, longing to return to industrial working-class life where work was coded as masculine and the home and child rearing as feminine (Chodorow 1978). Men base their narratives of who they are and what they want to become on cultural definitions of men as providers—even as their loss of earning potential prohibits them from translating these visions of (masculine) adulthood into reality. As Zerubavel (2003: 39) elucidates, "We feel particularly nostalgic about those parts of our past that seem most hopelessly irrevocable. . . . We likewise experience nostalgia during periods of dramatic change." On another level, through conjuring up nostalgic images of white picket fences, the *Dick Van Dyke Show*, and love that lasts forever—which stand in sharp contrast to their own pasts, characterized by family dissolution, economic hardship, and a pervasive sense of social unmooring—they also reveal a sense of profound dissatisfaction with the flux and instability of modern family life.

Deeply forged cultural connections between economic viability, manhood, and marriage proved especially devastating for black men who, struggling with long bouts of unemployment and discrimination during the Great Recession, often avoided committed relationships all together.[5] Without a stable economic foundation, young men forsake the possibility of commitment because the idea of taking care of someone else feels too perilous. As Brandon, the thirty-four-year-old black man who manages the night shift at a women's clothing store, explained, "No woman wants to sit on the couch all the time and watch TV and eat at Burger King. I can only take care of myself now. I am missing out on life but making do with what I have." These men avoid monogamy not because they reject marriage and family but because cultural definitions of masculinity as economic viability remain at the core of their visions of adulthood. Watching marriage and children pass them by triggers feelings of loss, revealing a deep cultural anxiety concerning the fluidity of adulthood and the uncertainty of the future. Douglas, a twenty-five-year-old black man said wistfully, "People used to get married at twenty-one. You don't see that anymore. Trust is gone. The way people used to love is gone." At the same time, knowing they are being evaluated shrewdly for their earning potential breeds a sense of resentment, one that makes marriage morally question-able. Nathan, a twenty-five-year-old black man who works the night shift as a medical biller, began the interview by joking that "twenty-five might be the year for monogamy." But he grew serious when I probed him about the meanings and possibility of marriage: "Nowadays, it seems like more of a hustle, honestly," he fumed. "'I need a ring' and everything, like you don't need that really. Why do we need to be legally bind, you know what I'm saying? It's a hustle."

"What Are You Going to Do as My Man?"

Black men's profound economic disadvantage, which often translates into an aversion to monogamy, profoundly affects black women who seek future-directed and committed men. Grace, a twenty-five-year-old black woman who has worked as a temp since graduating from college, sees herself as an entrepreneur, and she is driven and determined to start her own sneaker company as soon as she can find the financial backing. While she describes herself as "career-focused" right now, she would like to eventually get married, but has not dated at all in the past year.

> JS: What would you say that you are looking for in a person?
> G: His ability. The last guy I was with didn't know, like, he didn't have a brain or something. He didn't know what he wanted to do. In five years he was just kind of annoying. Just floating. I can't deal with that. I need some answers, you know.
> JS: You want some direction?
> G: Right. He had no direction. And he was almost ten years older than me. That really bothered me.
> JS: Yeah. That's what I hear a lot from people. Either that they want someone stable or they want someone they can trust.
> G: Right. He lied a lot too.

While the men in this study like Brandon and Nathan experience the labor market as stultifying, extinguishing their hopes of upward mobility over and over again, women read men's failure to move forward in life as a character flaw, often deciding they are better off alone. As Hill (2005: 111) explains, "For more privileged Blacks . . . marriage may make sense economically, yet poor women are not apt to want to sacrifice what little autonomy they have in exchange for a man who is unable to improve their standard of living."

While avoiding commitment, for men, is justified as an outcome of their inability to fill traditionally masculine obligations, it is experienced by women as pure selfishness. Women bemoaned the lack of commitment among men their age. As Sasha put it:

> It's like guys aren't on the same level as females when it comes to dating. It's like they can't be happy with just a slice of cake. They have to have like four or five slices of cake even though they're full off of the one piece. You can do the same thing with that one slice of cake that you do with all the other slices. I don't know if it's just a maturity thing, like guys don't fully mature as quick as females, but I have certain standards that I have when I wanna be dating someone.

Humorous cake analogy aside, deep fears of not being deemed good enough—and ultimately of betrayal—leave Sasha wary of committed relationships.

Candace, another young black woman, explicitly addressed the race-based inequalities that frame her experiences of dating. Reflecting on her past romances with working-class black men, she explained, "They were extremely nice to me. What little they did have, they did give. Time and being around and listening. That stuff is all good, but I was like, any average Joe can do that. I have friends who can do that. What are you going to do *as my man*? Because I'm doing everything as your woman, what are you going to do?" Setting herself apart from the women she grew up with—"I got my stuff together and I ain't knocked up and ain't on drugs"—she demands a relationship in which both partners contribute equally, both emotionally and financially. While she recognizes that existing social inequalities make it so that white, middle-class men are more likely to be able to meet her needs, her one attempt at dating a white man from college left her unsatisfied:

> There's this white guy who really, really likes me. First of all he's not like a black man. So, like, he pretty much has his stuff together. Except that he just, like, he is just emotionally needy. And I can't deal with that. I'm, like, you are worse than my mama. And I'm telling you I don't want a boyfriend, but I'll be a good friend. And you're telling me, oh I don't meet a lot of girls in college and I think you're special. That's all fine and dandy. But I don't want nobody right now. I can't take nobody right now. And you obviously couldn't even take it if I broke up with you. I went to Ruby Tuesday, Jen, and I never seen a black man cry. In public, [this white man] cried at Ruby

Tuesday, Jen. I told him I didn't want to be with him, like I've been telling him for the past months, and he cried at Ruby Tuesday.

Like Grace, Candace views herself as fiercely independent and simply bursting with potential; she therefore wants a partner who can contribute to a relationship both economically and emotionally. Deeply critical of black men—her anger only thinly veiling an intense sense of betrayal—she believes that dating a middle-class white man she met in college might be her only chance at achieving both security and equality. At the same time, she remains attracted to a very traditional working-class masculinity, as evidenced by her shock and disgust at her admirer's public crying. She mused, "I know what white families look like and how they have it together. But I want to be . . . I would want to have a black family. But then I don't know if that's racist of me, or if that's just me being, like, inconsiderate, or me just being stuck in the past, or me just being unfair." In this scenario, Candace's romantic desires do not match her financial interests. She is avoiding committed relationships until she can figure a way of out this trap.

Protecting the Fragile Self

White women also expressed fears of commitment, though these revolved around fears of losing the *self*. Kelly, a twenty-eight-year-old line cook, told her coming of age story as a long process of learning to trust and rely only on herself to survive. Over the past ten years, she has struggled to survive, living off and on in her car and battling a drug addiction that was memorialized by the faded scars that lined her arms (see Chapter 5 for an in-depth examination of narratives of addiction). Kelly has fought hard for her present sense of sobriety, independence, and security. When our conversation turned to relationships, she said that while she liked "the idea of marriage," she was not actively pursuing it:

K: I like the idea of being with someone, but I have a hard time imagining trusting anybody with all of my personal stuff which is a really big part of being in a relationship. It's being able to share and trust and that's something that I do when I'm in a relationship is I try to edit out things, not like facts but parts of my personality. And I found that I was just turning into someone I really didn't like. Like in the process of editing out the crazy parts of myself, I was also editing out the interesting parts too and just found like I was becoming someone who was just really bland, insecure, and that's not what I wanted to be.

JS: OK, so you'd rather . . .

K: I'd rather be alone and be fierce than be in a relationship and be milquetoast.

Kelly's relationship ideal is based on therapeutic notions of sharing one's deepest self; she will not sacrifice this ideal—or the "crazy parts of [her] self" it upholds—in order to ensure that a man stays with her. Her sense of self, while hard-won, is also tenuous, and she cannot risk losing it in a relationship with someone else. For working-class women who have grown up shouldering immense social and economic burdens on their own, depending on another person feels too perilous. Thus, they view therapeutic ideals of romance as liberating (Illouz 2007)—even if it means being alone.

This fear of losing oneself also came through strongly among the three white women who identified as lesbians. Monica, a thirty-one–year-old art student who previously worked as a truck driver, has decided to postpone committed relationships until she feels more stable with who she is.

JS: So you don't want a lifetime partner right now?

M: Not at all. Because I get, like, too wound up, and spend too much time in the relationship and then kind of lose track of what else is going on in my life. So yeah, I really need to be single right now. It's hard. I get so meshed and like . . . I even lose sight of what I like to do. All things that are, like, true to me. And then when I get out of the relationship I'm like . . .

JS: Where am I?

M: Where am I? Why do I sew now? I don't even like to sew.

Similarly, Lauren, who has been on her own since her father kicked her out of the house for being gay, did not want a partner who would threaten the autonomy that she had fought so hard for: "I want someone who has, you know, similarly overcome their respective obstacles and learned and grown from them, rather than someone who is bogged down by it and is always the victim." Thus, while she longs for a "Princess Charming" to share her life with, she will not risk being with someone who will drain her emotionally. When lesbian women lose their family's (and the larger society's) support, they learn the vital importance of being able to make it on their own.

For other white women, however, this seeming freedom paled in comparison to the imagined stability of the past:

> Like I said, I'm one of those women . . . not a lot of women want to be barefoot and pregnant and be a housewife, and that's what I wanna do. I would love to meet a man who wanted to work all day and come home and have dinner, and I could stay home and garden and take care of the kids. I love to do all that, so being a woman to me is . . . gender issues are not a problem. I'm happy being a woman and I'm happy being taken care of, and hey if you don't want me in your club because I'm a girl, who cares; I'll go join a girl club, whatever.

In this passage, Delores gives voice to a backlash against feminist promises of egalitarian gender relationships. Indeed, the "unsettling conditions of postindustrial society and the global economy only seem to have intensified cravings for security," fueling a desire to return to both the restrictions and the protections of the industrial family (Stacey 1998: 260).

Commitment as Risk

Working-class young adults learn early on that commitment, rather than a hedge against external risks of the market, is simply one demand too many on top of the already excessive demands of the post-industrial labor force. Many remembered watching their families torn apart by the strain of underemployment, disability, illness, drug and alcohol abuse, and prison. Women in particular often spoke of learning relationship lessons from their mothers' mistakes. Wanda, a twenty-four-year-old black woman, has watched her parents continually separate and get back together for the past decade. As she described them: "My dad is a con artist. He's like a . . . you know what I'm saying? So my mom, she's real weak towards that and just seeing what kind of man he is, what kind of man all those people are, I just was never really looking for a relationship." Amber, who is in a relationship but choosing to delay marriage, mused, "I would say my mom is somebody who never had a chance to grow up and kind of got sling shot, like she started having kids when she was eighteen, didn't have any idea what she was doing. And kind of got sling shot into being an adult." With their own families in the background as cautionary tales, fear of investing time and emotional energy into a relationship that could ultimately fall apart prevented many young people from pursuing romantic relationships.

Jillian, a twenty-five-year-old white woman, felt regretful and somewhat embarrassed by the fact that she had never had a serious boyfriend. Intensely focused on saving money, paying the rent on her own apartment, and buying a car, Jillian has worked seventy hours a week at a local tavern since she graduated from high school, leaving her little time or energy to date. The only steadily employed member of her family, she has also helped keep her relatives afloat, paying the rent on her mother's ice-cream shop in the winter when business was slow, sending money to her sister when the car broke down or the kids needed school clothes, and even paying her brother's college tuition on her credit card (he was supposed to pay her back but hasn't yet, a source of deep family strain).

Emotionally and financially drained, Jillian finds it "very scary to not have a future planned out yet" but is too afraid to lose what little stability she has to take out school loans or move to a city with more employment opportunities. This fear of taking risks extends to the realm of intimacy, where she dreads investing time and emotional energy in a relationship that may ultimately fail: "Because I feel I'm in it for the long haul. I don't get like the one-night stands and stuff. You're either in it, or you're not." Having spent her life fighting to keep economic and social insecurity at bay, Jillian views the modern relationship ideal—in which partners must negotiate the meanings of commitment, love, and sex at every stage—as too risky (see also Beck and Beck-Gernsheim 1995; Bellah et al. 1985; Giddens 1992). Reflecting on the meanings of adulthood, Jillian explained:

JILLIAN: I've really been focused on work and saving money, to be able to go out and get a car and get your own apartment or something. So that's where I've been. But now I'm like, yeah twenty-five and you know. I never really wanted to get a boyfriend. Because I feel I'm in it for the long haul. My friends are like, oh just have a boyfriend for a week, who cares. That's just not fun for me. If I'm in a relationship, I'm in a relationship. Whether it's a friendship, a working relationship, a boyfriend. I can't do it half-ass or like sometimes. You're either in it, or you're not. So maybe when I move. It's definitely lonely not having a boyfriend and would love to have a boyfriend, but if I want to move, I just don't see how I could make a relationship work.

JS: Do you have ideas about the kind of guy you'd like to find?

JILLIAN: Yeah. My friend really makes fun of me for that. She says, well if you're looking for that you need to go to church. Because I'm looking for a guy that, like, you know, I think sex comes in a relationship once it's solidified and means something and it's long term. So I need a guy that's going to be patient and wait, and that's extremely difficult to find in a mid-twenties guy. You know, that's willing to make the relationship work before sex, so that's difficult. I want a guy that's romantic and is in it for the same reasons I am. You know, wants to make it work and long lasting. You really don't find a guy in their twenties that's looking for, like, a deep meaningful relationship.

Like the vast majority of respondents, Jillian watches anxiously as conventional milestones of adulthood pass her by, keenly aware that she has veered sharply off the taken for granted path to adulthood: "It is very scary to not have a future planned out yet. And being twenty-five, it's like okay, in a few years I want to start a family. You know, I don't want to be a first-time mom at forty. You want to be a young mom. So starting a family around thirty or so, it's like I have five years to get my shit together. So yeah, which is definitely not going to happen."

Paralyzed by Fear

Fear of losing what they already have also keeps young men and women from moving from cohabitation to marriage.[6] Andrew, the white mechanic highlighted earlier who has always dreamed of "just being able to get old with somebody and know[ing] that you did the best you could," moved in with his girlfriend but has no plans to propose:

A: That's kind of touchy too because I have had a lot of really great women, and the problems I have had are commitment issues that I needed to work on. I have had a lot of great girls and you know I got rid of a lot of great girls. Women are tough. It is tough. Because, like, just the type of family I have been brought up with, they all get married and stay married, you know, so when I get married I am only going to get married once. So, you know, I think I have lost one really great girl because, you know, I had doubt issues and stuff like that and it is kind of tough. Finding girls is easy; making sure they're the right one is tough.

JS: Do you think as you get older, you become more trusting?

A: No. I don't think so. Like, I mean I have less commitment issues but I still have the same problem where I really pay attention to the way somebody is because the big picture is long term and I only want to do it once so . . . it's tough. Like the commitment issues I guess are, I mean I have become easier, like, I am not the type of person to cheat and there are so many people out there, it's be single or be with somebody but if you are with them, give them everything you've got. If you don't do that, you probably don't want to be with them.

He stays with his girlfriend for the time being because he does not want to be alone, but he is not convinced she is the "right one." When I asked him to define the qualities he is looking for, he replied, "I really think that the biggest things are trust and somebody that is caring, genuinely caring, cares about themselves as much as they care about other people. Really confident in who they are." In desiring a partner who is self-confident, Andrew echoes therapeutic relationship ideology, which holds that "only by knowing and ultimately accepting one's self can one enter into valid relationships with other people" (Bellah et al. 1985: 98). Yet the therapeutic logic also holds that "no binding obligations and no wider social understanding justify a relationship. It exists only as the expression as the free selves who make it up. And should it no longer meet their needs, it must end" (ibid.: 107). Because Andrew simultaneously longs for the unquestioning commitment his parents seemed to have, he is trapped between two competing cultural logics of romance—traditional and therapeutic—that leave him perpetually seeking (Swidler 2001).

Elliott, a firefighter who lives with his girlfriend and their two-year-old son, is afraid of solidifying his commitment to his girlfriend in marriage: "We are both, like, if it ain't broke, don't fix it, and we're fine. You don't have to be married to file your taxes even, not in Massachusetts anyway. So what's the point?" Similarly, when I asked Heather, a twenty-six-year-old bartender who has been with her boyfriend for nearly ten years, if she wanted to get married, she replied, "No. I like the way it is right now." Heather went on to say that she might consider getting married if she could find a job that was more stable; as it is, she works six nights a week, often not getting home until 4 A.M. For her, holding onto the stability of her relationship, especially in light of her uncertain work hours, is more important than marriage.

From the Nuclear to the Negotiated Family

For the eighteen informants who are married, troubles with intimacy do not magically stop at the altar. Marriage became less of a stable ending and more of a constant negotiation. Couples find themselves trapped between two competing logics of what love should be (Swidler 2001), yet unable to put either into practice.[7] On the one hand, they attempt to create traditional, two-parent households with clearly divided gender roles, only to find that they do not have the economic means to realize this goal. On the other hand, they also try to forge therapeutic relationships that foster the growth of their deepest selves, yet quickly learn that self-realization requires resources that they do not have. In a cultural context in which marriage is voluntary and ultimately terminable, couples must decide daily whether commitment and permanence (for themselves and for their children) is worth the sacrifice of their individual desires and needs.

Maintaining a traditional nuclear family in today's precarious labor market is difficult and sometimes impossible. Kiana and Curtis are a young black married couple I met while conducting interviews at a National Guard drill weekend. When Kiana became accidentally pregnant after dating Curtis casually for a few weeks, she panicked: "Me personally, I was gonna get rid of my baby; I know that sounds awful, but at the time, I was like what do I do? I had all these other plans."[8] Yet after talking with her best friend, who had had an abortion and regretted it, Kiana decided she could not go through with it: while she could separate sex from marriage, and love from sex, she still maintained a belief in the primacy of motherhood. For Curtis, marrying Kiana and being a father to their child confronted him as the obvious and only choice:

> Well, when she got pregnant it was just more of . . . My father has taken care of me all of my life. My father had a meal on the table every night for us to eat. It wasn't though that I had a father who just had, you know, he did what he could; no, my father gave his all into making sure he raised us and did a good job in doing it. So I can't be that one to just sit there and have my own and not do the same thing and give it my all. So once she was pregnant it was just, I got . . . It is not even . . . I love her but at the same time I just felt I had to be for what was my . . . I brought that into the world, so I can't just call it and that be OK. No, that is not me. I need to see that, I want to be there from the time she opened her eyes until I'm gone. I want to be there. So, I mean once she got pregnant she was pretty much, yeah, you're mine.

Here, he struggles to find the words to express a deep and unquestioning belief in marriage and fatherhood. As he explains, it is not simply "love" that anchors his commitment but a deep sense that he owes his child everything that he is and has.

The traditional nuclear family structure, however, continues to elude this couple. Curtis has been unemployed since his last deployment, and while his status as both a minority and a veteran should help him attain his goal of becoming a police officer, hiring freezes in the civil services have kept him on the reserve list. Kiana is trying to get into nursing school, juggling community college classes with a job at a medical billing firm that fortunately allows her to bring the baby to work. The couple has moved in with Kiana's mother, and the three adults pool their resources, with some additional help from WIC, just to stay afloat.[9] It is clear that working-class people who privilege traditional gender roles and family obligations over individual autonomy in this uncertain and risky labor market do so at a permanent disadvantage. Furthermore, while currently happy in her relationship, Kiana still allowed for the possibility of its ending:

> I don't have qualms now; it is what it is, make the best of the relationship, you know. If it ends, it ends, but I am going to be happy, because I got my daughter, and I am glad I found somebody to be happy with. Because, say, even if I died and he lived and remarried, or if we split up or whatever the situation is, I will always still be his friend, because he gave me my daughter.

While Curtis looks backward to the past to explain his commitment to her family, Kiana looks forward to the uncertainty of the future: it is only her relationship with her daughter that she sees as unquestionably permanent.

Married women also spoke of sacrificing earning potential in order to make some semblance of the nuclear family possible (Waldfogel 1997). For Toni, a twenty-seven-year-old woman with a degree from a historically black college, making her marriage work was more important than finding the job of her dreams. Thus, she decided to work as a low-paid medical biller while her husband, who had to drop out of college, completed basic training in the army and waited to find out where he would be stationed: "Right now I am withholding from trying to find a career of my dreams for the simple fact of my husband; I don't want to find my job here and then have to leave it. So I'm not really where I want to be right now."

Liberated and Lonely

Despite the desire for both partners to feel self-actualized at work, only one couple was truly able to make this work in practice. Neil, a thirty-two-year-old black man who started his own educational consulting business and makes almost $80,000 a year (by far the biggest earner in the sample), has been married to his wife Celeste for almost four years. Neil is from Flint, Michigan, the de-industrializing, economically devastated community made famous by Michael Moore's (1989) *Roger and Me*. His mother, who divorced his father before he was born, migrated from the South during the automobile boom and worked on the factory line at General Motors. When his older brother went to prison for robbery, Neil's mother was determined to set Neil on a different path. He earned a scholarship to a state college and became a teacher. He now lives in Virginia and runs a consulting business.

As a couple, Neil and Celeste share many activities: they run together, play tennis, volunteer for Habitat for Humanity, and put on college fairs at the local high school. At the same time, they are passionate about self-growth—Neil just finished reading an Oprah Book Club favorite called *A New Earth: Awakening to Your Life's Purpose*—and support each other's quests to be firmly autonomous individuals by spending hours discussing their personal goals. In response to my question about perceived risks, Neil—who is sheltered from nearly all the risks faced by other respondents because of his strong foothold in the labor market—mused:

> Risks . . . good question. Um, I guess just doing what we're supposed to do, as far as what we are working for . . . making sure our lives are full of purpose, not accepting just anything but really making sure it's in line with the goals and visions we both have. Picking something that's not in line would be a risk. You know, for a time my wife didn't work for three months; she was trying to find what she wanted. I said, take your time, don't just take anything, decide what you want. Don't settle. If you get complacent, it will spill over.

Part of what Neil values about his wife is that she freely expresses what she wants and pursues it, even if this means she has to take three months off from work. Within the therapeutic logic, "The ironic consequence of passively adapting to others' needs is that one becomes less valuable, less interesting, less desirable" (Bellah et al. 1985: 92). While most couples put children at the center of their marriages, Neil and his wife have put off the decision to have kids, explaining, "Lately, because she travels so much and her job . . . now our little running joke is that we don't talk about kids unless other people bring them up. We're good. When we moved to our house, we were, like, this could be the baby's room. It is now the relaxation room; we go in there and journal and read." Cultivating their selves alongside each other, rather than anchoring their commitment in shared obligation, gives this marriage its strength and propels it forward. They are the embodiment of the pure relationship.

For most couples, however, early childbearing and acute economic hardship lead to a marriage rife with conflict and confusion. Sandy and Cody provide a telling example of this trap. On the one hand, they each want to grow as individuals, meeting their own needs even if that means sacrificing those of the family; in this way, they consider divorce as a solution to marital dissatisfaction. Painfully recalling the day when she found pornography on Cody's computer and a box of condoms in his car, Sandy steeled herself against the possibility of future betrayal: "I'm definitely in a place in my life where I would just be done, and I'm okay with it, and he knows, which I think is why it's over. I wouldn't be crying in the corner wondering why."

Through intense counseling, they have learned to communicate in the therapeutic language of individual needs. Sandy elaborated: "He had to do a lot of what he had to do . . . a lot of becoming okay was, I am gonna do me and what I need to do, you're gonna do what you need to do, and if we figure it out, we figure it out. We have kids to worry about. We can't keep fighting. Physical fighting, verbal fights, a lot of stuff that shouldn't have happened in front of children that definitely did. It just became a point where . . . we are gonna do what we have to do, and if it works, it works." Cody now describes their marriage as the best it has ever been.

On the other hand, however, Sandy and Cody long for a commitment that transcends individual choice, viewing their relationship as their only safeguard in the storm of family chaos that threatens to destroy the precarious stability they have achieved for themselves and their children. Both grew up in families scarred by violence and alcoholism and have literally no one to depend on but each other. Describing a typical family holiday, Sandy remarked, "I mean those functions, for me, for twenty-four hours before and twenty-four hours after, I am a mess. I need Xanax because I am a mess. I just can't take it. I really . . . think that I need Xanax when I am around them. They are just horrible people. When you go to a house and they're like, Kill that nigger, fuck that bitch, telling the kids the goddamn dog should die . . . they're saying, what the fuck happened to you, you got fat this year!" Cody and Sandy are thus determined not to replicate their painful family experiences, and this means creating a lasting marriage for their children, even if it entails sacrificing their individual needs.

Reflecting on the therapy they received at their young parents' support group, they said:

C: They made us worse, they made us fight more. Some of the worse fights we ever had were when we were going to counseling.

S: They hear your side and are there for you! He was thinking, I am allowed to watch porn, I am a man; he got this frigging macho bravado attitude. And I'm, you know, thinking about my issues with my father and trying to become an independent woman away from that kind of man. So I was coming home thinking, I don't like you, and he was coming home thinking, I really don't like you, you're inhibiting me from what I am allowed to do!

C: So we ended up actually sitting down with each other and saying, this is what we need to do. Let's just do it.

For this couple, pure expressive individualism confronts them as unfeasible, costly, and laughably preposterous. Unlike Neil and his wife, who have the emotional and financial resources to make the therapeutic relationship ideal into a reality, Sandy and Cody do not have the means to pursue self-actualization and growth, nor do they want to risk it if it means potentially losing what little stability they have. Instead, they fuse elements of therapeutic and traditional marriages, which results in constant conflict.

While the therapeutic or pure relationship has been critiqued, especially by social conservatives, for promoting narcissism and selfishness, Beck and Beck-Gernsheim (1995) convincingly argue that autonomy should be understood as a by-product of an uncertain, competitive, and precarious labor market that forces individuals to navigate their life trajectories on their own in order to survive. That is, the more our futures seem uncertain and unknowable, and the more individualistic we are forced to become, the greater our need to find and express our authentic selves. Paradoxically, the more we are required to construct ourselves as individuals, to write our own biographies, the more we realize our utter inability to control the trajectories of our lives. Thus, the need to grow as individuals develops alongside an equally pressing need to anchor our lives in relationships with others: "When men and women are released from traditional norms and search for 'a life of their own,' they are driven into seeking happiness in a close relationship because other bonds seem too tenuous or unreliable. The need to share your inner feelings with someone . . . is not a primary human need. It grows the more individual we become and notice the losses which accompany the gains" (24). People are at once more liberated and more lonely, turning to intimate relationships as tenuous shelters from the storm of risk and uncertainty. The need to grow as individuals exists alongside an equally pressing need to form a lasting connection with each other, pitting individual needs against obligations in a never-ending battle between autonomy and dependence (Beck 1992). In this vein, Sandy and Cody's relationship often consists of two warring, yet mutually dependent, selves.

As the interviews reveal, in constructing their adult selves, married people find themselves trapped in a liminal space between the rigidity of the past and the flexibility of the present: they are haunted by the myths, rituals, and images of the traditional, gendered family even while this model confronts them as both untenable (economically) and undesirable (socially). Because marriage is considered to be ultimately terminable, it represents less of a stable and clear marker of adulthood and more of a temporary, contingent one.

Children: The Last "Stable Ending" of Adulthood?

Despite the increasing uncertainty surrounding the meanings and practices of adulthood, for those who have children and are actively caring for them, adulthood is clearly demarcated: they are adults because they are responsible for their children. Existing literature (e.g., Edin and Kefalas 2005; Marsiglio and Hutchinson 2002; McMahon 1995; Silva and Pugh 2010) has established that economically disadvantaged mothers and fathers experience parenting as a vehicle for achieving maturity and adulthood; indeed, with unequal access to traditional markers of adulthood such as higher education, stable jobs, or marriage, parenting remains attractive as an available source of self-worth, social integration, and lasting commitment.[10] Children, though almost always unplanned (in my sample, only two informants said that they meant to get pregnant) have become the last "stable ending"—the one promise young people, whether single or married, "can keep" (Edin and Kefalas 2005). While there are competing logics of romance for working-class men and women to draw from, there is only *one* logic of child rearing—intensive, devoted, and self-sacrificial (Hays 1996)—that provides parents with a sense of dignity and self-worth.[11]

When pregnancy occurs, men and women attest that their worldviews, relationships, and expectations of themselves and their futures undergo a radical transformation. Indeed, twenty-six respondents construct a coming of age narrative in which their previously unsettled and nebulous lives take shape and direction only after they embrace the identity and ongoing work of parenting. Sherrie, a thirty-year-old white woman hoping to get into nursing school, captured the spirit of this process: "I didn't have any dreams until I had my daughter." Parents attest that caregiving has changed them in core ways, leading them to erect barriers (against problematic relationships), aspire for more (than they did for just themselves), view parenthood as a second chance (for them to prove themselves as honorable), hew a new path (in contrast to their own childhoods), and make wider or deeper connections to others (Silva and Pugh 2010). As Sherrie, whose pregnancy gave her the courage to break up with her abusive boyfriend, continued: "You have a baby to take care of! That is what I say; my daughter is the reason why I am the way I am today. If I didn't have her, I think I might be a crackhead or an alcoholic or in an abusive relationship!"

These changes mainly occur when respondents draw upon memories of their own childhoods, which prompts them to think about the kinds of parents they want to be (see Chapter 5 on the significance of the family past). Swidler (1986) states that "to adopt a line of conduct, one needs an image of the world in which one is trying to act." For young parents, this "image of the world" in regard to parenting is created by imagining the *opposite* of their own unpredictable and painful childhoods. As Ashley put it, "My goal in life was not to be my mother." Parenting gives rise to a strong need to protect their child from behaviors like drinking and using drugs, from unsafe or unstable relationships, and from the uncertainty and insecurity they experienced as children. While these mothers and fathers did not have dreams for themselves before parenthood, embracing the identity and work of parenting has led them to forge new aspirations and goals, hoping to provide stable lives for their own children. They become accountable, fearing the disappointment of their children, and thus striving to transform their lives; to some degree, they gain a real sense of accomplishment and meaningfulness when they watch their children's lives unfold in a more stable fashion (Silva and Pugh 2010).

Yet the social institutions in which young adults create families can work against their desire to nurture and protect their children. Rachel, a young black single mother, joined the National Guard in order to go to college through the GI Bill. However, working forty hours a week at her customer service job, attending weekend army drills, and parenting has left her with little time for taking college classes. Hearing rumors that her National Guard unit may deploy to Iraq for a *third* time in January, she is tempted to put in for a discharge so that she is not separated from her son again. However, her desire to give her son everything she possibly can—including the things she can buy with the higher, tax-free combat pay she receives when she deploys—keeps her from signing the papers:

> I am kinda half and half with the deployment coming up. I could use it for the money. I could do more for my son. This last deployment, the money, I ended up coming home with $10,000 because I was sending $900 home every month to help with the bills and for my son. It's a matter of me budgeting and only sending home a certain amount and then the rest, don't touch. I am looking forward to the deployment because I would know what I needed to save up. That is why I am kinda happy about it and kinda not. I missed the first two years of my son's life and now I might have to leave again. It's just rough. You can't win.

Knowing that "there are people ten times worse off" than she is, she stays in the National Guard. Her obligation to and relationship with her son have changed her outlook on life so that she wants to achieve more for him; yet the only path to economic stability and a better life for her son requires her to put her life in danger and to leave him.

Becoming parents opens up a new world of dreams—of economic security, higher education, and home ownership—geared toward giving their child a better life than they had, yet simultaneously exposes the limits of these dreams as they struggle to make ends meet in an increasingly competitive and risky service economy. Most parents end up tied to jobs that hold little promise of advancement, lacking the time, resources, or skills necessary for higher education, and often unable to find a trustworthy and stable partner who could ease the responsibility of parenting. Their narratives of hope can take on a desperate quality. "My daughter, she is going to college, I don't care what it is," said Janisa, a thirty-three-year-old black woman whose oldest son dropped out of high school. "I don't care if she doesn't pick a major. I'm like, you're going, I don't care." While having children allows respondents to create narratives of self that allow them to look to the future with hope and direction, structural barriers work against their efforts to transform their lives.

Shifting Ideologies, Persistent Inequalities

As this chapter demonstrates, both the material and cultural resources to achieve happiness and security in the private sphere are essentially out of reach for working-class young men and women. These findings speak to the potential of not only financial scarcity, but also culture, to *constrain* choices, particularly the achievement of emotional well-being in the sphere of intimacy (Cherlin 2009; Gerson 2009; Hays 1994; Swidler 2001). That is, rigid visions of what a relationship should be, combined with extreme vulnerability to market forces, renders the risk of commitment too high. In an era when economic and social shocks such as job loss, illness, or disability are the responsibility of the individual alone, the field of intimacy becomes yet another arena of struggle. Single working-class white and especially black men who subscribe to traditional gender ideology but do not hold stable jobs, for example, believe that their inability to support a wife and children precludes the possibility of monogamy. They cannot think outside of these traditional gender arrangements (Gerson 2009).

For women who have grown up with extreme economic and family instability, the need to hold onto hard-won independence makes them wary of commitment; they do not want to squander the selves they have painstakingly constructed on a partner who will be unfaithful, directionless, or needy, but instead want someone who will nurture their deepest selves. Both men and women intensely fear pouring time, emotion, and energy into a relationship that will fail. Feeling overburdened by the task of taking care of themselves in a precarious labor market and unable to meaningfully plan for the future, for them commitment becomes yet another risk. Ultimately, young adults base their notions of successful intimate relationships on criteria that are structurally unavailable, leaving them resigned to being alone or perpetually seeking the one person who could magically meet their needs. Marriage, at least so far, is in these cases less of what Cherlin (2009) calls a "go-round"—an endless cycle of marriage, divorce, remarriage—and more of a nonstarter.

Married respondents must negotiate the tension between autonomy and dependence (see also Bellah et al. 1985; Cherlin 2009). Without the resources to pursue their individual needs and assailed by both economic and family turmoil, Sandy and Cody decide daily if their mutual dependence and desire to give their children a stable home outweigh their personal happiness. Lacking the bargaining power that comes from social and cultural capital, they have little control over their fates in the labor market, which exacerbates feelings of individual powerlessness and increases mutual dependence. The therapeutic relationship style works in some in-stances (e.g., Cody's porn addiction) but fails in times when the cost of asserting their individual needs was too high (e.g., their experiences in counseling). Clearly, the pure relationship is an economic and emotional luxury they cannot afford. Young parents alleviate the disappointment in their intimate relationships by devoting themselves to their children—the only people who cannot betray them. While obligations to their partners may be uncertain, respondents know that they must take care of their chil-dren, finding a sense of purpose and meaning in this unquestioning commitment.

Marx and Engels critiqued the institution of family as a "sentimental veil" for "mere money relation" (2002: 222), arguing that it has disap-peared among the property-less proletariat. Yet these interviews reveal that while the traditional form of the working-class family may be dissolving, its emotional significance is not. While middle-class men and women may have the linguistic, material, and cultural resources to negotiate flexible forms of work and family arrangements (Cherlin 2009; Gerson 2009; Illouz 1997), working-class youth lack the tools and resources to achieve this kind of success. Indeed, the counterexample of Neil and his wife—whose flexible work, gender, and family arrangements, linguistic skills, and material resources allow them to continually re-envision and perform their visions of a successful marriage—throws into relief the unequal access to intimacy that the vast majority of my working-class informants experience.

This often overlooked form of inequality has had, and will continue to have, profound consequences for working-class men and women. And they will not only suffer from disillusionment, feelings of failure, and loneli-ness; they will also miss out on the concrete economic and social benefits of lasting families: "Unfortunately, those who have the least resources to overcome the costs of family dissolution are experiencing the highest levels and the most increase in the risk" (Raley and Bumpass 2003: 256). Ironically, while children have become the last bastion of hope and commitment—the one remaining "stable ending" of adulthood—the institu-tions in which young parents raise children consistently work to *destabilize* their families. As long as working-class young parents' efforts to create families remain unsupported by social institutions, it is likely that they will pass down their own troubles with intimacy to their children, despite their very best intentions.

Taken together, Chapters 2 and 3 demonstrate the impossibility of tra-ditional pathways of adulthood. In the realms of work and family, young men and women learn that they cannot simply follow in the footsteps of their working-class parents or grandparents, even as older models of adulthood continue to cast a long shadow over their expectations, desires, and practices. In the remainder of this book, I leave the past behind, examining how economic insecurity, uncertainty surrounding gender, family, and race, and deepening inequality seep into the lives of young working women and men—and how they, in turn, are recreating not only what it means to be an adult but also to be a worthy person (see Lamont 1992, 2000).

4 | Hardened Selves
THE REMAKING OF THE AMERICAN
WORKING CLASS

O
N A CHILLY MORNING IN January, I interviewed two sisters: Carley, who works the morning shift at a water park, and Alyssa, who works nights at a hotel parking lot. I met with both of these young women in their parents' three-bedroom ranch house on a quiet, tree-lined residential street where they both still live. Carley has not yet been able to save enough money to move out, while Alyssa left to go away to college but dropped out and returned home after two years. After spending the morning with Alyssa, a bubbly twenty-four-year-old with big green eyes who kindly woke up early after pulling a late shift, I was welcomed into the cozy living room and offered coffee and muffins by their parents, Anne and Steve. When Carley came home from work a few minutes later, she said hello, grabbed a muffin, and collapsed on the couch with the family's bulldog at her feet.

Steve, Anne, Carley, and Alyssa went to great lengths to make me feel welcome in their home, warmly and generously drawing me into the light-hearted banter that fills their household. As I slowly realized, however, their cheerfulness belies the precariousness of their economic situation. Since the housing market crash of 2008, Steven—a contractor—has not been able to get enough work and contemplates putting the house on the market as a short sale. Meanwhile, Anne struggles to balance three part-time jobs with keeping up with the housework: "Excuse my laundry," she laughed apologetically as she unloaded a large pile of clean clothes from the drier onto the coffee table to fold. Their daughters move from one minimum wage job to the next, often borrowing money from each other to make their car payments and cell phone bills. No one in the household has health insurance, and while both daughters once hoped to get college degrees, their high schools offered them no knowledge of financial aid, leaving them with the impossible task of paying tuition.

On a sixty-five-inch television that stood as the focal point of the living room, *Fox News* was covering a story on the cap on bonuses for senior executives whose firms received government (i.e., taxpayer) bailout money following the economic crisis of 2008.[1] Steven, whose construction company has been floundering since the crash, leading him to fall behind on his own monthly mortgage payments last month, shook his head in disgust. "Why shouldn't they get their bonuses?" he demanded. "Those bonuses were part of their original contracts. The government can't step in and take those away! And they shouldn't tax them either!" As his daughters murmured their agreement, the image changed to President Obama delivering a speech in favor of universal health care, and both parents looked away from the screen, shielding their eyes with their hands. "They can't even look at him anymore," Carley confided in me as she picked up some laundry to fold. "They are very patriotic, and he wants to make this a socialist country. That is not what this country is about." Somewhat daunted by the tension in the room, I felt a sense of relief as the news anchor moved on to a seemingly less provocative topic—"Martin Luther King Day Sales—Crass Marketing Move by Retailers?"[2] To my surprise, the room erupted in anger. "What? Why?" Alyssa demanded. "No one cares when there is a Columbus Day Sale, and Columbus did a great thing too," her father replied. "Is it just because he's black? This is just stupid," Carley concluded.

In less than ten minutes, these fleeting and colorful snapshots of news epitomized the central debates surrounding privatization, deregulation, and individualism that would lead Congress to come within minutes of shutting down the government in 2011. For this family, the solution to all their troubles lies firmly and unequivocally in the neoliberal utopia of unfettered markets and untrammeled individualism—hence their impassioned defense of big business and their hostility toward the merest hint of affirmative action. They long to return to an imagined past in which the government did not interfere with markets, thus allowing individuals—understood as *transcendent of race*—to determine the course of their own lives.[3] As an outsider—observing from a vastly different social location—the first question that came to mind concerned how and why this family, who have clearly not reaped the rewards of deregulation and privatization, believes so deeply in their promise. Why has the American working class embraced the free market as its own justification?

It is tempting to decry and then dismiss this scene as false consciousness, a family duped by neoliberal ideology into speaking and acting against its own material interests. But the sheer force of these emotions—of vehement anger, defensiveness, and profound betrayal—throughout my interviews demands a more complicated explanation, one that starts from within the processual, contingent, and ongoing meaning-making of informants. That is, rather than stand outside as an "objective" observer with a particular political agenda, my goal is to study the cultural pathways through which my informants figure out who they want to be, negotiate their relationships with and obligations to others, and come to terms with what it means to live a worthy, dignified life in twenty-first-century America.

Within the powerful emotions that saturated the room and drove the conversation forward, I argue, are important clues to understanding how the post-industrial working class imagines itself and its relationship to others. Seemingly pre-reflexive, personal, and internal, emotions derive their power from their *social* origin; that is, emotions concern the relationship between oneself and another, containing all the hopes, expectations, needs, and desires lodged within it (Illouz 2007).[4] In other words, emotions can be understood as an outcome of a particular configuration of historical meanings and social relations, "*as they are actively lived and felt*" (Williams 1977: 132; see also Elias 2000).[5] Looking more closely at the moments when my respondents were most impassioned, then, can make visible the often unnoticed architecture of social relations and cultural meanings in which they live out their lives, revealing what it means to become working class in an age of neoliberalism (Chauvel 1998; Mannheim 1952; Williams 1977). Accordingly, this chapter interrogates the consequences of the neoliberal turn at the level of the *self*. I ask, What does it mean to become working class in the post-industrial economy? What kinds of identities—whether in terms of work, race, family, or gender—are these young men and women growing *into*? And how do they draw boundaries between the worthy and unworthy, deserving and undeserving, as they stake out what it means to be an adult (Lamont 1992)?

Over and over again, the men and women I interviewed told me that growing up means learning not to expect anything from anyone (see Putnam et al. 2012). They told stories of investing their time and energy in relationships and institutions, only to find that their efforts were one-sided. I demonstrate how experiences of betrayal, within both the labor market and the institutions that frame their coming of age experiences, teach young working-class men and women that they are completely alone, responsible for their own fates and dependent on outside help only at their peril.

They learn to approach others with suspicion and distrust.[6] Many make a virtue out of necessity, equating self-reliance and atomic individualism with self-worth and dignity: if they had to survive on their own, then everyone else should too. In an era of short-term flexibility, constant flux, and hollow institutions, the transition to adulthood has been inverted; coming of age does not entail entry *into* social groups and institutions but rather the explicit rejection *of* them.

In turn, working-class men and women draw harsh boundaries against those who cannot make it on their own, revealing deep animosities toward others—particularly African Americans—who are perceived as undeserving of help. In the end, by rejecting solidarity with others, insisting that they are individuals who can define their own identities and futures, and hardening themselves against social institutions and the government, working-class men and women willingly embrace neoliberalism as the commonsense solution to the problems of bewilderment and betrayal that plague their coming of age journeys.

The Mismeasure of the Social Contract

Nearly all of my informants emphasized their commitment to hard work, loyalty, and generosity toward their employers, their customers, and their fellow workers. They view their labor as a measure of their character, far more than just a paycheck. Describing her restaurant server job, for instance, Rebecca said, "The best part, well, besides counting your money at the end of the night, it is when you have that little old person finally smile at you, you know, that has finally made some kind of contact or smile or expression with you." Her least favorite part involves "being . . . rushed or overwhelmed, or thinking that I am not giving good service." In a similar way, Craig, a twenty-five-year-old white server, feels a "rush" when he successfully completes a dinner service and pleases his customers:

> It's so stressful! But that is why I like it, because I kind of love the feeling after I have pulled my ass out of the fire, like I was all stressed out and crazy and I deal with it. Sometimes you just kind of get by, but when you deal with it well, and it's over, and you made those people as happy as you could, and then they might come back later, there is definitely a rush in making things go okay. When it ends up fine and you find out how much money you made, it's awesome and it's so worth it! Such an accomplishment. And it feels very grown-up.

Despite its increasing contingency and insecurity, work is made meaningful as a space of personal accomplishment and real human connection. Informants also stressed their loyalty to their fellow workers, such as when Rachel, a young black woman who works in customer service, described her work environment as a family: "Once I get to know you, I open up, and I would give you the shirt off my back if I knew you needed it more than I did. If I had $10 in my pocket right now, I would give you the $10. I don't like to see people hurting and I know what it's like to struggle so I am gonna help you out. They all know they can ask me for anything and I would give it to them."

But informants also spoke of realizing their commitment was one-sided, that they were putting in more than they were getting back, that their co-workers were not pulling their weight, that the employer they tried so hard to please would cut them loose without a backward glance. Toni, a twenty-eight-year-old black woman who is counting the days until her husband finishes basic training and she can quit her job and move onto the army base, was promoted last year but never received her raise: "But I feel like I'm basically getting used for what I am getting paid. And it's difficult to go to work every day and deal with a stressful environment and know that, well, this is what I'm supposed to be making and you keep saying you're going to give it to me, you're going to give it to me and then you're constantly asking me to do more." She continued: "I try to be humble. I'm not a difficult person. And I feel like you know and I know, so I'm not going to ask you again. And that's just how I am. And I say, you know, God bless me that I get it before I leave." Her sense of self—as a humble, pleasant person who works hard and does not cause tension—compels her to fulfill her side of the bargain, even while she watches her employer skirt hers.

Yet part of growing up for these young people means learning that depending on, trusting, and investing in others will only hurt them in the end. This lesson was learned painfully by Jillian, the twenty-five-year-old white woman from Chapter 3 who recently quit her job at the local tavern. Jillian began working at the tavern as a prep cook, making $5.50 an hour the year she graduated from high school. Under the guidance of her manager, Bill, a man she looked up to like a father (and who was very different from her own alcoholic and abusive father), she worked her way up the line until she was Bill's "right hand man," running the line by herself and making sure everyone cleaned up their stations at the end of a long day. Jillian's whole world revolved around the tavern: she arrived at five every morning, sometimes didn't go home until eleven at night, and lived for the moments when the restaurant would break its nightly earning record: "When it all comes together and it clicks, it's a great feeling knowing that everybody came together. Everybody is communicating. Everybody worked hard and this is what we got for it," she remembered, a hint of past exhilaration lingering in her voice. Jillian approached her work like a calling, defining the success of the business as her own personal success, and investing a great deal of time and emotional and physical energy into its running. For her efforts, she was able to save enough of her $11 an hour wages to buy her first car, a $7,000 used Toyota.

Then one weekend, Bill fell ill. His doctor diagnosed him with late-stage cancer of the liver and gave him "days, not months" to live. After his death, the owner waited over a year to hire a new manager, during which the tight ship run by Bill slowly dissolved into chaos: "People realized that it didn't matter if they came in late," Jillian explained. "It didn't matter if they didn't clean what they were supposed to clean. It didn't matter if they weren't doing their job responsibilities because there was no one there to tell them otherwise. So I begged and pleaded for a manager. Waving my arms, like, we need help! But they just didn't care to hire." After a year of skeleton crews and back-breaking seventy-hour work weeks, Jillian threatened to quit, but the owner persuaded her to stay: "They promised me that they understood where I was coming from and that things were going to change. That they had put rules in place. So I felt that I was heard and that things were to change. But they never did, and things fell right back into the same slump."

When I asked Jillian about the hardest part of growing up, she reflected:

> After Bill died and the tavern was collapsing, it was definitely very difficult. Because I wanted it to work so bad. And there was just no reason why it shouldn't. But I think respect and appreciation is very important to me. It's the basis of all relationships. So for them to not . . . just total of lack of respect between everybody at the tavern, lack of communication and lack of the support of the ownership. Like I wasn't asking for a promotion or a raise or anything. I was asking help to get the crew back to where it needs to be. Yeah, things were falling apart and it just wasn't working. It was very, very difficult to let go of that. Because I had worked there for over six years. And with me and Bill, I was able to be a part of management stuff. He depended on me to do a lot. So when he wasn't there I didn't have that relationship with the ownership, so I went back to square one at the job. Everything was falling apart and yeah, it was hard.

Jillian knew that she was lucky to have forty hours a week to work, especially in the recession: "You basically worshipped the ground they walked on because they gave you a job. You had to keep your mouth shut." She therefore didn't ask for a promotion or a raise—simply for the owner to value her work experience and to hire a new manager to supervise the kitchen. But instead, Jillian felt betrayed—by the rest of the staff, who did not put in as many hours as she did, and more sinisterly by the owner, who treated her like "just another line cook"—and once even snapped, "You won't get respect anywhere else, so why expect it here?"

With her self-respect at stake, Jillian quit. "Everything crumbled when I lost my job at the tavern," she said wistfully. "I thought I had it going good for awhile there. But everything really came to a screeching halt, and I bought the car, and now not having a job. So I feel like I'm starting over." Since then, she has learned to put on emotional blinders to protect herself from investing emotion and time into ventures that could disappoint her in the end: "I know it's her restaurant and she could do whatever she wants, but I said I can't be a part of that anymore." Jillian is focused on taking care of herself now.

The Endless Cycle of Betrayal

This mood of betrayal that dominates young people's experiences in the labor market is reproduced in the powerful institutions that shape their paths to adulthood. In light of their disappointments in the realm of education, for example, young people moved beyond self-blame and expressed profound feelings of anger toward the school system, which they believe betrayed its implicit promise to prepare them for the future.

Several women informed me that the failure of their grade schools to accurately diagnose their learning disabilities had derailed their educational pursuits, thereby taking college out of the realm of possibility. Amber, a twenty-eight-year-old white woman who works in a bakery, revealed:

> I knew I was smart and that I wasn't a straight C student, yet all my teachers, you know, we had thirty kids in the class, and the teachers were just too busy . . . unless you were destructive, you really didn't get attention. I guess knowing, once I knew that I had ADHD,[7] knowing if somebody had seen it in me earlier, I could have gotten so much further. Now I am medicated, which makes a world of difference. It is just bad. If somebody had just known . . . *sometimes I feel cheated out of life, I could have been in college by now. I could have had a real live career that is not just a cook.* That sounds terrible.

As she spoke, I too was overwhelmed with sadness and regret, wishing that someone could have set Amber on a path to a happier, easier life. Of course, it may be simplistic to believe that a simple ADHD diagnosis would have changed the course of her life so drastically; but in her eyes, it is *the* source of her current struggles, the reason the month always seems to end in a "search for change to buy ramen." Amber has since turned to self-help books to cope with her learning disability, teaching herself strategies to stay focused at work: "Now I have a lot of ADD coping mechanisms. I am a big self-help reader. It is a lot cheaper to buy [a book] and memorize it and figure it out. Like ways to change my actions and the way I do things to make it easier. But it is still a challenge, staying focused." She has, in short, learned to rely only on herself.

Others pointed to the failure of their high schools to prepare them for college, whether by neglecting to transmit the skills necessary for navigating its bureaucracy or simply by judging them to be inferior. When I asked Alyssa about whether her high school had offered college preparatory programs or guidance counselors to help her learn the ropes of applications or financial aid, she replied: "They had some [college prep classes] but they didn't do enough to help you prepare for those classes. They didn't tell you much about them, like how to sign up even. It was a big mess. All the guidance counselors were not good. I knew who he was and he was not good at all." In other words, it was his job and he failed. The responsibility for deciphering the rules of the game thus fell squarely on Alyssa and her family—none of whom had the knowledge to fill out the FAFSA. In a similar way, Alexandra bitterly recalled her guidance counselor in high school warning that she would not get into her top three college choices. She applied anyway—on her own, without institutional support—and was accepted to one of them, proving to her that she should not trust the school for support or guidance.

Vanessa, a thirty-year-old white woman who works as a nanny, recounts several experiences of being profoundly misunderstood by the administrators at her elementary school:

> In second grade, I took balloons from a PE shed and gave them out. I didn't know it was wrong to steal; no kid did at that age. I thought it was just having fun but they thought it was stealing—I saw the envelope of balloons and took it and got in trouble for that. And then in third grade, I took a teacher's little stationery set that had a little ball of glue and a little thing of tape, but it also had a razor blade in it. I didn't know at the time that it had a razor blade; it had a pen and a pencil, and I was like, what little kid

wouldn't want something like that? I took it because I liked it, and I got in trouble for that, and I guess my parents never really sat down and said, "Hey look, you can't take things that aren't yours." They were upset, and I knew they were upset, but I didn't know why. And then the last thing that happened which was the most severe to everybody . . . do you remember those pencils that were natural, that didn't have any paint on them? They came out and all the kids had them? Well, I still had my yellow pencils. So in second or third grade, my dad dropped me off at school, and he always kept this pocket knife on the dashboard, and you know it was bothering me so bad that I didn't have a natural pencil like everyone else that I was like, I will just shave the paint off my pencil and I will have one like everyone else. And I was sitting there at my desk shaving it off, I was doing it during math, and the teacher was walking around and she caught me with it, and I really don't remember, she didn't yell at me or anything, I just went to the principal's. My dad came in and they sent me out and they suggested my dad, with all these incidents, to go to a psychiatrist. And if you look back at it, they were thinking I brought the knife to school to hurt somebody. I brought it to school because I was having issues with my pencil. I needed to go so the psychiatrist knew why I brought the knife to school and not that I was gonna hurt somebody.

In some of these instances—such as her professed ignorance that it was wrong to steal in elementary school—we might question the accuracy of her recollection. But her coming of age narrative is colored by her current mood of resentment, and she frames the principal's inability to listen to her—to instead see her as disruptive, dangerous, and in need of psychiatry—as a cutting betrayal. Furthermore, while middle-class parents have been found to assertively intervene in school settings where their children face obstacles (Lareau 2003), Vanessa's father and mother—a field machinist and a medical biller—deferred to the authority of the school, unintentionally teaching their daughter to distrust both her family and the educational system.

To provide another example of educational betrayal, Jay, a twenty-eight-year-old black man, struggled through college partly because he failed several classes after his mother suffered a severe mental breakdown. After being expelled from college and working for a year, helping his mom get back on her feet, he went before the college administration and petitioned to be reinstated. He described his experiences of powerlessness and humiliation heatedly: "A panel of five people who were not nice. It's their jobs to hear all these sob stories, you know I understand that, but they just had this attitude, like you know what I mean, 'oh your mom had a break-down and you couldn't turn to anyone?' I just wanted to be like, fuck you, but I wanted to go to college, so I didn't say fuck you." When I asked Jay if he eventually graduated, he replied:

> JAY: Yes. When I was twenty-five. And you know, I was so disillusioned by the end of it, my attitude toward college was like, I just want to get out and get it over with, you know what I mean, and just like, put it behind me, really. I didn't even walk [across the stage to receive a diploma]. I ended up not even walking at the end of it.
>
> JS: Did you see it as meaningless?
>
> JAY: I felt like it wasn't anything to celebrate. I mean I graduated with a degree. Which ultimately I'm not even sure if that was what I wanted, but there was a point where I was like I have to pick some bullshit I can fly through and just get through. I didn't find it at all worthwhile.

Since graduating three years ago, Jay has worked in a series of food service and coffee shop jobs, remaining completely baffled when it comes to using his communications major to get a professional job. Reflecting on where his life has taken him, he fumed:

> Well, to be honest, *one of the great lies that I was fed was the magnificence of my brilliance.* I feel like, you know, I was always straight A's and honor society and stuff like that. They were just blowing smoke up my ass—the world is at my fingertips, you can rule the world, be whatever you want, all this stuff. When I was fifteen, sixteen, I would not have envisioned the life I am living now. Whatever I imagined, I figured I would wear a suit every day, that I would own things. I don't own anything. I don't own a car. If I had a car, I wouldn't be able to afford my daily life.

Scholars have argued that the educational system reproduces inequality behind the backs of actors by convincing them of its legitimacy (Bourdieu 1977). But Amber, Vanessa, and Jay do not simply internalize the logic of institutions; instead, they approach education (as well as other institutions) with suspicion, seeking out the ways in which their schools and teachers not only failed to help or understand them but also even maliciously lied to them. That is, they each testify that they upheld their end of the social contract—they worked hard, they were honest, they were smart—but got nothing in return.

Even extracurricular activities were remembered as a site of betrayal. Sam, a twenty-four-year-old white bank teller, often wonders whether his future could have unfolded differently if his junior high school baseball coach had only believed in him and given him a chance to prove himself:

> I always think that I could have been a sports player. . . . My last year of baseball was the toughest because it was like the level right before high school and I was the first baseman but it was so much harder. People would throw the ball faster and I couldn't always catch the ball. I kinda resented my coach at the time because he just moved me into the outfield. It was like, "oh you're not a good player in the infield, you just play outfield." He didn't really coach me on how to be a better first baseman. I kinda think he gave up on me there, so I kinda just . . . after that year I was like, I'm done with this game. I can't, I don't want to be here left in the dust.

Sam is struggling: his minimum wage job cannot even cover his student loan payments; he does not know how to sign up for state-subsidized health insurance; and he knows that the house he lives in with his mother and two siblings is on the brink of foreclosure. His childhood memories of baseball suggest that another kind of life was possible for him—if only someone had believed in him instead of leaving him behind "in the dust."

The Treacherous State

Encounters with the state—whether the legal system, the military, or government aid—also bred confusion and anger, leaving young people with the conviction that the state could not be trusted to act justly on their behalf. Instead, taking the law into their own hands became the only way to survive. Two young men, for example, served time in prison, one for stealing when his father became an addict and could not provide food, and one for assaulting the man who molested his sister. Simon, a twenty-four-year-old black man who currently works as a groundskeeper, explained, "*I had to do what I had to do.* When my dad left, I stole a car and some guns, the whole nine. Got locked up from sixteen to nineteen." Mike, a twenty-four-year-old white man whose stepbrother molested his younger sister but was never prosecuted, recalled, "I just kind of just blacked out and, yeah, it wasn't good. It wasn't good at all. So I did two years of juvie which ain't nothing. There's no way I could get out of it because I assaulted him. He didn't provoke it, if that's what you're asking.

He didn't say anything to me. It was totally unprovoked." Both of these informants express the feeling that they were completely alone; they could not count on other avenues—like the state or the police—for care or justice. For their efforts, they spent many of their teenage years locked away.[8]

In another realm of the state, men and women who joined the military for the financial incentives often did not read their contracts and thus did not know that the signing bonus would be divided up over several years, rather than paid at one time, and expressed some regret over this lack of knowledge. Travis, a twenty-five-year-old National Guard weekender who has been on two fourteen-month deployments in Afghanistan in the last four years (and was about to leave for a third, at the time of the interview), recalled bitterly, "Yeah, I just needed extra money and they flashed the bonus in my face. I was like, I'll take it."

Fear of the government taking away what was rightfully theirs (see also Hays 2003) was passed down through generations, taking new forms when new opportunities arose. Isaac, for example, hoped to attend community college after high school. He explained solemnly, "I wanted to go to better my education and knowledge. I knew quite a bit, but not as much as there is out there to know." Isaac's mother, who raised him and his brother alone as a prison guard, could not afford to pay his tuition, so he attempted to apply for financial aid. To his surprise, however, his mother would not provide him with the necessary parental financial information for the FAFSA:

> I: The thing is, really to be honest with you, my mom, she wouldn't give out her financial information. Like she didn't feel comfortable giving it out. So without that, I couldn't do anything. Even though I came here and I talked to the head people, even the financial aid office, I even talked to them. And they told me without her being willing enough to give that information up, I can't do anything.
>
> JS: Did you ask her why she didn't want to give it to you?
>
> I: Yeah, I asked her plenty of times. She just said that she just doesn't want to give it out because she doesn't feel comfortable telling people how much she makes. I don't know why honestly, but that's how she feels as of right now. But hopefully maybe next year I could do something to make her change her mind a little bit, and make sure that her information will be safe and nobody can see it but the financial aid office and the head people. And it's not like they're going to go tell anybody anything.

Currently, the federal government considers students under the age of twenty-four to be financially dependent on their parents for college and thereby requires students to submit proof of parental income when eligibility for financial aid is determined.[9] This holds true even if parents do not claim the student as a dependent for income tax purposes or if the student is completely self-sufficient (see Dear Colleague Letter GEN-03-07 and page AVG-28 of the Application Verification Guide). In adopting the view that it is the parents' responsibility to pay for higher education, the US Department of Education does not consider parental refusal to contribute or to provide financial information as grounds for an override.[10] In Isaac's case, his mother's own feelings of distrust toward the federal government prevented her from filing a financial aid application. Isaac, in turn, feels like *both* his mother and the government are working against his efforts to build a successful life for himself.

"I have this problem of being tricked"

Feelings of betrayal are woven through the smallest everyday interactions and practices. Christopher, for instance, is a twenty-four-year-old black man who was laid off nine months ago and has still not found another job. He grew up in a state group home for children after his parents divorced, an experience that has left him deeply jaded about seemingly benevolent government services: "I can't say it was positive. I seen a lot of shit going on there. Staff members punching kids in the face. *It opened up my eyes to how the world really works*." When I asked him if he had any debt, he confessed, "Well, I have this problem of being tricked":

> Like I will get a phone call that says, you won a free supply of magazines. And they will start coming to my house. Then all of a sudden I am getting calls from bill collectors for the subscriptions to *Maxim* and *ESPN*. It's a runaround: I can't figure out who to call. Now I don't even pick up the phone, like I almost didn't pick up when you called me.

Simply answering the phone confronts him as risky and uncontrollable, an opportunity for deception. In another instance, Christopher was "tricked" by a man looking to rent out his apartment: "The guy thought I had agreed, even though I hadn't, but I didn't want to say no, so I moved in. Then the guy also had his son and cousin move in, and I felt like I didn't belong. That was fucked up. I would not agree if I could go back. He tricked the shit out of me." He resents his roommate for taking advantage of his lack of confidence and for later violating his perceived agreement. Most recently, Christopher was taxed $400 for not purchasing mandatory health insurance in Massachusetts (see Chapter 58 of the Acts of 2006 of the Massachusetts General Court, entitled "An Act Providing Access to Affordable, Quality, Accountable Health Care"), which he could not afford because he was unemployed and did not know how to access free health care. This was a common occurrence among the Massachusetts service workers and sparked resentment toward universal health care. Christopher tells his coming of age story as one incident of deception (as evidenced by his usage of the word "tricked") after another—each of which incurs a heavy emotional and financial cost.

Even when the state seemed to support their efforts to get ahead, informants remained wary, as what they got was never as good as what they were seemingly promised. Sandy and Cody, a white married couple, won a lottery for low-income housing in a wealthy suburb, where they now live with their three children. This couple explicitly viewed the lottery as a battle against other low-income families. Cody explained, "Twelve people out of eighty-nine got one and we were number thirteen, but then one family didn't qualify for their mortgage so we lucked out. We were so excited." But owning a low-income house turned out to be little better than renting, as they explained with a savvy born of deflated hope:

> s: The only thing is that it comes with a deed restriction that when you go to resell it, you got it at a third of the value it was worth, but you resell it at that same rate . . . you can only collect, after you pay back the town, you can only collect a third.
>
> c: It has to go to a low-income family first.
>
> s: We bought it at $116,500. Now the houses are worth $400 something. So now the low-income family can buy it at $165. We get a third, after paying the mortgage off, of the $165. So you really can't resell it for anything.
>
> c: That's why we've decided to stay.
>
> s: There is no resale value in buying it; that is one thing about buying low income.

This is not to make light of their gratitude at having a home in a safe suburb with a good school system in which to raise their children. But at the same time, their hope that someone—in this case, the personified state—would reward their efforts at keeping their family together against all of the centrifugal forces that threatened it (see Chapter 3) was not quite fulfilled. In a sense, they were given enough to be comfortable, but not enough to take control over their lives or to get ahead.

Hardened Selves

As interviews with these young men and women reveal, the standard life course has grown increasingly uncertain, unpredictable, and risky; as a result, they must themselves remain "flexible," altering their life trajectories according to the constant fluctuations of the labor market (Beck and Beck-Gernsheim 1995). That is, they learn that they should not expect commitment, loyalty, or fairness from their employers or colleagues but should rather come to terms with their lack of bargaining power and support; recalling Jillian, "you basically worshipped the ground they walked on because they gave you a job, you had to keep your mouth shut."

The dictionary defines "flexible" as "capable of being bent repeatedly without injury or damage."[11] The men and women I spoke with cope with their disappointments in the labor market by actively fostering a kind of flexibility within themselves, bending with the constant disruptions and disappointments in the labor market, and staunchly willing themselves to be unbreakable. Kiana, a young black woman, describes how she reacted when her husband, Curtis, was laid off from his first job:

> You can't sit and sulk about it. What do you get out of that? Where do you go from there? *Nowhere, you either decrease or stay the same, keep moving, and as long as you keep moving, you see more improvements*. My husband, I mean getting laid off from your first job, who expects that? That was a slap in the face for him, and he was thinking this is the best job he had ever had, and that hurt him. And of course you let the person hurt for a while, but then you gotta pick them back up, you can't just leave them down there, like, come on sweetie, let's do something else. If he had seen me down, he would have done the same thing.

As she explains, young adults learn to "keep moving," as if to adjust their expectations and behaviors so quickly that their feelings can't stick to them and weigh them down with pain.

However, while they can actively manage their feelings of betrayal in the labor market—coming to terms with the idea that short-term flexibility and flux are the natural order of things—they have a much harder time managing betrayal in institutions such as education, the state, or the law, where they expect to find people who will help them. Yet their lack of knowledge within these powerful institutions serves to solidify their wariness and distrust, thereby confirming their deep-seated beliefs that they have only themselves to count on. Even everyday activities like answering the phone or finding a roommate become risky, yet another opportunity to be deceived.

In turn, those who are "flexible" in the labor market become hardened outside of it, turning inward as a way to steel themselves against the possibility of disappointment and hurt. While the market is seen as private and asocial, institutions are not; and this difference was made abundantly clear when informants spoke of the state, to which they ascribed human qualities of heartlessness and duplicity. Allan, a twenty-six-year-old white emergency medical technician (EMT) from Richmond, explained:

> I have a buddy of mine who has something called spina bifida. And his parents have brought him up babying him, giving him everything he wanted, and everything else. Then I have a buddy who only has one leg. This other guy's parents [his friend who only has one leg], they said, you only got one leg, deal with it. We're not going to baby you. Which I think is the right way to do it. *Because there's nobody in this world that's gonna baby you. When you get out from under the wing of mommy and daddy, the government doesn't care if you're disabled. They're gonna tax you just like everybody else.* You gotta make a living. Be it however little you can make or whatever.[12]

Expecting sympathy or care, he believes, will come back to haunt you in the end. Interestingly, Allan viewed unions as one space where the social contract was still alive. He said: "Unions have somebody who will go and fight your employer for you, and here you don't. It has its pros and cons. I worked in a union before and I think they are a little steep on their charges, but what they promise you is what you get. You don't get nothing more, you don't get anything less." But his job is non-unionized, leaving him up against his employer alone.

Vanessa, who felt so profoundly betrayed at school, has developed virulent feelings of distrust toward the government, which she uses to justify her own hardened attitude toward others. Her suspicion was broad, targeting Muslims, President Obama (and the "birther" controversy over where he was born), and the state more generally (which she believes monitors her phone conversations). She elaborated:

Right in our building, there is a Muslim couple, her name is Islam, and for a while I didn't want to talk to them, but I ended up talking to them, and they are nice people, and I know there are nice ones out there. *But I make them guilty until proven innocent, if you get what I mean; that is how the government works anyway.* I am looking at Obama as guilty until he proves himself innocent.

Experiences of profound uncertainty and betrayal in their childhoods teach young people that trusting others is a dangerous game, prompting them to construct an image of the world as a hostile space in which they can depend only on themselves. Indeed, Vanessa's reversal of the classic phrase (and legal right)—"innocent until proven guilty"—captures the lens through which working-class young people understand social bonds and their place within them.

Because most respondents have had to survive on their own without safety nets, they come to see their struggle as morally right. To put it in Bourdieu's terms, they "'cut their coats according to their cloth,' and so [become] the accomplices of the processes that tend to make the probable a reality" (1990: 65). That is, they make a virtue out of not asking for help, out of rejecting dependence and surviving completely on their own, mapping these traits onto their definitions of adulthood. Emma, a twenty-five-year-old white woman who works two bartending jobs while taking community college classes part-time, said proudly:

> My grandfather dug ditches. For a gas company for thirty years. He has a fat-ass house and a pool and a barn. They lived in that house for thirty years and made it what it is. They worked their asses off. People today don't use what they have—that is a lesson people don't get. My parents did it on their own and they expect me to, too.

Elliott, a twenty-four-year-old black firefighter, echoed, "I'm like a rock. I like to figure things out myself, so I really don't go looking for help."

But these heroic tales of self-sufficiency have a darker side, one that entails cutting ties, turning inward, and numbing oneself emotionally. Christopher, for example, acknowledges that he has not achieved traditional markers of adulthood but still believes that he is at least partially an adult because of the way he has managed his feelings of betrayal. He remarked: "I ended up the way I am because of my experiences. I have seen crazy shit. If people could only see what I have been through. Like staff members taking a chain saw and cutting holes through walls at group homes. And hospitals strapping kids down for hours. *Like now if I see someone beating someone up in the street, I don't scream. I have no emotions or feelings.*" Through constructing a narrative of self that is completely hardened against and detached from the social world, dependent on no one and completely and utterly alone, Christopher protects himself from the possibility of betrayal.

Taking stock of his life, he mused, "I should have my own place, take care of myself like a man. But I can't. This is not a situation that an adult should be in. I need a break; the hardest part about being an adult is finding a real fucking job." He paused, then continued: "I am not gonna give up. I am not gonna end up like the bums on the street. It is all about who's around you. Me being in those programs has led me to have certain kinds of friends. If I was around successful people, that would make me have more motivation too. My friends don't do shit. I was the first one with a job." Rejecting all forms of dependence and connection becomes the primary channel to adulthood. That is, when others perpetually weigh you down and hold you back, you are better off without them.

Through this process of meaning-making, the logic of neoliberalism comes to resonate with their experiences as deeply personal and individual—in short, as commonsense reality. Neoliberalism, then, reigns not only as an abstract and removed set of discourses and practices in the economic sphere but also as a lived system of meanings and values in the emotional sphere (Illouz 2007; Williams 1977). Taken together, these two spheres are mutually confirming, creating a world where self-reliance and rugged individualism are the only categories that these young adults can grasp to think with. The power of neoliberalism is thus not only top-down, forced upon them, but also deeply embedded in "a whole body of practices and expectations, over the whole of living: [their] sense and assignments of energy, [their] shaping perceptions of [them]selves and [their] world" (Williams 1977: 110).

The Boundaries of Solidarity under Neoliberalism

So far, I have demonstrated the ways in which betrayal serves as the lens through which young working-class people construct their coming of age narratives. That is, labor market flexibility combined with unsuccessful interactions with institutions bolsters young people's visions of themselves as completely alone, teaching them that they can depend on no one but themselves. This heightened sensitivity to betrayal and the concomitant reverence for individualism and self-reliance also shape the ways in which they draw boundaries against others, marking their community boundaries and demarcating where their obligations to others end (Lamont 1992).[13] For the post-industrial working class, I argue that the logic of neoliberalism—of atomic individualism, self-reliance, and government distrust—underlies the kinds of boundaries they draw against others, especially in the realm of race. This process of neoliberal boundary-making holds grave consequences for the social, economic, and political future of the American working class.

The Promise—and Limit—of Color-Blind Individualism

About a third of white respondents, both men and women, answered my questions about the importance of race in shaping their life trajectories by explicitly stating that race does not matter in their daily lives. Like Carley and Alyssa's family, they see themselves as *individuals transcendent of race*, as evidenced by Mike's response: "Race has never . . . I don't care about race. Just people. I see heart and soul, I don't see color."[14] These respondents are committed to ideals of meritocracy, individualism, and equal opportunity in such a way as to equate sameness with equality. Indeed, as Joan Scott (1988) points out, most Americans rely on a discourse of fairness that structures equality and difference as oppositional, so that recognizing socially produced differences is understood as antithetical to equality. In some cases—particularly those in which whites and blacks worked together, whether as firefighters or paramedics or soldiers— respondents understood racial division as dangerous to group solidarity and thus adopted strategies to neutralize difference. Ariel, for instance, explained that soldiers realize in basic training that succeeding as a unit necessitates group solidarity and thus rely on humor to manage difference (see also Black 2009):

> We kind of make jokes about it here. Like, um, this is kind of bad. Like we pick on each other. Like the nitpick brother sister thing. There is a girl in my platoon, she is Chinese, or Korean, Asian, I don't know, because none of us care (laughs). We joke back and forth with her about being Asian, about eating rice and singing little Chinese songs. We all make fun of each other about everything. We have another guy who has eight fingers—Mac Eight! We have a guy whose last name is McMahon who has all ten fingers, and we have MacKenzie who only has eight fingers, so there's Mac 10 and Mac 8! And we walk by him and are like, Hey Mac! High Three! You know, and

high five him with three fingers. *It is almost like pointing out, not what is wrong with people, but their differences and then exploiting it and making it funny, so that it's not an issue.*

Anything falling outside the norm—of whiteness, of physical ability—was promptly recognized and then explicitly negated, thereby removing its potential divisive effect while also reestablishing the line between "normal" and "abnormal." White respondents committed to this ideology of sameness were also willing to challenge other whites who were explicitly racist against their peers. Rob, for instance, once testified in a military court against higher-ranking officers who made racist remarks to his black and Jamaican colleagues. In this context, the logic of individualism allowed Rob to see himself and his fellow soldiers as individuals united by a shared social contract rather than divided by race.

Using humor to neutralize difference was also employed by black respondents in these contexts. At a National Guard training meeting at weekend drill, the commander announced that the unit would be training in Tennessee for the summer. Rachel, a young black woman, immediately called out, "Is that black friendly?" drawing attention to race in a way that defused potential tensions and perhaps even warned her colleagues to watch out for her in the South. Similarly, while I was interviewing at the firehouse one Thanksgiving morning, I observed a group of firefighters feeding breadcrumbs to pigeons on an adjacent rooftop. Noticing the lone brown pigeon among a sea of white ones, a Puerto Rican firefighter—well-aware of the tensions surrounding affirmative action hiring in the department—joked, "Look, the minority, like me!" evoking laughter from his colleagues.

Working within a discourse that creates an impossible choice between equality and difference, one that treats any kind of dissimilarity as potentially divisive, black and white respondents who feel secure in their positions and united in a common goal strive to convince each other that they see only individuals rather than social categories. These strategies for denying the social weight of difference, however, are imperfect, as they leave in place a false neutrality that reproduces the hegemony of white culture and ignores the unequal social structures underlying the social production of race (Scott 1988). Additionally, in traditionally masculine spaces like the National Guard and the firehouse, black and white men are able to diminish the importance of race mainly by uniting against their "common enemies"—homosexuality and femininity. In this way, they harness masculinity as a sort of "bonding capital" (Putnam 2000: 22) that forces others out.[15] When I was interviewing Rob at the army base, for instance, several of his friends—two white, one Puerto Rican—interrupted to mock Rob's (homo)sexuality ("did he tell you he's gay?") and simultaneously assert their own masculinity. "Hey, why don't you show her that tongue-rolling thing you do? *In her mouth?*" snickered a white soldier to his Puerto Rican friend. In this incident, racial difference was neutralized through humor, while masculine domination was reinforced.[16]

But ideologies of racial sameness begin to unravel when respondents must compete for jobs, particularly in the civil service realm, which takes an explicit "pro-active approach to affirmative action" (yet does not publicly release their policy for doing so, thereby creating confusion and bitterness among civil service test-takers).[17] Again, the notion of government as acting against one's interests, as taking away something they have earned, sparked feelings of betrayal. Within this framework, being black emerged as a seeming advantage in the fight for scarce resources.[18] White respondents waiting for increasingly scarce hires as police officers, postal workers, and firefighters conceive of affirmative action as "reverse discrimination," arguing that "individual merit" rather than race should determine hiring decisions. Eric, a twenty-four-year-old white EMT who still lives in his parents' basement, remarked bitterly, "I don't feel [minorities] are entitled to anything. In general, the whole reparation thing is bogus. I never owned slaves. I get annoyed by those people." Clearly, Eric sees racism as an artifact of the past. Joseph, a white firefighter who was hired in part because of his veteran status, does not resent his minority colleagues, yet still wants his own son to be hired one day, preferably without military service: "I am not prejudiced at all. I don't think it is, I just think that maybe . . . when does it come to a point where they are not the minorities any more? There are so many on the job, sooner or later there aren't going to be minorities; it's going to be half and half."[19]

Whites outside the civil service sector also feared that black managers gave preference to black job applicants who were less qualified than whites. Craig, a white server, told the following story:

> The assistant manager became the manager and he—this is gonna sound racist, but deal with it—he was black and all the new people he hired were black. Some of them were better than others. I mean, there was one girl who got accused of stealing money, and I stood up for her, but then I found out she had been accused at her last two jobs too. He fired people who had been there for like eight years. I finally realized he was weeding his way through to start over. I got in a fight with him.

In telling this story, Craig goes to great lengths to cast himself as a non-racist person, showing how he gave this young woman the benefit of the doubt, only to learn that she was indeed unworthy of the job. He creates an image of black people deviously infiltrating the workplace, displacing loyal, honest, and upstanding white workers who have proven their worth. Because he frames his critique in terms of individual merit and morality, though, he absolves himself of racism.

"Playing the Race Card"

Whites also expressed hostility to minorities who "play the race card," resulting in "reverse discrimination." Usually this accusation was accompanied by personal stories of black people unfairly accusing white respondents of discrimination. Tara, a twenty-five-year-old white woman who worked as a police officer in a low-income section of Boston (and who joined a Facebook group called "I Support Cambridge Police Sgt. James Crowley"), recounted, "Somebody was always throwing the race card down. You're just doing this because I'm black, you're just doing this because I'm you know whatever. Whatever! You just kind of take that and deal with it as it comes, but there's definitely a lot of that out there." In her view, everyone is an individual; individuals who happen to be black break the law and get arrested more frequently. She continued: "I would love it when I was able to . . . like there was this white guy who was doing something stupid in the bathroom or whatever, because that makes me not look like a racist. You know what I mean? So I would love it when I could like toss some white guy up into the bus stop or whatever across the street." By arresting a white man, she could prove to herself and others that she was fair and unbiased.

Rebecca, a white server, expressed anger and frustration at being unfairly labeled a racist by black customers: "I have had people accuse me of being a racist when I know they are just projecting blame. My little cousin used to live with me for a while, and she was biracial, so I think that is one of the last things you can label me, being racist. It's just people saying, you didn't get to me first . . . in the order the food came along, stuff like that." Upholding a view of herself as reasonable, individualistic, and meritocratic, Rebecca approaches her black customers with suspicion, viewing their accusations of racism as thinly veiled attempts to "play the race card" and get more than they deserve (in this case, getting their food served first). As the clearly identifiable Jim Crow racism of the past evolves into an unsettling murkiness, interactions between blacks and whites unfold laced with anxiety and suspicion (Bonilla-Silva 2003).

The Race-ing of Resentment

In sharp contrast, a small group of white respondents drew strong and vehement boundaries against other races, particularly African Americans. Anti-black racism was expressed through two major frameworks: blacks as immoral, and blacks as dangerous. In both cases, white informants drew upon personal experience to justify their claims that black people take what is rightfully theirs (thus feeding into existing feelings of betrayal) and break their trust (thus resonating with resentment over the broken social contract).

Eileen, a thirty-three-year-old white woman, complained about her inability to collect welfare or WIC when her daughter was born. Because she inherited a house when her mother committed suicide, she was deemed ineligible, despite her low income as a biller at a property management firm. She explained:

> Like I said, I do have issues with black people that don't want to work and we have to pay for stuff, but there's white people like that too, and there's Mexicans, and then the other people that come in that want something for nothing. Coming from where I came from. I tried to get welfare or child health when my daughter was born. They wouldn't give it to me because I owned a house. So I have a big issue with that. I was like, you got people over here on [a predominantly black street] and they're out playing basketball, my tax dollars are paying for it and you know . . . it sucks, it bites that you've got people out there like that that are able bodies that can get out there and work and you know. Like I said, whether it be black or white but mostly what I've seen is black and that's just my opinion.

Eileen recognizes the political incorrectness of accusing all black people of being lazy welfare cheats and thus makes sure to ground her accusations in real-life observations. But she clearly believes that she was denied welfare because the system privileges black people who refuse to work over hard-working white people like herself, thus drawing racial boundaries to sort out the morally deserving from the non-deserving.[20] That is, her feeling of betrayal within an institution that was supposed to help *her* leads to anger that it helped someone less deserving. Allan, in a similar way, spoke of the difficulties of watching black mothers neglect their children, a phenomenon he witnesses in his role as a paramedic: "You see a crack head lady that has a baby hanging out, and she's saying she's not pregnant." Tim, the most openly bitter and angry white respondent, complained about "African Americans of a certain dialect" who threaten the order and stability of his neighborhood:

> There's a couple of families in my neighborhood, they park in their yard, they leave trash in the yard, they don't maintain their house. There's a lot of them living in a small space, so you know it's got to be cluttered in there because there's a lot of people living in a small area. And I see that, and I don't like it. I see them outside just in groups. A group of the same type of person interacting with the general population. So not really causing trouble, but acting as they normally would with each other, but in a public setting that annoys me. Because they are being a nuisance to society.

Tim resents the presence of blacks in what he views as *his* space, yet frames his racism in terms of protecting and preserving moral order (Lamont 2000). Like Eileen, Tim also subscribes to an ideology of individualism and knows that it is therefore wrong to judge a person solely based on race; yet he contradicts himself in the process: "I hope you're not taking this wrong, with me calling them 'them.' Just that type *of individual*, and it's not all of them, so I don't consider myself racist. Mexicans are the same way. Well, I shouldn't say Mexicans, most Latin Americans. So yeah, all of Latin Americans in general."

Other respondents admitted to being afraid of black people, whether as children or as adults. Daniel recalled being "picked on" by black kids at school, where he was targeted for being overweight and weak: "The Civil War never really ended. It's still going on. And those are the kids who were picking on me, that tried to kill me, it was all people that said at some point, you know, after years of slavery this is something or other like that. And it's like, that's over and done with." He believes that these children at school unfairly used slavery as an excuse to torment him, thus constructing himself as a victim of a broken contract. In a similar way, Ashley looks at African Americans with a mix of fear and disdain:

> I have always had issues with black people. Only because trusting the ones that I did didn't work out so well. I have always been, you know, wary and just very like . . . And I remember when I first met Jeff, we would go into a 7–11 and if black people were there, I would freak out, and he was, like, you can't do that, you're gonna get me beat up. Like why, I don't understand the whole pants around the ankles thing, I can't look at you with a straight face if you have to stand with your legs apart to keep your pants up. They think they are in Gangster-ville. What are you doing? Like girls come into the

store with them and I am just like . . . you are a pretty girl, you can't get a guy that has pants that fit? No? It irritates me. I am just very trust-cautious of a lot of people.

Ashley justifies her fear of black people by drawing on personal experiences of betrayal (although her coming of age narrative is full of betrayals by white people, she does not see whiteness as raced). She also mocks and disparages black men who do not conform to middle-class white, mainstream aesthetics of self-presentation, suggesting that their clothing choices warrant social exclusion. As if to protect me from the moral chaos that blacks represent to him (see Lamont 2000), Will, a white nurse, confidently assured me that I did not want to interview any of the black nurses' aides he works with (despite my protests): "You don't want to talk to them. They'd be like, 'you be talkin' to me?'" In other words, he demonstrated his moral superiority (and masculinity) through shielding me from these women.

This anger at those who do not subscribe to white social norms extended to those who do not speak English. Sandrine, for instance, fumed: "To turn around, then, and speak another language while in public, not only are you disrespecting and being rude to the country, but you are doing that to yourself too. It means you have no respect for yourself, no common courtesy for yourself as well as others. That is just how I was brought up. So it has nothing to do with race." Visibly flustered and angry, Sandrine shrouds race in terms of patriotism and cultural membership. She understands a refusal to learn English as a direct assault against the American way of life—the explicit breaking of a shared social bond.

Broken Solidarities

Black informants embrace many of these frameworks as well, precariously balancing race-blind visions of meritocracy, individualism, and self-reliance with real-life experiences of racism (Bobo 1991; Newman 1999; Smith 2007). Black men working in civil service jobs told me upfront that they were hired because they are minorities, even though they *all* had active-duty military service and several tours in Iraq under their belts. These respondents were ambivalent about affirmative action, believing in the dominant ideology of individual merit and equal opportunity. As Elliott, a twenty-four-year-old black firefighter who served in the Marines, pragmatically put it, "I will be the first person to say that it's stupid to get preference for the color of your skin. It should be who did the best on the test. But don't get me wrong, if it's there, I am gonna use it, because I don't get too many handouts in life, and that was a handout and I took it. It was there and I took it." Benefiting from affirmative action is thus recast as his one opportunity to take something back from a system that set him up to fail. Black respondents have a contradictory set of ideals, in which they both recognize the systematic force of racism but also resist seeing themselves as its victims; in the words of Katherine Newman (1999: 266), they reveal how "the dilemmas of race, intertwined with the power of a common cultural ideology and an economy that has privileged some at the expense of others, has produced a refracted and contradictory set of belief in most of us: the powerful pull of meritocracy, with its race-blind vision of equal opportunity, and the recognition that race intervenes to shape lives in the most profoundly unfair fashion."

The commitment to meritocracy, however, was far stronger than the belief in race as a system; as Julian, a twenty-seven-year-old black man, confessed with tragic earnestness: "Ethnicity plays in people, but I don't look at it as a part of my shortcomings, if that makes sense. Every day I look in the mirror, and I could bullshit you right now and tell you anything I wanted to tell you. But at the end of the day looking in the mirror, I know where all my shortcomings come from. *From the things that I either did not do or I did and I just happened to fail at them.*"

Indeed, all black respondents shared experiences of blatant and vicious discrimination, yet have developed powerful images of themselves as masters of their own fates, resilient in the face of those who would make them victims. Rather than view racism as a structural force, black men in particular viewed it a challenge, one which they had a moral imperative to conquer on their own. Douglas, a twenty-five-year-old black man who runs the athletic department at a local Boys and Girls Club, hesitated when I asked him how he identified racially. "*I* don't identify racially. But I would be identified as African American." He continued, "Growing up in the neighborhood, always heard about 'the man.' Growing up I realized that race really needs to disappear. There are successful African Americans and successful Caucasians." He steels himself against racism by refusing to put into words—and thus bear witness to—its impact on his life. In a similar way, Nathan, who attended a historically black college for a year and a half before failing out, broached the subject of race, only to retract it quickly: "We actually had, they actually had a white valedictorian there. I used to see that cat here and there around campus. He seemed cool." "Oh yeah, I remember the news about that," I replied, trying to gauge his reaction to it.

"That was kind of weird . . . " But he refused to discuss it further: "Yeah, let's move on," he shrugged.

Speaking about race meant giving it too much power as a system, when the real task was to manage it on their own. John, a twenty-seven-year-old black man whom I approached at a Richmond community college, explained: "Society lets it [race] affect me. It's not what I want to do, but society puts tags on everybody. You gotta be presentable, take care of yourself. It's about how a man looks at himself and how people look at him. Some people use it as a crutch, but it's not gonna be my crutch." Learning how to code-switch (Anderson 1999) becomes essential for mitigating powerful cultural images of black people—and black men in particular—as threatening or deviant. John continued: "I can dress like a hustler or like I'm in *GQ*. I refuse to be told no for a job. I know how to speak. I mean I can talk Ebonics, but I can also talk so you can understand me. I don't forget where I come from, but I can talk proper."

These respondents also draw boundaries against black people who view code-switching as "selling out" and thereby circumscribe their own agency by acting, as Kiana put it, "ghetto." Simon put it most harshly: "If you wear baggy jeans and talk like an asshole, you are not gonna get ahead. It's not racism, it's you. I hate black people who say it is racism." Navigating the perils of a neoliberal social order becomes an individual, rather than a collective, game of cunning; to admit that racism holds you back is to admit weakness, both in terms of ability and in terms of character.

Thus, disdain for minorities who cannot pull themselves up by their bootstraps prevails among both white and black respondents. Candace, a young black woman, explained her ability to leave her public housing project behind and attend a four-year college in terms of willing herself to have the right "mind-set":

I don't let myself have a low-income mind-set. That's why most black people don't have no money. Like at income tax time, they get these $4,000, $5,000 refund checks. And then they've never seen money until . . . I mean the whole month of December they're already planning on how they're going to spend that $5,000. So the money is already gone once it gets here. Oh I'm gonna buy jewelry, and I'm gonna buy my kids all name brand stuff, and I'm going to get my hair and nails done. And, you know, never realistic stuff. They do stuff that makes them feel good. Never stuff that, never necessities. So my cousin, she got two checks. One for $5,000 and one for $3,000. And I mean, the one for $5,000 was gone in a week. I thought it was powder dust. I was like, you know you ain't got no job. You could have paid your rent for a year. What was you thinking? Your children are going to outgrow these clothes.

As she attempts to move up the social ladder, Candace draws sharp boundaries against the community where she grew up, blaming its residents for their short-sighted greed and lack of planning, hard work, and self-reliance. Indeed, she attested that part of the reason she agreed to the interview in the first place was to prove to the world that she is not just another "negative statistic": "I wanted your dissertation to speak for those who succeed despite obstacles. I do not communicate my experiences for pity or sorrow but for resilience and triumph. There are so many negative statistics about minorities and poverty. However, very few people listen to those who do not assimilate to the stories."

In this way, informants distance themselves from those who are closest to and just below them in the social structure. Bourdieu (1990: 137) argues that "minimum objective distance in social space can coincide with maximum subjective distance." With the exception of one interviewee, who defines himself as a "revolutionary socialist," no one railed against wealthy people (except for one mechanic who doesn't like the "rich Jews" whose cars he services) or acknowledged class, race, or gender-based injustice as true obstacles. By constructing boundaries against those closest to them in the social hierarchy, respondents articulate an awareness of the struggle for resources—like jobs, welfare, and self-respect—that defines their coming of age experiences. However, the kinds of boundaries they create negate the possibility of class consciousness because they effectively divide those who share the most dismal life chances.

Becoming a Neoliberal Subject

At the time of this writing, distrust for the government is higher than it has been in decades: the Pew Research Center (2013) reports that the majority of Americans believe that the federal government threatens their own personal rights and freedoms Over 40 percent say that the government has a negative effect on their daily lives—an alarming jump from thirteen years ago when only 31 percent expressed such sentiment. Government leaders on both sides of the political debate rail against government waste and prioritize draconian spending cuts. Meanwhile, CEO bonuses are expanding, large corporations openly flout tax laws, and corporate leaders who just a few years ago begged for government aid boldly proclaim that new forms of government regulation unfairly curtail profits. To wit, Jamie Dimon, CFO of JP Morgan Chase, recently wailed that restrictions on debit card fees would prove the "nail in the coffin for big American banks." As capitalism has reduced human dignity to individual ability (Sennett and Cobb 1973), neoliberalism has distorted liberal ideals of freedom into self-sufficiency in the marketplace (Slater 1997). The "common sense" of our time (Schutz 1953) dictates that structural inequalities—sexism, racism, unemployment, lack of access to the tools to navigate one's future—can, and should, be individually overcome.

At first glance, it seems counterintuitive that the young people who would benefit most from social safety nets and solidarity with similarly disadvantaged others cling so fiercely to ideals and practices of untrammeled individualism and self-reliance, not only as the way things are but also as the way they should be. I argue that their deeply held convictions are not simply imposed from above but that they are grounded in their everyday experiences of humiliation and betrayal, their recognition that the social contract they depended on has been severed—or simply never existed in the first place. Over and over again, working-class youth learn that they can depend on others only at great cost. In turn, they numb the ache of betrayal and the hunger for connection by seizing upon cultural scripts of self-reliance, individualism, and personal responsibility. The more "flexible" they must become in their interactions with institutions—that is, the more they learn to manage short-term commitment and disillusionment—the more "hardened" they become toward the world around them.

Through this process, they become acquiescing neoliberal subjects, rejecting all kinds of government intervention, and affirmative action in particular, as antithetical, and thereby offensive, to their lived experiences. In this way, potential communities of solidarity are broken apart by the strain of insecurity and risk. Men hold fast to the few remaining public sector jobs by vigilantly policing their boundaries against women and gay people. White people draw moral boundaries against blacks for taking government money and wasting their tax dollars. Black respondents draw even stronger boundaries against other blacks who cannot get ahead through hard work alone. Ultimately, young working-class men and women believe that if they have to battle through life alone, then everyone else should, too. Hacker (2006b: 1) writes, "Risk can bring people together, creating communities of shared fate. Yet risk can also split people apart." For the post-industrial working class, the necessity of taking care of themselves breeds resentment, fear, and distrust, thus making the possibility of community too risky.

In recognizing the ways in which institutions repeatedly fail them, informants exhibit what Willis (1977) terms "partial penetration," or a sense of the conditions of their social existence and their position within the social whole. They realize that they are denied the tools to succeed by the very institutions that they believed in to help them. But this awareness becomes subsumed under dominant definitions of reality in such a way that the hegemonic logic of neoliberalism is reaffirmed rather than fundamentally challenged (Williams 1977).[21] That is, their deep distrust leads them to embrace widely available neoliberal ideas and policies, believing that it is in their own best interest to live in a society that privatizes risk and privileges the individual over the collective. As a deeply saturating, hegemonic cultural framework, neoliberal ideology resonates with their lives, concealing the "social organization of [its] production and plausibility" (Ewick and Silbey 1995: 214). In translating their experiences of loneliness, uncertainty, and betrayal into stories of staunch individualism and absolute self-reliance, informants create personal narratives that not only express but actively constitute and ultimately reproduce the hegemony of neoliberalism (Ewick and Silbey 1995: 212).

Even seeming acts of resistance are incorporated within an individualistic logic, as evidenced by informants' reliance on popular culture to ease their anxieties and rage. Interestingly, many of the young people featured in this chapter—Amber, Jay, Vanessa—read and sometimes even write, fantasy, science fiction, and self-help books. When I asked Amber what she liked about these genres, she replied without a moment's hesitation, "the escapism. Getting to escape. I like fantasy!" Jay is currently in the midst of what sounds like a fascinating science fiction novel that is explicitly about class struggle:

JAY: The protagonist is a skinhead neo-Nazi who acquires a time machine. Nazis fascinate me. In the first draft, it was actually a hardcore Republican, and I felt like it wasn't interesting enough so I went further and found the most degenerate conservative you can come up with. I mean, aren't we all fascinated with things that disgust us? I am hoping . . . you know what transgressive art is? I feel like it's gonna be transgressive art, like people will really hate the protagonist. He acquires a time machine and him and his gang rewrite history to make it like a white paradise. And then they get to live in their white paradise and it's never enough. Even though they have it all, they want more, they want more, and the real issue is not about white power; it's something else. He sees the error of his ways but his gang members don't.

JS: So if it's not about white power, what is it about?

JAY: It's about class struggle. Because ultimately people who join groups like that, I mean there is another character who has to put up with a militant black, like a modern day Black Panther, and, uh, eventually they realize that, um, each other's hatred is based on the same thing. They are poor and angry and uneducated.

But the awareness of injustice is channeled through popular culture in a way that renders it individual (a matter for "self-help") or solitary (writing a novel); they see exploitation as something to be resolved on their own. And this makes sense, given their inability to navigate bureaucracy and fundamental distrust of others.

Cobb (in Sennett and Cobb 1973: 271) writes: "When the structure of society appears as permanent or beyond human control, when what human beings have created comes to seem immutable, 'natural' transformation becomes individualized. How *you* are going to interpret the world moves to the front of consciousness, how you can transform it in accordance with your needs ceases to be a real question." In this way, working-class youth affirm their commitment to self-reliance and individualism by devising individual solutions to overcoming obstacles. In Chapter 5, I will demonstrate how adulthood itself becomes an individual project.

5 | Inhabiting the Mood Economy

S ITTING IN AN ICE-CREAM SHOP in a student-filled, bustling, and artsy neighborhood in Boston, Massachusetts, I immediately recognized Monica by the large camera slung over her shoulder and the relief in her eyes: at thirty-one, she had just survived her first day of art and design school. With her short, ruffled hair and plastic rim glasses, Monica exudes a boyish charm that perfectly complements her flannel shirt and cigarette jeans. But in her own mind, she still feels like the "super shy," awkward girl from the farm who, wrestling with her sexuality and unable to talk to her conservative family, survived the lonely days of high school only by turning to drugs and alcohol.

Monica grew up on a dairy farm where her mother traded milk for doctor's visits and sometimes hid food stamps from her proud father to get the family through the long winter months. After graduating from high school, she found her first job in a nearby toy factory where she spent long shifts packing dolls in boxes before they were shipped out. When the factory closed, she moved to an electric plant, where she sat for eight hours a day installing tiny springs inside electrical switches with tweezers. This factory, however, soon closed also: "The machine that I was using got shipped to Mexico, and I got laid off." When I asked her where she worked next, she furrowed her brow; she could not keep track of her long and disorderly work history: "Then . . . this is where it gets tricky." She has since worked as a waitress, a truck driver, a field hand, a telemarketer, and a hospital aide, returning in her late twenties to live with her parents and help her father in his logging business after yet another long-term relationship fell apart.

Like many of the "prisoners of the present" chronicled in Chapter 2, Monica never envisioned herself having a future. "There was no five-year plan," she laughed. "I started using really, really young and really didn't think I would live to see thirty. I was just like, I just want to have fun today, right now. So whatever it takes for me to get out of myself, like, with a drug or alcohol, like, I'm going to do that so that I feel good. Whatever the consequences were I just didn't think about it."

Monica described one earth-shattering moment when she realized that her life was going nowhere, prompting her to get sober:

> I definitely had one moment. It was the very end of working for my dad. I was in the truck and I was at a woodlot and it was a freezing cold morning and I was waiting for them to be ready to fill the truck. So I was just sitting, and I was, like . . . the radio was off and I was journaling, and I was hung over and I felt horrible. I was just like, what am I doing with my life? It's such a mess, it's so unmanageable and I'm a mess and I'm not happy in any way. I'm not doing anything I want to do. Working for my parents and been working for my parents for years and it's just not . . . nothing in my life is working. So I kind of, like, said a little prayer and asked for help and made a pact with myself that I was going to change something. So yeah, that was the turning point.

Monica found a therapist who diagnosed her with depression, started her on anti-depressant medication, and convinced her to go to an Alcoholics Anonymous meeting. This therapist also encouraged her to "find something that you're passionate about." Although she has relapsed a few times and had to stop taking her medication because she could not afford health insurance, Monica continues to attend AA meetings. She feels optimistic that she has turned her life around. Monica challenges herself to see the positive aspect of everything that happens to her, believing that happiness is within her control: even when her bike (and sole form of transportation) was stolen last spring, she "was like, that's all right, I needed to get rid of my mountain bike and get a road bike *(laughs)*. You really just have to keep it positive today."

Monica's parents, while very poor when she was growing up, have finally achieved some financial stability through her father's logging business. Reflecting on the difference between herself and her parents' generation, she mused:

> I know that they were, like, real working class, pulled themselves up by their bootstraps. Like they worked hard for what they have and they totally deserve what they have. I have those strong work ethics, but at the same time I'm not going to slave away at a job that I hate. So I really feel like I've

found my passion in life and it happens to be in the arts. I know it's going to be a struggle to make a lot of money or make a living so that's a huge difference. And they have had a hard time supporting me because they're scared I'm not going to be able to make a living. And they've seen me move and change jobs so often.

Unlike her parents, who view economic security, financial stability, and family as foundational to a worthy life, Monica has redefined success in terms of passion and creativity. Her string of short-term jobs and relationships, and years of constant flux, have taught her that depending on work or family to center her sense of self would leave her constantly seeking.

Instead, she has created a different kind of coming of age narrative, one that hinges not on *any* of the traditional (and deeply gendered) markers of adulthood but instead on discovering her personal demons, overcoming her addiction, and realizing her authentic self. She reflected:

> I think that having more time in sobriety has taught me to grow up in a lot of ways. I mean there's tons of stuff that I don't feel proud about that I've done, like tons of stuff. But I can't change that, and I wouldn't be who I am today if I didn't go through everything that I did. And I feel like I've had a very, like, live-out-loud, colorful growing up and maturing, and you know a lot of life's lessons that I had to learn and I had to go through *myself*.

Today she is beginning an undergraduate degree program at the art college, taking out nearly $30,000 in loans to pay her tuition and living expenses in the hope of becoming a professional photographer. Despite this enormous risk, her narrative of suffering and self-transformation keeps her hopeful: she has resolved the structurally embedded uncertainties, tensions, and failures of her life at the most intimate level of her *self*. That is, even though she is "just hanging on by a thread all the time financially" and is postponing long-term relationships for the time being, she has faith in her abilities to stay on the right path—just as long as she stays sober: "Because if I don't, you know, I could drink and that would mean losing everything."

Adulthood as an "Unsettled Time"

As Monica's story reveals, working-class young men and women are learning that the performances once relied upon to construct an adult identity—to *feel* like an adult—have become structurally unavailable and sometimes undesirable. In such unsettled times, as Swidler (1986: 279) argues, people "reorganize taken-for-granted habits and modes of experience" into new rituals that better fit the changing ethos. Accordingly, in this chapter, I explore the emerging ways in which young people ascribe meaning, order, and progress onto their dislocated and de-institutionalized experiences of coming of age (see also Silva 2012). In doing so, I uncover what it means to be an adult in an age of insecurity and uncertainty.

About a quarter of the men and women I spoke with told their coming of age narratives as journeys of having achieved traditional milestones or of hoping to progress toward them. They viewed adulthood in terms of clearly defined role transitions structured by external sources of authority such as traditional gender roles (as in the example of Joseph) or God (as in the case of Rachel). For the vast majority, however, understandings of adulthood bore little resemblance to the normalized progression of leaving home, completing school, finding a steady job, getting married, and having children that so clearly demarcated the split between childhood and adulthood in the decades following World War II. Instead, in the absence of traditional rites of passage, these young men and women were in the process of reconstructing adulthood as *therapeutic*—inwardly directed and preoccupied with psychic development. As I will demonstrate, this alternative, therapeutic coming of age story ends not with marriage, a home, or a career, but with self-realization gleaned from denouncing a painful past and rebuilding an emancipated self (see Illouz 2008). These working-class men and women employ the therapeutic narrative to recast their dislocated experiences of work and family as a triumphal narrative of overcoming a painful past.[1]

I make sense of the phenomenon of therapeutic adulthood through the concept of the *mood economy*. I argue that working-class men and women inhabit a social world in which the legitimacy and dignity due adults are purchased not with traditional currencies such as work or marriage but instead through the ability to organize their difficult emotions into a narrative of *self*-transformation.[2] The mood economy replaces more traditional forms of organizing the self, such as those invoked by Monica's working-class parents; it is articulated and instantiated through the telling of a therapeutic narrative. Within the mood economy, *emotional management* has become the new currency of working-class adulthood, promising transformation—and longed-for progress—in exchange for a public denunciation of pain: "The suffering person is compelled to make her pain a compelling narrative of identity, to work on it and make it into a meaningful life project" (Illouz 2003: 161). When Monica, for example, takes stock of her life, her inability to find a steady job or maintain a romantic relationship are eclipsed by the suffering she endured in her personal struggle to defeat her addiction. By enabling her to tell her coming of age story *backward*—to start at her present, "transformed" self and work backward through the emotional trials she has undergone to construct it—the mood economy allows for the possibility of self-worth, meaning, and progress. Yet there is also a darker side to the mood economy, one that threatens to make self-reliance—and severing social ties—the only imaginable path to a life of dignity.

The Triumph of the Therapeutic?

For the vast majority of the men and women I spoke with, coming of age has been reimagined as a psychic *struggle to triumph over the demons of their pasts*. These "demons" take several different forms: pain or betrayal in past relationships; emotional, mental, or cognitive disorders (e.g., depression, dyslexia, or anxiety); or addiction to drugs, alcohol, or pornography.[3] Hurtful and agonizing betrayals within the family lie at the root of these torments, grounding their adult identities in the quest to heal their wounded selves. Through telling their stories of confronting a difficult past, working-class women and men stake a claim to dignity and respect, based not on traditional markers of adulthood but on having undergone emotional trauma and emerged, triumphantly, as survivors.

Haunted by the Past: Pain and Betrayal in Intimate Relationships

Some informants made overcoming painful past relationships the arc in their narratives of becoming an adult. For these men and women, themes of breaking free from pathological family patterns and liberating themselves from their disturbed pasts anchor their adult identities in suffering and self-transformation. Family pathology is invoked both to explain (to themselves and to others) why they have not achieved traditional adult milestones and to map meaning, order, and progress onto their experiences of stagnation in the present.

Eileen is a thirty-three-year-old white woman who describes herself as having "old, traditional Southern views." Eileen grew up in a trailer park about an hour outside Richmond. When I asked about her parents' occupations (a seemingly easy question I often used to break the ice), Eileen took a deep breath and stated resolutely, "I have to keep telling myself they're no reflection of me. That's what I keep telling myself, and you know, I am still trying to learn all this, trying to make sense of what I'll never make sense of." Holding back tears, Eileen explained that her father had spent his life in prison for armed robbery and soliciting sex from a minor; her mother, who was only fifteen when Eileen was born, committed suicide when her daughter was in her late teens. Struggling to come to terms with her mother's death—her sorrow amplified by guilt over discouraging her mother from taking anti-depressants—Eileen fell in love with Scott, a man whose brother had also committed suicide recently, and soon became pregnant. When their daughter Elizabeth turned four, Eileen realized that Scott was molesting her, and she called the Department of Social Services and the police in a panic. After several harrowing years, "the monster" finally gave up his fatherhood rights, but for reasons that Eileen does not comprehend, Scott was never convicted of his crime (see Chapter 4 for a discussion of betrayal and confusion within institutions).

Eileen is now married and has another daughter, Sophie, who is four. She is looking for a new job, having recently left her "accounts billable" position at a property management company because there were no opportunities for advancement. A firm believer in hard work, self-reliance, and the American Dream, Eileen will do "anything to better myself. You got to take those chances. I know with the economy and everything right now, people say hold on to your job, but I think I'm one of those persons that likes to take a chance, to better myself for my daughters." But after months of fruitless searching, Eileen is losing hope: "I am definitely feeling not so optimistic about the future, because I have been without a job. My own doing. It was a risky move and I thought for sure I would have a job within a month or two. No luck. I have applied everywhere, except fast food chains. I have even applied for housekeeping positions." The family is living paycheck to paycheck on her husband's truck driving job, which keeps him on the road five days a week and makes it difficult for Eileen to search for job openings.

Looking back on her life, Eileen reflects, "I always wanted to get married and then have children and you know, go to college. But it just, it didn't happen. I keep saying I want to go back to college or go to college rather, but it's just, it just doesn't happen." Eileen locates the source of her inability to achieve these goals within her childhood: "I always said that I wanted to do things right, as far as not following in my mom's footsteps. But I think it's just the lifestyle that I had growing up. I think, like I said, I don't want to blame that lifestyle for my actions, but I think it does play a part of the way things turned out." Today, Eileen admittedly spends most of her time reliving the past, trying to come to terms with the horrifying tragedies that have befallen her family. Speaking of her ex who molested her daughter, she reflected:

> After my mom passed, I was looking for something. People like that [Scott], they leech onto things and, I learned later, that they leech on and that's how they, I guess, come into things like this. They can sugarcoat stuff and then they aren't what they are. So I just, you know, I think as I'm making sense of all this just the way that my childhood played out. I didn't see this person, you don't see people for who they are until after you get to know them. And I beat myself up a lot because he just was a horrible person. I'm finally getting myself out of that.

For the past two years, Eileen has been seeing a free counselor at Children and Family Services who diagnosed her with post-traumatic stress disorder and treats her with medication and therapy. She is slowly learning to tell a narrative of selfhood—of becoming—that hinges on self-consciously confronting her difficult family past and setting herself free from destructive family patterns. In taking responsibility for "getting [her]self out of that," Eileen has staked out an adult identity founded upon intense suffering and self-transformation. Pondering the kinds of lessons she would like to teach her daughters, she summarized: "As with their mother, sometimes we have to learn the hard way about life. To realize we aren't perfect, that we make mistakes and we try to learn from it. We keep chugging along and not give up."

Battling (Internal) Disorder

Others told their stories in terms of the cognitive, emotional, or mental disorders that have plagued them throughout their lives, threatening to keep them from achieving their true potential. These disorders cover a wide range of conditions, from self-diagnosed "anger management" issues to obsessive compulsive disorder (OCD) to depression. When respondents construct a narrative of battling these disorders, they emphasize the process through which they came to understand their symptoms as legitimate diseases, re-envisioning their life histories through the lens of this previously unacknowledged problem (Martin 2007). Respondents also emphasize the betrayal they felt from their families who allowed their problems to go undiscovered. In conceiving of disorder as something internal—stemming from biological, chemical, or emotional dysfunction—informants construct their problems as controllable, rewarding themselves with a sense of accomplishment when they overcome their demons.

George, a thirty-three-year-old black man, is in countless ways a success story. Raised by a single mother who works at a meat processing plant, George moved thirty-eight times (he counted) between the ages of seven and eighteen, living everywhere from rooming houses to abuse shelters to crowded efficiency apartments. He laughingly recalled sleeping in a walk-in closet in high school. Because he finished high school in a city with strong public schools, George learned how to apply to college and for financial aid from his guidance counselor and his peers. Sharp, insightful, and engaging, he graduated from a public university in the South, then secured a stable government accounting job that he still holds today. A few years ago, feeling bored and unsatisfied in his job, George attempted to go back to school for a master's degree in psychology. However, he soon dropped out, finding himself unable to cope with the stress of graduate school.

G: Do you want to know why I really left?

JS: Yes, definitely.

G: OCD [obsessive-compulsive disorder].[4] It still sucks for me. It was really, I don't know if this is off the topic but, when I left I was like at the bottom of a complete downturn. It took about a good . . . I think it was January or February. It took until about May, April or May of that year, to actually be pretty good with it. I was on a program. I was on meds, whatever. And then, like a lot of people, I just didn't want to be dependent on them, so I stopped taking them. I thought I was fine, but then I went down again. I started taking them, I felt better. I stopped taking them again, and now I feel shitty. It's one of those things where unfortunately psychiatrists don't really have credentials to subscribe to health insurance plans, so you have to pay out of pocket and then get reimbursed. So I mean, I have to pay 250 bucks per visit, sometimes it's twice a month. So I got kind of tired of that.

George is currently not seeing a doctor because he dreads haggling with insurance companies for coverage. Instead, he has committed himself to learning as much as he can about his condition. He continued, "I went to this conference two falls ago, *The OCD Foundation*. I met this guy, Jonathan Grayson, he is like a prominent OCD psychiatrist. He's the end all. He's been actually on Oprah et cetera. . . . He was just fabulous. I bought his book."

By reading about obsessive-compulsive disorder, George has learned to organize his past experiences of flux, uncertainty, and betrayal into a coherent and intelligible narrative, thus solidifying his identity in suffering and self-transformation. Looking back on his life, he reflected:

> I've always had it. I didn't know what it was until college actually when I read about it. It started when I was about seven. Like I remember just pulling my hair out. It's hard to explain. I think it's called trichotillomania. It's hair pulling and so that's one of the reasons why I keep my hair short all over. Because I still do it, but not as much as I was when I was in school and stuff. I didn't know what it was. I just thought it was something to do. But the thing is, my mom wasn't really educated, so she just told me to stop it. When I was in middle school I noticed a whole fear of rust thing and cleaning disorder thing. When I was in high school it got worse, and I remember telling my mom about it. Like I remember she had this white car, and on the passenger side I guess the window paneling or insulation was gone. It was removed and there was some steel there and it was all rusted. So anytime I wanted to get into the car I had to go like that [he shields his body with his hands]. I could never roll the window down. So there was one time when she was living with my brother in some townhouse. Anyway, I was trying to like get between the car and a concrete wall and go into the garage and trying to avoid the car. She was like, "What are you doing?" I couldn't really explain to her, and she just got mad at me. Instead of asking why, she got mad at me. She said, "You have a problem." I said, *"Yeah, I know, I've been trying to tell you about it for twelve years."*

In this painful recollection, George expresses resentment and anger that his mother did not help him, regretting that his lack of resources and knowledge as a child prevented him from putting a name on, and in turn managing, his disorder.

Tellingly, George understands his illness as existing entirely within himself. The social context in which his extreme anxiety and compulsion to control his environment developed are not viewed as relevant to him (especially interesting when considering that the subtitle of Dr. Grayson's self-help guide to OCD: *A Personalized Recovery Program for Living with Uncertainty*).[5] For George, it is his *illness* that has prevented him from building a better life for himself, but it is also the one constant presence in a life full of upheaval and flux. As something to be controlled and managed, it has become a meaningful, consistent piece of his adult identity—and an enduring symbol of his mother's betrayal.

The most common disorders mentioned by respondents were anxiety and depression.[6] Respondents spoke at length about their trials to overcome these problems in order to achieve true emotional well-being. Vinny, a twenty-seven-year-old white man, started out at an $8 an hour security guard job after graduating from high school. Driven and competitive, Vinny took as many overtime shifts as he could, first working his way up to manager, then to shift supervisor, and finally to account manager. Vinny feels extremely lucky to have stayed with his company for almost ten years, especially without a college degree. Terrified that he will not measure up, he pushes himself daily to the brink of exhaustion:

> As I said, there's a lot of responsibility and the job is pretty stressful. There was a point where I really let it get the best of me. I ended up working myself into getting really, really sick. I ended up developing all sorts of anxiety problems over work. I would be literally awake for three and four days at a time and it was all because I was pressing so hard to try to do more and be the best. I'm very driven by my numbers, because that's what I'm marked on. I have it in my head, we have these monthly meetings we often present our numbers, and even to this day I still have it in my head where I got to be the best.

Vinny eventually had to take a two-month leave of absence to recover. He was forced to start over as a shift supervisor when he rejoined the company, which only intensified his concern over his "numbers." While he continues to struggle with anxiety, he has developed personal coping strategies to calm himself down:

> The actual anxiety attacks, *you just got to figure out that it's all in your head and you almost got to talk yourself out of it.* You know, get a cup of water, go take a deep breath, and just let it pass. . . . Because if you feel like you're going to pass out and you don't know why, you start to panic and then it's just like a ridiculous cycle that never ends until you're in the hospital with Ativan [a fast-acting anxiety medication]. But if you can just kind of get a grip on it, you know what it is, there's no need to panic over it.

Being aware of and managing his *emotions*—rather than the precariousness of the labor market itself—becomes the only way to get through the day.

"Hitting Bottom" and Redemption through Sobriety

The third type of therapeutic narrative pivots on fighting the pull of addiction to alcohol, drugs, or pornography. Addiction is construed as a coping mechanism for deep psychic wounds originating within the family. Like Monica, who opens this chapter, these men and women center their stories on "hitting bottom," weaving a linear narrative that leads to the realization that they must surrender to their powerlessness over the disease of addiction itself (Denzin 1987). Yet they also express a sense of hopefulness, of redemption through sobriety, painstakingly measuring their forward progress through life in the number of days, months, or years they have gone without a fix.

Lauren is a twenty-four-year-old white woman who has been on her own since her father kicked her out of the house at age sixteen for being a lesbian. At the beginning of the interview, she warned me that she might need to step out for a cigarette break; after a few minutes of one-word, terse answers to my questions, I asked her if she wanted to take the conversation outside, and her pale blue eyes lit up: "Yes, please!" As we stood outside her favorite coffee shop, sharing my umbrella to shield us from the pouring rain, she inhaled cigarette after cigarette, shakily recounting her story of addiction and recovery:

> I suffered from a lot of depression and social anxiety and . . . just a lot of emotional and mental issues growing up. I saw psychiatrists and then I turned to drugs. That's why I didn't do well in high school, I was too busy smoking pot. . . . I did everything. Everything but like free-basing . . . well, actually I smoked crack so I did free-base. Everything. I did . . . um . . . cocaine was my favorite in all its forms. Every day, I spent all my money on it. I was unemployable because of it. I started taking classes and then I would drop them, and then I would take more classes and I would drop them. I kept trying to get on my feet but I never could. Addiction runs in my family. My mom is an alcoholic, my dad is an alcoholic, my mom's brother stuck a shotgun in his mouth and pulled the trigger because of drugs. There's a lot of addicts in my family and I am one of them, I found out.

Lauren came to the realization that she needed to seek help after not eating or sleeping for six days. When a treatment center turned her away because she did not have health insurance, she found Narcotics Anonymous (NA) and began to turn her life around. "The moment I decided to seek help for my addiction was the moment my obstacles became growing experiences, learning experiences," she stated resolutely. In NA, Lauren has learned a new language of empowerment-through-suffering for conceptualizing her sense of self. As she declared: "Everybody's life sucks, get over it! My mom's an alcoholic, my dad kicked me out of the house. It's not a handicap, it has made me stronger." Despite the fact that Lauren is unhappy in her job as a barista and cannot afford to go back to school, she feels that she has made great progress in overcoming her addiction and has forged a meaningful identity as a survivor.

Through Alcoholics and Narcotics Anonymous, informants learn to encounter the world *as addicts*, making sense of their past disappointments and failures through the lens of their addiction and the underlying pain that fueled it (Denzin 1993). Looking back on her inability to get along with her coworkers at one of her service jobs, for instance, Monica mused, "Now I think they were just used to banter, but then I took offense to it. Like I took it personally. And I think part of that is being an alcoholic. You just take things personally. It's like a defect of character that you have." Informants thus connect the seemingly unrelated events of their chaotic past lives through the creation of a forward-moving coming of age narrative of self-discovery and change (Illouz 2007).

To provide another example of redemption through sobriety, Kathleen is a twenty-five-year-old white woman who was asked to leave her small private college (where she was funding her education with loans) after her first year because of excessive drinking and failing grades. Too embarrassed to tell her friends and family who believed she was still in college, she spent a year and a half living at a sober house.

JS: How does that work? Do you have to pay to go there, or do you go there for free?

K: No, they let you go there. The state will fund it.

JS: Can anyone sign up for that?

K: Yeah, you have to be . . . They'll interview you and see like if you really want to make a change in your life and things like that, and they put me in. And I was the youngest by I think at least twenty years so . . . I mean, it was a struggle but that's the same with growing up. You know, I started drinking because I didn't want to feel the pain, almost like the abandonment issues with my mom? And with my dad working all the time, I never really saw him. So school has always been a struggle, and after that I decided I was going to make something of myself.

Kathleen came to understand her drinking as a response to the emotional trauma inflicted by her mother's neglect. Her father, whom she idolizes, often worked overtime shifts as a prison guard to keep the family afloat, leaving Kathleen alone most of the time.

In her reconstructed narrative, Kathleen gives voice to a sense of pride and empowerment: she was able to work through the trauma of her childhood and give herself a fresh start at a sober, meaningful life. Importantly, Kathleen sees her recovery as a *choice;* she is emphatic that people can find happiness and health if they are strong and determined enough to face their difficult emotions (Morrison 2011). Indeed, while I labeled working-class youth "prisoners of the present" in Chapter 2, it may be more accurate to describe them as "prisoners of the past"—*who must set themselves free*. Comparing herself to her mother, Kathleen reflected:

> I think she has it so embedded in her head that she won't, that she's in a way given up. It's hard for me because, for me if something happens to me or whatever I may be down for a day or two but I get right back up. You know, and it's hard to see someone not like that. I pray to God that she does; I would never want her to live a life like this, but I've also learned you're not going to get better if you don't want to.

Here, Kathleen draws a strong moral boundary against people who cannot will themselves into health, functionality, and happiness; her sense of self depends entirely on framing her emotional progress as an individual choice.

Kathleen has now been sober for three years and is currently going back to school (this time to a less expensive public one) to become a counselor for children: "I'm looking towards working in a hospital in a Psych Unit. I want to more target children. So instead of having the problem already presented and trying to fix it, trying to get it before the problem gets there." Her addiction becomes the thread that weaves together her disparate experiences of family disruption, failure, and redemption, ultimately pushing her life forward in the goal of helping others like herself.

Making Sense of Suffering

In interpreting the stories of suffering and self-transformation told by the working-class young men and women I interviewed, I begin with the assumption that the therapeutic narrative predominates not because it allows informants to articulate the whole of "what really happened" but rather because it allows them to organize their complicated feelings and experiences in a way that makes their lives comprehensible and meaningful. Following Illouz (2008: 69), I argue that the therapeutic narrative provides a culturally available tool kit for "mak[ing] sense of their difficult emotions and help[ing] put them 'to work' by eliciting a narrative of suffering and self-help." In this way, the therapeutic narrative has become a vital coping mechanism for combating the chaos, hopelessness, and insecurity that threatens daily to strip working-class young people's lives of all remnants of meaning and order.

To clarify, at the center of the therapeutic coming of age narrative are not more traditional sources of identity such as work, religion, or gender, but instead the *family*—as the source of one's individuality, the source of the self, *and* the source of the neuroses from which one must liberate oneself (Illouz 2007). For post-industrial working-class young people who are nostalgic about the past, crippled by the present, and wary of the future, learning to tell a *past-centered* therapeutic narrative feels like finally unveiling the long-awaited hidden truth of their experiences. Addressing the commercialization of intimate life, Hochschild (2003: 39) argues that "the more the commodity frontier erodes the territory surrounding the emotional role of wife and mother, the more hypersymbolized the remaining sources of care become." Through an analogous process, the more the market renders the future unimaginable and the present unmanageable, the more hypersymbolized the *family past* becomes.

Within the mood economy, working-class young people make uncertainty, disruption, betrayal, and failure *meaningful*, especially those who find no intrinsic meaning or hope in their jobs or futures. As their interview transcripts reveal, therapeutic discourse is deeply ingrained in the institutions that frame their coming of age experiences: school psychologists, social services, self-help literature, free drug trials, and Alcoholics and Narcotics Anonymous. In a time when suffering is plentiful and work and family unreliable, the mood economy allows competent adulthood to be defined not in terms of traditional markers like financial independence, a career, or a marriage, but rather in terms of psychic development: achieving sobriety, overcoming addiction, fighting a mental illness, or simply not becoming one's own parents.

When Eileen tells her story, for example, she organizes her experiences of relationship failure, guilt and regret, institutional confusion, and labor market stagnancy into a linear narrative of emotional *self*-transformation. She measures her progress in her ability to discover why she was attracted to "the monster," to heal her wounded psyche, and to become a stronger person for her daughters. Thus, when I asked her if she would call herself an adult, she replied:

> Yes, though I still like playing games and doing stuff with my girls. And I think, too, like with my mom I don't remember a whole lot of that stuff with her. . . . I want to be, not so much different from her, but just [to] take more responsibility in . . . I guess that is being an adult. I guess I just answered that question after going around the mulberry bush (laughs).

In Eileen's eyes, adulthood is reconfigured through the lens of the therapeutic narrative to signify emotional growth. Indeed, while her response begins with a joke about being an adult despite her enjoyment of children's games, she is immediately drawn toward the past, invoking memories of her own mother's lack of involvement in her childhood to show how she has set herself free from these destructive family patterns. Triumphing over individual and family pathology and pain, and ultimately realizing one's true and emancipated self, subsumes her coming of age narrative even when she starts to tell another kind of story. Within the mood economy, the active remembering of suffering is the only path to self-emancipation; as Illouz (2008) explains, "the therapeutic narrative only works by conceiving of life events as the markers of failed or thwarted opportunities for self-development. Thus the narrative of self-help is fundamentally sustained by a narrative of suffering" (173).

Like Eileen, Candace also connected adulthood to realizing her authentic self through suffering:

> c: So I will say coming into adulthood is, when you are a person who has so many disadvantages you tend to construct yourself based on what people want and what people expect and what people think is good of you. Which has benefited me well. Because I take people's suggestions very seriously. The real Candace is not based on what people expect of me, what people do with me. I think the first decision that I really ever made was not to run track [in school]. So it was like my first real decision for, like, my happiness, and it's been wonderful.
>
> js: I know you mentioned having a hard time in school.
>
> c: Hard time ain't the word, man. My therapist actually wanted me to withdraw. And I told her I'm not a quitter. No, I'm not going to withdraw. Because then I won't be able to come back for a year. No

way, I'm doing that. And I think just like a little side note, I think one of the hardest things is just looking around you when I'm coming into age at college. And just knowing that I won't have like a strong . . . that my strongest family support is not my real family. So when my mom got out of jail she asked me like what year in school I was. Which broke my heart, because she didn't know what year I was in school. And that was almost like three years ago. And now we're starting to get back on pretty good terms. She came to my apartment to help me move. And I had to basically take two photo albums and a yearbook and walk my mom through my high school years, because she didn't know anything about my high school years. So that was bittersweet. That's also difficult just being the adult and having to show the adult that's supposed to be taking care of you.

Within this coming of age story, Candace works through the disappointment, pain, and betrayal rooted in her mother's drug addiction and emerges as stable, healthy, and whole. Through its telling, disruption, betrayal, and failure born of everyday life in an unequal and risky society are imbued with a sense of extraordinariness, thus granting her life meaning, dignity, and coherence.

The Transformation of Working-Class Adulthood

These coming of age stories of emotional trauma and self-transformation may challenge popular conceptions of the American working class; indeed, it is difficult to imagine the iconic industrial steelworker or coal miner articulating, let alone opening up about, his psychic pain. Similarly, the coming of age narratives constructed by my informants sound dramatically different from those found in earlier studies of the American (usually white and male) working class chronicled in the work of Willis (1977), Rubin (1976), or even more recent scholars like Lamont (2000). In these studies, dignity was born of economic self-sufficiency; rugged masculinity; commitment to God, family, and country; and upholding moral order. Illouz (2008: 235) explains:

> As the British sociologist Paul Willis has shown in his ethnographic study of the shop floor, blue-collar work mobilizes an ethos of bravery, strength, and distrust of words. . . . The individualism of the working-class men and

women is characterized by narratives of struggle with adversity; it is a rugged individualism that emphasizes distrust, toughness, and physical strength.

There was no place for therapeutic discourse within industrial working-class work and family life, which required an emotional style of taciturn stoicism. In contrast, my research suggests that working-class understandings of selfhood are in flux, with therapeutic notions of personal self-growth and emotional expression melding with, competing against, or replacing these older, more traditional forms of defining the self.

Within my sample, remnants of more traditional understandings and performances of adulthood did exist, hinging not on therapeutic self-expression but instead on hard work, taking care of one's family, and devoting oneself to God. The male firefighters in my sample invoked traditional masculine conceptions of adulthood most coherently. When Joseph, for example, was growing up, his father was in and out of prison for using and selling drugs while his mother struggled to raise their five children. The moment Joseph graduated from high school, he enlisted in the Marines and took his first plane ride ever to boot camp. When he came home for a short break, he married his high school sweetheart at nineteen, and they had their first child two years later on the military base. He is committed to building a solid nuclear family: when the city eliminated all overtime pay at the start of the recession, he took a second job monitoring a cell phone tower, and his wife runs a day care out of their home—which they own—to make ends meet. His adult identity is deeply gendered, founded on being a good father and a good husband: "I had my priorities straight. I'm not going to go sit at a bar and drink with my friends when I got my wife and kids at home."

Joseph's family life was not less fractured or difficult than those of others in the sample. But Joseph doesn't view the painfulness of the past as central to his identity; he holds no grudges against his own parents, believing that his own generation has no idea how hard their parents' or grandparents' lives were. He has allowed his father back into his life, repairing their relationship not through words but through building an addition on Joseph's house together. He describes himself as focused on the future, his belief in upward mobility through determination and hard work propelling his narrative forward:

They were both pretty much poor, well, maybe my father wasn't poor, they needed all their kids to work but that is what family did back then. But now compared to them, I feel like kids' goals should be more . . . that is why when I graduated I wasn't gonna mess around and see what comes, I just went ahead and did it; it's the most important thing you can do in your life. I don't think they had that. But I didn't want to have to struggle to live like they did. I just went out and did what I had to do.

What separates Joseph, and his fellow firefighters, from the therapeutically inclined informants, I argue, is the fact that they have stable, public sector jobs in traditionally masculine fields. They have futures that are manageable and certain, and have not needed to develop a language of the self rooted in past suffering and redemption. Furthermore, in fields such as firefighting that strictly police the boundaries of masculinity and femininity, there is little to be gained in expressing emotion. Indeed, during *every* interview I conducted at the firehouse, a fellow firefighter would pop his head into the room and say something along the lines of, "you know he's gay, right?" eliciting peals of boisterous laughter from outside the door. Rather than view the interview as a sacred space for telling one's story, as the therapeutically inclined informants like Monica did, the young firefighters construed it as a site for male bonding, teasing, or perhaps even flirtation with a female interviewer. As this example demonstrates, young people construct their selves according to the available cultural resources of the institutions in which they come of age.

A small number of black women used their religious faith as their primary way to make sense of their delayed transition to adulthood. Rather than abandon traditional markers of adulthood, these women trust that they will come in God's time. Rachel, a twenty-seven-year-old black woman I interviewed at the armory, works forty hours a week as a customer service representative at an electronics store. She was kicked out of her mother's house at sixteen for refusing to abide by her rules. Rachel "bounced around" for a few years, sleeping on friends' couches and relying on her credit card to survive. She recalled, "For two years, if I had to go to the hospital, I had to pay for it. I was working odds and ends jobs, sometimes I wasn't even working, so I didn't have the money to pay for the bills at the time. They just racked up and racked up and racked up. It brought my credit to the floor. It's horrible because of that." On the day she turned eighteen, she enlisted in the National Guard and shipped out to basic training, hoping to finally pay off her thousands of dollars of debt and to use the GI Bill to go to college.

Ten years later, her debt has grown to $20,000. She has moved back in with her mother, and she still hasn't found the time to go to school. While she fondly refers to the military as "the dad and brothers [she] never had," she admits that her two deployments in Iraq took a serious emotional and physical toll on her. "Every day I would get up and say, God, please let me make it home safely," she recalled shakily. "It's like, please don't let it be today. Every time I was on the road, driving my truck, I would say please don't let this be the night that something happens." Her four-year-old son Mark is "the thing that keeps her going." Rachel is raising him alone, describing his father as "not even boyfriend material. . . . He didn't have a job, he was selling drugs, just a lot of stuff under the rug that I didn't know about until it was too late." With little hope of finding a husband and father for her son, Rachel knows that her only chance at providing a better life for Mark requires deploying to Iraq yet again to take advantage of the combat pay. She remains "half and half" about it: "I am kinda happy about it and kinda not. I missed the first two years of my son's life and now I might have to leave again. It's just rough. You can't win."

When I asked Rachel if there have been times when she wanted to give up, she leveled with me:

> When it rains, it pours, you know that expression? No matter how hard I try, I take one step forward and get punched back ten steps. Like no matter what I do, I just can't seem to get ahead and make things work out for me. *Like I said, I kinda just leave it up to God, you know what I mean, because He has a plan for me and that is what I believe. When He wants me to go a certain direction or be stable or have wealth or whatever he wants me to do, it will come when he wants me to have it and I am just trying to think about that whenever I get down.* I do still have days when I want to go to sleep and I don't wanna get up. And then I think of my son and I know if I'm not here to help him and protect him, nobody else will protect him. God and my son are the only things that are keeping me going. That's when I feel hopeful; that's when I think to myself that I am doing it for a reason.

Rachel's life experiences provide plenty of raw material for a therapeutic narrative of suffering and self-transformation. However, within the institutions that frame her transition to adulthood—the military, her family, and her church—she has learned to tell a different story. Rather than understand happiness as something within her control, like Monica does, she puts it in the hands of God: "He has a plan for me and that is what I believe." Here, suffering is not interpreted as a sign of psychic wounds that must be healed within herself but rather as part of a larger plan that she does not understand.

Indeed, Rachel admitted that she does not know how to communicate her emotions, nor does she view her feelings as manageable or controllable.

> I don't cry, and I am not the type of person to break down and cry unless it is like when I just don't want to get up anywhere, which are the only times I have broken down and cried. The only vent that I have is through my iPod. That centers me and brings me back down and puts me in a mellow mood. I don't open up well and my family, my mom and I, like maybe it's a military thing, we are not the "I love you" type and hug and kiss and all that. We know we love each other. We just don't say it. We are not the lovey-dovey type. She is not the easiest person in the world to talk to, so I feel like I have no one to talk to. I keep my emotions bottled up and deal with them on my own, and then I let them keep going and going and then I break down. My iPod is my release. It doesn't even matter what it is, I just throw on the iPod and it always tends to bring me back down to a place where I can handle everything.

As this passage reveals, suffering is something to be endured rather than psychically resolved. She sometimes feels besieged by her emotions, with no idea how to manage them: "I keep my emotions bottled up and deal with them on my own, and then I let them keep going and going and then I break down." In other words, outside of the mood economy, she cannot exchange her suffering for a sense of progress or meaning.

The contrast between the industrial working-class selfhood depicted in earlier studies (and in a small number of my interviews) and the pervasive therapeutic conception of adulthood in my sample raises the question of how cultural definitions of selfhood and dignity change over time. Here, it is helpful to draw upon a central insight of the sociology of emotion: that one's place within social structures—and the everyday linguistic skills, embodied practices, and interactions that sustain it—produces the very capacity to feel and express emotions. These emotions—whether anger, pride, or desire—are then experienced as pre-reflexive and unmediated (Collins 2004; Goffman 1959; Hochschild 1995; Illouz 2007; Williams 1977). To put it simply, what is outside continually constructs what is inside; emotion can thus be thought of as the least conscious part of the internal-external feedback loop that is *habitus*, constituted by and constitutive of not only social structure, but also social inequality (Illouz 2007). Indeed, the very ability to feel—as well as to express and manage—particular emotions is shaped by and in turn shapes one's position in the social structure, whether by gender, social class, or race (Hochschild 2003; Illouz 2007, 2008; Lively and Heise 2004).

Connecting emotion to social structure suggests that emotions may have profound consequences for the reproduction of social inequality. Pioneering this line of thought, Illouz (2008) argues that working-class people may lack the linguistic and emotional skills necessary for organizing their intimate experiences of disruption and betrayal into a coherent therapeutic narrative.[7] Consequently, differences in emotional capacity and expression should be viewed as "inequalities in the chances of obtaining access to ordinary forms of well-being" (2008: 235). Recall Rachel's inability to "open up" and deal with her emotions, leaving her so overwhelmed that she would "break down."

While Illouz's interviews were conducted in the late 1980s and 1990s, my interviews conducted several decades later document that many young working-class men and women can and do create self-conscious narratives of personal suffering and self-realization. This profound shift in working-class emotional expression points to a broader generational divergence in what it means to experience working-class life at the level of the *self* (Chauvel 1998; Mannheim 1952). For the post-industrial working-class men and women in my sample, it is not the shop floor, but rather the struggle to come to terms with its *disappearance*, that characterizes their life-worlds. They have come of age amid the decline of blue-collar factory work, and they have personally experienced the insecurity and uncertainty wrought by de-industrialization and the rise of neoliberal policies and ideology. At the same time, the increasing availability of therapeutic discourse within the institutions that shape their lives has prompted the adoption of a new set of discourses and practices for conceiving of the self and its relations to others (Illouz 2007).[8] While therapeutic institutions may allow the professional middle classes to achieve emotional self-realization and well-being (Illouz 2008), they appear to serve a different purpose for the working class. That is, the therapeutic narrative allows working-class young adults to temporarily keep anxiety and risk at bay, anchoring their lives in self-management amid the insecurity of the service sector and the fragility of personal relationships and public commitments.

The Unforgiving Mood Economy

A great deal of scholarly work has critiqued the therapeutic ethos for promoting narcissism, engendering weakness, and destroying the social fabric (see, for example, Hoff Somers, and Satel 2005; Lasch 1979; Rieff 1987). Such critiques often veil a politically regressive agenda, one that yearns for a return to models of selfhood and sources of authority that would delegitimize the very selves—of women, of people with alternative sexual identities—which the therapeutic narrative makes possible. As my interviews reveal, telling a therapeutic story about oneself can be both liberating and meaningful, as when Monica breaks free to love whom she chooses or Kathleen embarks on a career to help abandoned children. As Illouz (2008: 224) explains, "the therapeutic ethos appears to be a cultural resource that helps actors reach forms of well-being *as they are socially and historically constructed.*" For working-class youth, the mood economy provides the very possibility of selfhood and self-respect in a world where suffering is plentiful and work and family unreliable.

Yet the mood economy also has a darker side, often leading young adults to draw harsh boundaries against their families, to become suspended in the narratives of suffering they believed would bring them promise, and to construe the *self* as their greatest risk in life. The mood economy's imperative to heal oneself leads to a new kind of symbolic boundary construction: boundaries against those who do not have the *will* to be healthy, happy, and strong. Candace, the young black woman introduced in Chapter 3 whose life was turned upside down by her mother's drug addiction and her father's abandonment, reported that she had suffered from depression for years. She confessed, "I just . . . man I was just so depressed. I was just so unhappy. I was just crying all the time, or not crying all the time because I held my emotions in." When she was placed in a foster home in twelfth grade, Candace got a chance to focus on her own life: "so it was definitely the only time I was able to feel like a child. The first time probably since I was, like, nine." She recalled:

> Which I think helped me because this was the first time, um, probably for the last time I remember that I'm not depressed in the winter. Yeah. I mean . . . I don't even think I want to call it seasonal depression anymore just because of what's going on, how I'm feeling, like, right now. I think part is seasonal depression and I think part of it is just me worrying about stuff that I couldn't control. And just not doing things for me. So now I do a lot more stuff for me, even though I'm probably almost staying in the house just as much as I used to but I'm still seeing my friends. I'm still doing things if I want to do them, so it's equaling out for me to be just a lot more happy which has definitely been a new experience for me just to be genuinely happy.

After years of trying to help her mother, whom she describes as a "fallen star," Candace explains that she finally learned to consider her own needs. By systematically dividing her life into compartments that she can and cannot control, she has superimposed cognitive order onto the structural chaos of her life. With the support of her foster family, Candace now feels empowered to leave her days of depression and hopelessness behind. While she is still angry with her father—"Till this day I tell him don't tell people about me. Don't tell people I run track. Don't tell people I have a nice car. Don't tell people I went to college. Don't tell people about me"—she has learned to see herself as independent from him. Cutting family ties is the conduit to freedom from depression and genuine happiness.[9]

To provide another example, Ashley, a beauty supply store clerk, told a story of working through her painful childhood, in which her mother, a hotel chambermaid who neglected her in favor of a boyfriend who would leave opium on the kitchen table and drive her to school with a "bloody Mary between his legs." She recalled, "She chose many things over me. I am like, there is so much resentment and hatred in there that I just can't let go of. It's hard to explain, you know? My mother doesn't like the responsibility of being a mother." A self-described alcoholic and drug addict by thirteen, Ashley got in trouble with the law and was sent away to an all-girls' school for a year. Upon returning, Ashley recounts, she vowed to be nothing like her mother. While she still resents her mother deeply, Ashley has forged an adult identity as a survivor who managed to overcome her childhood of abuse and neglect:

> I got to the point where I was, like, there is nothing I can do about the way my life was, there's just nothing you can do about it. It made me who I am today. So I figure I am a stronger person for it. . . . I just think it has to do with who you are. Like I am a strong person. I just, like, I look at things that happened to me when I was younger, and the same things that happened to other people, that you know aren't strong. You either go one way or the other. Keep going or not.

She believes that her life is exceptional and meaningful because she was able to survive a painful childhood that would have crippled others; indeed, it is others' failures that throw into relief her own success. Within the unforgiving mood economy, there is no place for empathy: dignity is earned only from willing oneself to be healthy and happy.

Longing for Human Recognition

As these stories reveal, the therapeutic model of adulthood lends meaning and purpose to young people's lives not through marriage, home ownership, or a career, but instead from self-realization gleaned from denouncing a painful past and reconstructing an independent, complete self. However, simply constructing this alternative narrative—with its individualized markers—was not enough for them to feel like adults. The very act of telling calls for a *witness*, a recognizing subject who listens to and validates one's hard-won but tenuous self (see Taylor 1989). Like traditional adulthood rituals that mark the transition from one status to another in a socially recognizable way, then, therapeutic markers *also* required the participation of others.[10]

Justin is a thirty-one-year-old black man who works as a server at a casual dining chain restaurant. The son of a factory worker and a secretary, Justin spent six years at a historically black college, finally earning a degree in finance, which he paid for with loans ("It was $17,000 my first year, and then it kept going up, so . . . "). Upon graduating, Justin found a job as a death claims clerk at an insurance company in central Virginia and fell in love with a coworker named Stan. After four years, however, the relationship fell apart, dragging Justin into a deep depression that left him unable to get out of bed for three months. Justin finally moved to Richmond in search of a fresh start, and took his current service job after spotting a "Now Hiring" sign in the window. He described: "I'm just kinda like at my rope's end. I've been working here so long that I'm just like . . . I'm tired of hearing from my mom and my family like everyone is like, you've got degree, why are you working at Applebee's?" Barely breaking even every month as it is, however, Justin is afraid to leave this job in case he can't find another: "It's nerve-racking to me sometimes because what's preventing me from leaving this job is what's keeping me. It's like, I want a new job but I'm scared of leaving this job because I don't know if that job is going to work out, then . . . " Justin is trapped, unable to move forward in his journey to adulthood through traditional conduits because of fear of losing what little he has.

Taking stock of his life, Justin ascribes meaning, order, and especially progress onto his stunted experiences of coming of age through an alternative ritual: the construction, and public telling, of his story of family suffering and self-realization. Justin narrates his adult self through his struggle to "come out" and claim his true sexuality. As he recounted, "There were a few things that hindered me growing up. One of them was, growing up my family doesn't talk about stuff. Like we're a very hush, hush family . . . sex, we never talked about sex, never, ever, ever. And then me being gay, first of all I don't know what sex is. I don't know how to say sex or talk about sex, you know so . . . " Convinced by his religious upbringing that homosexuality was evil, Justin prayed every night that he would wake up the next morning and be straight. After many agonizing years of unanswered prayers, Justin decided that it was time to accept his sexuality as an undeniable part of himself: "I had no choice. You can't. No matter how long you try to repress these feelings. If you're gay, you're gay. That's how I know you're born this way." While he struggles to pay the rent on his studio apartment and has yet to find a long-term romantic partner or a lasting career, he feels a sense of accomplishment that he has faced a painful upbringing and found the strength to claim his authentic self.

Justin's pride in having found the strength to become the person he wants to be, however, is tempered by the fact that he cannot come out to his conservative religious family: "Like no way. No way, José." Tragically, Justin believes that his father, who recently passed away from cancer, might have been his only chance for affirmation:

JUSTIN: And before he passed away, he actually, I think he was trying to give me a sign that he knew. Because he gave me this big card and it had like a bowl of candy on it, and it said, "No matter how sweet you are I will always love you."
JS: So you think he was trying to communicate with you?
JUSTIN: Yeah.
JS: Even though he maybe didn't know how to say it to you?
JUSTIN: Yeah.

Here, Justin constructs a narrative of suffering and *almost-redemption*. That is, his redemption remains incomplete because he has no one to witness and affirm that his suffering yielded something meaningful: the brave discovery of his adult self.

This lack of recognition informs the stories of many respondents. Some young people attested that their parents suffer from mental illness, alcoholism, or drug addictions that have left them unable to provide the kind of support and recognition that respondents needed from them. Others simply state that their families or partners do not understand their pain. Vanessa, an unemployed twenty-seven-year-old, constructs her coming of age narrative around a psychiatric diagnosis of bipolar disorder. Following her second divorce, she explained, she went to a party, where she began to hallucinate, perhaps as a result of mixing beer and anti-depressants. When she was hospitalized, she was diagnosed with bipolar disorder and has since reinterpreted her past experiences through the lens of this illness. During our three-hour interview, Vanessa searched her past for signs of her illness, linking the painful events of her life—being bullied at school, fired from jobs for stealing, getting divorced twice, and losing custody of her twins—with the common thread of her disorder. As traditional markers struck her as unsustainable, understanding her past and breaking free from unhealthy relationships became central to her definition of adulthood: "Since my divorce, I have been on my own for the first time in my life. I have not had anybody controlling me but myself. . . . I have only been an adult for six months (*sobbing*). I have learned a lot along the way."

But Vanessa's parents—a field machinist and a medical records coder, whom she described as traditional, religious, and Southern—viewed their daughter with a mixture of sadness, bewilderment, and disdain: "They just look at me and say, 'What is wrong with you? Why can't you get a job, why aren't you taking care of your own kids?' And I am like, you grew me up doing certain things, and this is what has happened because of it, so you can't blame me." Her parents—as potential witnesses—did not judge her performance of adulthood as authentic. Unable to afford therapy, she joined an online bipolar support group but soon quit because she felt ignored: "It was all about [the founder of the group], you see, she would take up most of the time to talk. She didn't think the other people there would need people to talk to as well." Today, Vanessa continues to search for sources of validation.[11]

For Justin and Vanessa, their chosen witnesses could not identify with their performance; building on Illouz (2008), we can see how *generational* differences in emotional expression become an insurmountable obstacle to communication. That is, the categories they use to understand themselves are not shared by their parents who came of age just forty years before them and for whom "coming out," battling mental illness publicly, defeating a legacy of alcoholism, or choosing art school over a stable career or family are incomprehensible.

When young men and women cannot communicate their feelings of anger and betrayal to those who wronged them, their coming of age stories remain unvalidated. As Isaac, a twenty-four-year-old black man who works as a stocker at a discount retail company, confessed poignantly:

"When I would try to tell them what was really going on or things that I had on my mind, it's like I was talking to a brick wall. Sometimes like now with things, I have a lot of memories that I would like to forget in the back of my head. There are things that I've held inside that I wanted to tell them for a long time. But you know I've just held it in for so many years."

In telling their story to a witness—especially one who hurt or betrayed them—respondents imagine that their accounts will be honored, thereby allowing them to finally move beyond the painful memories that anchor their identities in the past. Within the mood economy, human recognition becomes the key to dignity and self-respect, in short, to finally appraising oneself as adult, complete, and fully human. Telling one's story is thus an interactional accomplishment, reliant on social recognition for validity and authenticity (Davis 2005). When a witness cannot hear their story—or discredits their account—working-class young people become suspended in a narrative of suffering, and the ritual fails to produce a newly adult self. These respondents thereby become trapped in the mood economy, unable to attain human recognition, dignity, or self-respect. Once again, the transition to adulthood is inverted, as coming of age means accepting that they are alone, dependent on others at their peril.

The Self as Risk

What makes the therapeutic narrative as a conduit to adulthood most problematic is that it transforms the self into one's greatest obstacle to success, happiness, and well-being. Indeed, the therapeutic narrative leads young people to make themselves the heroes, victims, and villains of their own lives (see also Furedi 2004; Moskowitz 2001). In teaching young people that they alone can manage their emotions and heal their wounded psyches, the therapeutic ethos dovetails with neoliberal ideology in such a way as to make powerless working-class young adults feel responsible for their own happiness. In a neoliberal world of unpredictable markets, fragile families, hollow institutions, and anemic safety nets, the self—alone and uncertain—is endowed "with the power to make or unmake itself" (Illouz 2008: 131). Indeed, the vast majority (n = 70) of informants reported that they viewed *themselves* as their greatest risk. As Kelly, a twenty-eight-year-old line cook, declared, "When I start feeling helpless, I just have to make a conscious decision to not feel that way. It sounds easy and it's really not. There's just no other choice. No one else is going to fix me but me."

Their foundational belief that they are completely and unconditionally responsible for creating a good life leads young people to examine their personal traits and behaviors for signs of weakness that could explain their precarious lives.[12] For many, the fear that they will not take the "right" risk looms as a logical explanation for failure. Candace, the young black woman who has overcome a family legacy of drug abuse and poverty, as well as depression, explained: "Um, the biggest risk is putting too much out on the line with my family. Being scared to fail. Being scared, the unknowing, yes. Because there will be certain things I won't do that could make me a stronger person, could make me more succeed, but I'm just afraid of doing it because it's a chance. It's a risk."[13]

But it is Delores, a thirty-four-year-old white woman, who most powerfully demonstrated the cruelty and injustice of the mood economy. When we first met, she was working the cash register at a bakery outside of Lowell where I often stopped for coffee on my way to an interview. Judging her to be a possible interviewee, I asked if she would like to participate in my study. A few days later, I returned to the bakery during her lunch hour to hear about her experiences of growing up.

Delores's father was laid off from a shoe factory when she was young and never found stable employment again. Learning from an early age that work is precarious and the future is unpredictable, she recalled: "The way I grew up, we grew up with nothing and we were never told what to do with it if we ever got it. In a lot of the ways, I feel like I'm living the same way that my parents are. Just . . . day by day." Delores explained that she had been struggling with depression since high school. A few years ago, she got pregnant and her boyfriend insisted she have an abortion, which led to a "downward spiral," a tumultuous breakup, and a spending spree that left her tens of thousands of dollars in debt.

D: I took a nosedive again. I decided I wanted to try medication. I went in and I was diagnosed. I went into a study because I didn't have any money. It was on the radio I think. But it was a study to test the effectiveness of concentrated doses of Saint John's Wort against Prozac. It was a study, so I didn't know what I was on whether it be sugar pills, Saint John's Wort, or Prozac. But after a certain amount of time if it doesn't work they take you out and put you on Wellbutrin, which has been shown to work on a wide variety of people. It wasn't working, so they put me on Wellbutrin, and I was on that for awhile and then they switched me over to Prozac. I guess it's not so bad if I remember to take my pill every day like I'm supposed to. But when I get off kilter I get very stressed and then I'll do impulse buying.

Like, oh I don't care, I'll just spend the money. So that kind of screws me. I would like to be good and do what I am supposed to do, but then I get so upset and I don't want to do anything, I don't want to think about bills, I don't want to pay anything . . . I just . . .

Like many informants, Delores explained her problems in the present through the lens of her mental disorder. At the time of the interview, she told me she was developing new ways of managing her depression with remedies found on the Internet: drinking copious amounts of caffeine, smoking marijuana, and illustrating children's books to relax.

A few months later, when I was back in Massachusetts for interviews, I stopped in at the bakery again, but Delores was not there. I asked her co-worker, Lindsay, whom I had gotten to know through my frequent visits, if she was still employed at the bakery. Delores, she informed me, was suffering from another debilitating round of depression: she had frequent migraines, could not get out of bed for weeks, and had eventually been fired for missing too many days of work (which meant she had also lost her health benefits). During her last few weeks of work, she had been caught drinking beer in the back kitchen and was suspected of stealing money from the cash register; there was no chance that she would be hired back. I left the bakery feeling confused and sad, trying to reconcile my memory of the soft-spoken, solemn woman who had kindly donated her time to me with the erratic, irresponsible behavior described by Lindsay.

Then, about a year later, after I had moved back to Boston, I ran into Lindsay again. "You'll never guess what happened," she said, tearing up. Delores, she informed me, had died just a few weeks before of cancer. Her intense headaches, extreme fatigue, and behavioral and emotional changes were in fact not caused by depression, but by a malignant brain tumor that went undiscovered until after her death. There are treatments for brain cancer, including surgery, radiation therapy, and chemotherapy, and there are also ways to improve one's quality of life. But Delores saw the world through the therapeutic lens, attributing all of her suffering to psychic wounds. When she lost her health insurance, she continued to treat herself with home remedies, trying until the end to heal *herself*. Viewing the world through the lens of the therapeutic narrative, it never occurred to her to see a medical doctor for her headaches, not that she could have afforded it. Delores's death is a tragedy, one brought about not only by the lack of material resources, but also by a cultural logic that makes self-management the taken-for-granted, and indeed only, solution to pain.

Neoliberalism, the Mood Economy, and Power

For the majority of working-class young people in the sample, the logic of neoliberalism and the logic of the mood economy are deeply intertwined, creating a mutually constitutive and self-enclosed reality in which self-reliance becomes the only path to success, happiness, and growth (Bourdieu 1984). On the one hand, as Chapter 4 reveals, their experiences of betrayal lead them to shun the thought of economic dependency or outside help. On the other hand, the therapeutic narrative—and its gospel of individualism, self-transformation, and personal growth—is deeply institutionalized within the spaces where they come of age, providing a discourse for taking sole responsibility for their own *emotional* fates (see Nolan 1998). Respondents do not want pity for their painful pasts; to quote Kelly, "Life doesn't owe me any favors. I can have a sense of my own specialness and individuality, but that doesn't mean that anybody else has to recognize that or help me accomplish my goals." On the contrary, in their interactions with the state (rehabilitation homes, support groups, social workers and psychologists, foster care), the media (talk shows, Internet blogs, self-help books), or the medical field (hospitals, free drug trials), young people learn over and over again that happiness is theirs only if they work hard enough to control their negative thoughts, feelings, and behaviors on their own. Like the market economy that exploits their labor, the mood economy forces these young adults to put their emotions to work in ways that can ultimately lead to more suffering.

The mutually reinforcing relationship between neoliberalism in the economic sphere and emotions in the personal one raises the question of how inequality is reproduced through the routine interactions and practices of everyday life—or how, in other words, working-class youth grow into working-class adults "by themselves" (Althusser 1970: 181).[14] The young people in this sample report that institutions such as family, education, or religion have little importance in their lives; on the contrary, they describe their coming of age journeys as the realization that they are alone, dependent on no one—and no institution—for their survival. In doing so, however, they do not see the ways in which the majority of the institutions that frame their coming of age journeys are steeped in therapeutic ideology. Their schools, for example, may appear to them as sites of betrayal that act against their interests; but they learn the therapeutic language through school psychologists and social workers that teach them to take responsibility for managing their emotions. Similarly, while the state may confront them as heartless and cold, whether stealing their hard-earned money or failing to protect their families, its subsidized alcohol and drug recovery programs or support groups reinforce the language of individual empowerment through accepting sole responsibility for one's self (Nolan 1998). Through everyday interactions and practices, these institutions foster a culture of neoliberalism *outside* the economic sphere (see Illouz 2007) which I argue is central to reproducing social inequality and exploitation at the most intimate level of the self.

The Political Is Personal

In social movements like feminism, self-awareness, or naming one's problems, was the first step to radical collective awareness. For this generation, it is the only step, completely detached from any kind of solidarity; while they struggle with similar, and structurally rooted, problems, there is no sense of "we." The possibility of collective politicization through naming one's suffering is easily subsumed within these larger structures of domination because others who struggle are seen not as fellow sufferers but as objects of scorn.

bell hooks's (1989) insights into the reduction of the political to the personal within the feminist movement are particularly apt here. She writes:

> This slogan ["the personal is political"] had such power because it insisted on the primacy of the personal, not in a narcissistic way, but in its implied naming of the self as a site for politicization, which was in this society a very radical challenge to notions of self and identity. . . [but] the radical insistence on a politicized self was submerged, subsumed within a larger cultural framework wherein focus on identity was already legitimized within structures of domination. . . . Popularly, the important quest was not to radically change our relationship to self and identity, to educate for critical consciousness, to become politically engaged and committed, but to explore one's identity, to affirm and assert the primacy of the self *as it already existed.* (106, italics added)

That is, "the personal is political" was intended to reveal the profoundly historical and collective nature of experience, *not* to create an endless array of individual narratives. Yet, without a collective sense of structural inequalities, the suffering and betrayal born of de-industrialization, inequality, and risk is interpreted as individual failure: their family members are seen as unworthy individuals and their addictions and illnesses as private vices. Ultimately, the predominance of the unstable and imperfect family past serves to obscure the shaping power of the unstable and imperfect market present. By dismissing the social forces that work against their attempts to create secure futures and placing responsibility for success only on themselves, this generation of working-class youth will experience coming of age as perpetually coming up short—yet have only themselves to blame.

Conclusion | The Hidden Injuries of Risk

THIS CLOSING CHAPTER DRAWS INSPIRATION from Sennett and Cobb's 1973 *The Hidden Injuries of Class*. Nearly four decades ago, this now-classic sociological exposé showed us life through the eyes of the working class, uncovering the invisible, emotional burdens of class inequality: "the feeling of not getting anywhere despite one's efforts, the feeling of vulnerability in contrasting oneself to others at a higher social level, the buried sense of inadequacy that one resents oneself for feeling" (Sennett and Cobb 1973: 58). At the time of their writing, as the 1970s ushered in a new era of politics that emphasized marketplace freedom over jobs, wages, and labor rights, collective working-class agency was dying the "death of a thousand cuts" (Cowie 2010: 236). The power of the postwar working class who had battled big business and won was decimated by the neoliberal turn of the 1970s, leaving the militancy that once fueled their collective movement nowhere to spread but inward. "The burden of class today is thus a strange phenomenon," Sennett and Cobb (1973: 172) observed, where "the logic of discontent leads people to turn on each other rather than on the 'system.'"

They explain:

> If I believe that the man I call "Sir" and who calls me by my first name started with an equal fund of powers, do not our differences, do not all signs of courtesy and attention given to him but denied me, do not his very feelings of being different in "taste" and understanding from me, show that somehow he has developed his insides more than I mine? How else can I explain inequalities? The institutions may be structured so that he wins and I lose, but this is my life. . . . Even though we might have been born in different stations, the fact that he is getting more means that somehow he had

the power in him, the character, to "realize himself," to earn his superiority. (255–256)

As power shifted from labor to big business, industrial work grew less and less secure and valued. This decline in the economic sphere was accompanied by a shift in working-class consciousness, leaving its members to believe that they had no right to demand equal opportunities because their own shortcomings were blamed for their lack of success.

In their conclusion, Sennett and Cobb draw attention to the post-industrial society that was just "coming into being" (259), speculating over its impending consequences for economic security, dignity, and meaning. Nearly half a century later, a great deal of scholarly work has examined the political economy of insecurity and uncertainty wrought by the demise of American industry and the rise of neoliberal ideology and policy. As we have seen through the stories of the young women and men in this book, the standardized work and life course of industrial society has given way to a fundamental uncertainty about how to navigate one's course through life (Beck 1992, 2000; Bourdieu 1998; Giddens 1992; Hacker 2006a; Sennett 1998). Jobs for life have disappeared, obliterated by a technologically advanced and global capitalism that exalts labor market "flexibility" above all else (Beck 2000). In turn, the institutions of marriage, religion, and family that once anchored working-class lives have shattered into ill-fitting pieces that each individual must consciously put back together on his or her own. In some ways, the fragmenting of these institutions offers the promise of emancipation, particularly for women or members of the LGBTQ (lesbian, gay, bisexual, transgender, and queer) community who now hold greater control over their romantic destinies. But in a larger social climate of insecurity in which risks are increasingly redistributed away from the state and onto the individual, the freedom from tradition more often leaves them longing for the connections—and constraints—of the past.

In light of these rapid and sweeping economic and cultural transformations, this book has attempted to continue the work of Sennett and Cobb by shifting attention to the hidden injuries of *risk*. This is not to imply that class is no longer relevant, but to underline the ways in which traditional conceptions of the "working class" as white, male industrial labor no longer capture the dynamics of division and inequality in post-industrial life. Rather, I draw attention to the ways in which risk—both as it structures people's life chances and shapes their sense of the kind of person they are and the kind of world that they live in—is reconstructing what it means to become working class. Clearly, what unites the men—and women—in my study as working class is no longer the shared culture of the shop floor, the indignities of demeaning and routinized labor, or a sharply policed division of masculine and feminine spheres of life (Rubin 1976; Willis 1977). Instead, the children of the nearly obsolete industrial working-class can be characterized primarily through their struggles to come to terms with the disappearance of the foundational aspects of industrial working-class life.

Both working-class men and women find that they are caught in the teeth of a flexible and ruthless labor market that promises little job stability, routine, or permanence. In a time when individual solutions to collective structural problems is a requirement for survival, these men and women experience a common lack of resources—whether knowledge, skills, credentials, or money—to protect themselves from economic and social shocks like unemployment, illness, or family dissolution. As traditional markers of identity and adulthood confront them as unattainable and even undesirable, young people learn that creating their adult selves is an individual endeavor; yet their lack of cultural, social, and economic capital means that they have few tools with which to undertake this immensely risky task. Insecurity and risk are thus daily burdens shouldered by the working class, injuring, in multiple ways, those who bear them.

The Sources of Injury

The structural sources of risk shouldered by the men and women in my sample are easy to pinpoint. By structural, I mean the ways in which the risks of modern capitalism, whether unemployment, injury, old age, or illness, are managed at the social policy level (Beck 2000; Hacker 2006a; Taylor-Gooby 2004). For these young men and women, risk is radically privatized. The majority bears the risk of unemployment and underemployment; they cannot find steady, living-wage jobs, nor can they afford to take the steps required by individuals—whether gaining new skills through higher education or moving to a city with more jobs—to make themselves more attractive in the labor market. As factories close one after the other and corporations use layoffs as a strategy for increasing short-term profit, working-class men and women describe how they "can't get their feet under them," bouncing from one temporary job to the next and turning to their credit cards as a safety net even though they know they will never be able to pay back their debt. For black men especially, racism in the service economy magnifies the risk of unemployment.

Because their jobs do not offer affordable benefits, these men and women also bear the risk of illness and disability on their own. When Rebecca needed stitches, for example, she was forced to use her credit card to pay her hospital bill, putting on hold her plans to go to college to become a teacher. Delores continuously searched for free drug trials or home remedies to treat what a doctor could have diagnosed as (and even possibly treated) a malignant brain tumor—not, as she believed, depression. Her untimely death stands as a tragic reminder of the dangers of privatized risk.

In attempting to protect themselves against the brutal labor market, some young adults turned to the military to save money, increase their chances in the civil service system, and pay for schooling. Only by risking their lives and leaving their families could a few men capitalize on their masculinity to earn stable civil services jobs that promise a better life. Others enrolled in college classes to increase their earning potential and job security. Social and cultural capital—specifically, having family members who completed college who could impart their knowledge and experience—enabled a few respondents to graduate from college and even achieve upward mobility, especially in fields like nursing or government administration. Most, however, found that they had neither the finances nor the skills required to earn a degree, their massive loans serving as an enduring reminder of their failures. Even those who did manage to graduate were left with a sense of confusion when they attempted to translate their degrees into a job or a better salary. Recalling Brandon, who opened this book, education confronts them simply as a system of "fake goods": "That sheet of paper [his degree] cost so much and does me *no good*. Sure, schools can't guarantee success, but come on; they could do better to help kids out. You have to give Uncle Sam your firstborn to get a degree and it doesn't pan out!"

The Self in an Uncertain World

Working-class men and women also suffer from more "hidden," but no less pernicious, injuries of risk. In this sense, risk encompasses the subjective experience of growing up with pervasive uncertainty—how it shapes their perceptions of time, the future, and their commitments and obligations to others (Bourdieu 1998; Giddens 1991 Putnam 2000). Many young people, who have grown up watching economic stability and commitment elude their families, and who have no grasp on the present because they do not have the tools to compete successfully in the uncertain labor market, are unable to imagine or act toward a future that holds little promise of hope. Some come to expect nothing out of life as a defensive strategy; to paraphrase Cory, the thirty-four-year-old bartender, you can't have fears if you don't have goals. It is little wonder when they turn to alcohol or drugs, drop out of community college, or become accidentally pregnant. Others like Rob or Jalen undermine the few opportunities for upward mobility that they have out of sheer disbelief that their investments in the future could ever come to fruition. *Having* goals, on the other hand, sometimes works against them, leaving young men and women even worse off than they would have been if they hadn't taken risks to get ahead. Alexandra had big dreams of being a psychologist with a big office and diplomas on the wall, but predatory lending in the real estate market turned her dreams of upward mobility into a nightmare of foreclosure, class action suits, and a legacy of poor credit that may keep her from going to law school.

As Hacker (2006b: 11) points out, the social costs of risk-bearing include a deep sense of insecurity, hopelessness toward the future, and an unwillingness to invest in oneself or the broader community: "When workers and families are faced with fateful economic choices that place them at grave risk—about, for instance, the level of education to get or whether to retrain for new jobs—they may be unwilling to take the socially desired level of risk. As a result, more people take the safe option." Fearful of losing what little they have, young people who shoulder immense amounts of risk find that they are unable to *take* risks; in turn, they blame themselves when they cannot seem to change the course of their futures. Working-class youth thus come of age lacking a basic sense of trust that they can control the trajectories of their lives. If growing numbers of today's youth are taking the "safe option," unable or unwilling to risk any kind of self-investment, there will be larger social consequences for the health and vibrancy of American communities.

Working-class young people also come to understand themselves as profoundly isolated from others. Early on, many learn that they cannot depend on their families to shelter them from the harshness of post-industrial life; battling their own demons, their parents have little support, knowledge, or comfort to give them. The loneliness and betrayal that young adults experience early in their unstable and chaotic families is replicated within the institutions that frame their transitions to adulthood. The field of education, which they believe will hand them the tools for success, proves to be nearly impossible to navigate: they are misunderstood or looked over by teachers, unprepared for schoolwork, and unable to translate the education they do receive into economic rewards. Many respondents leave school feeling inadequate or cheated. As they attempt to build lives for themselves, they find that the cultural logics of institutions continue to elude them. Christopher, for instance, felt that he was constantly "tricked" in his everyday life. Young people painfully discover that it is both unwise and perilous to rely on other people and social institutions. Being an adult means trusting no one but yourself.

Knowing that they are isolated ignites a hunger for connection. Both men and women yearn wistfully for enduring commitment that transcends individual desire, hoping to anchor their chaotic lives in connection with a partner. While nostalgia for a mythical past of white picket fences and love that lasts forever provides a temporary escape from the precariousness of the present and the uncertainty of the future, respondents cannot realize these fantasies and are left continually seeking. As their words reveal, they encounter several obstacles in the field of romantic relationships. Couples who attempt to create traditional marriages based on distinct gender roles and obligations find that their desires are at odds with the structure of the economy: Curtis, who wants to follow in his father's footsteps and provide for a family as a husband and a father, cannot find a job, let alone make a family wage. Again, for black respondents, the dearth of stable jobs for men makes monogamy even more difficult than it is for whites. On the other hand, couples who want to create relationships that foster the growth of their deepest selves find that self-realization requires resources that they do not have, and they must decide whether commitment is worth sacrificing their own interests and desires. For women, fears of losing the self predominate: their sense of self feels too fragile to risk in a relationship. Because many young people fear disappointment, betrayal, and dissolution, they often choose to be alone.

In a world where you have only yourself—hard-won through privation and suffering—to depend on, relationships feel overwhelmingly risky. Caught between two impossible ideals of love, many find themselves unable to forge romantic relationships that are both satisfying and lasting. Respondents thus numb the ache of betrayal and the hunger for connection by embracing cultural ideals of self-reliance, individualism, and personal responsibility. In doing so, they become acquiescing neoliberal subjects, rejecting all kinds of government intervention, and affirmative action in particular, as antithetical, and thereby offensive, to their lived experiences. As I demonstrated in Chapter 4, they become "hardened" to the world around them while families and potential communities of solidarity are torn apart by the strain of risk. Men guard the few remaining public sector jobs with hyper-vigilance, using weapons of sexism and homophobia to police the boundaries of their professions. White people draw moral boundaries against blacks for laziness and moral disorder. Black informants draw even stronger boundaries against other blacks who cannot navigate the perils of a racist society on their own; echoing Simon, "If you wear baggy jeans and talk like an asshole, you are not gonna get ahead. It's not racism, it's you. I hate black people who say it is racism." Ultimately, young working-class men and women believe that if they have to battle through life alone, then everyone else should, too. Children become the last bastion of hope and commitment, and young parents find meaning and structure in caring: yet the powerful forces of inequality often work against their efforts to provide stable homes and opportunities for their children (Silva and Pugh 2010). Their children may grow up to resent them for not giving them the tools they needed to succeed, despite their best efforts and intentions.

The Mood of Risk

Finally, I explore the effects of risk as it is managed at the level of the *self* (Furedi 2004 Giddens 1992;. These young adults are haunted by the meanings and rituals of traditional adulthood even while this model confronts them as unattainable, inadequate, or simply undesirable. While a few men with stable, public sector jobs are able to perform traditional adult roles and feel like adults, the vast majority of respondents find themselves "lost in transition" (Brinton 2010). For a few black women, religion proved to be a useful resource for justifying the delayed transition to adulthood. In the absence of institutionalized rites of passage, however, the vast majority of young adults searched instead for individual milestones to mark their progress going forward.

In taking stock of their lives, the suffering, pain, and betrayal they have survived become the foundation for constructing who they are and what they want out of life. In particular, the need to overcome legacies of suffering through emotional resolve lends order and direction to their lives. I argue that working-class young men and women inhabit the *mood economy*, an emerging system of selfhood that locates dignity in emotional self-management rather than in traditional accomplishments such as marriage or work. The mood economy makes virtue out of necessity, providing the very possibility of meaningfulness, progress, and coherency in the void of meaning wrought by the decline of traditional life pathways. Through the therapeutic narrative, young people "emplot" their adult selves in a forward-moving narrative of suffering and self-transformation (Illouz 2008), whether through overcoming an alcohol addiction like Monica, coming out and claiming one's sexuality like Justin, or struggling daily to not become one's own mother like Ashley or Kathleen.

Although cultural sociologists have depicted the working class as unable to use therapeutic language (Giddens 1991; Illouz 2008), I point to an emerging emotional habitus among the post-industrial working class, one that is both classed and generational. Therapeutic discourse is ingrained in the institutions that shape working-class lives, including social services, school psychologists, self-help literature, popular culture such as Oprah, free drug trials, meet-up groups and self-help sites on the Internet, and Alcoholics and Narcotics Anonymous. Indeed, these institutions are more prominent than more traditionally oriented ones (such as masculine jobs like firefighting, or religion) in the interview transcripts. These institutions structure working-class coming of age trajectories in unseen ways, reinforcing the culture of self-reliance fostered by neoliberalism in the economic sphere by teaching young people that they are responsible for their own emotional well-being in the private sphere. Happiness comes to be understood as the by-product of individual will, rather than structural circumstances—and this rising generation of working-class youth draws swift and unforgiving boundaries against those who cannot achieve self-change and contentment through sheer emotional resolve.

However, resolve is not enough: many do not have the tools or resources to stage their visions of healthy selfhood. Those who see their family members as the source of their suffering cannot communicate their feelings of anger and betrayal across generational lines to those who hurt them; their experiences of rejection and pain remain unvalidated. As Isaac confessed poignantly: "When I would try to tell them what was really going on or things that I had on my mind, it's like I was talking to a brick wall. Sometimes like now with things, I have a lot of memories that I would like to forget in the back of my head. There are things that I've held inside that I wanted to tell people for a long time." Respondents who frame their understandings of who they are around categories of mental illness cannot afford the medication and therapy needed to heal. And those who beat addictions feel the pull of drugs and alcohol when sobriety does not solve structurally embedded woes of unemployment, poverty, and hopelessness. Without the resources, whether material or symbolic, to put on their performances of adulthood—to show, through interaction with others, that they have indeed wrested control of their emotions and transformed themselves—they become trapped in the mood economy, unable to realize the visions of worthy personhood it sets forth. This is the greatest injury of all.

Standing at the Crossroads of Risk

In many ways, Wally, a thirty-year-old white man who lives in the South, has a life very similar to that of the other respondents featured in this work. Wally's parents met at a paper mill, which is now closed. His dad is an electrician, and his mom works in the service economy, changing jobs according to the demands of the market; they manage to "teeter on the edge" of middle-class status by "getting lots of credit cards involved." Wally describes himself as confused about his family relationships. As his once all-white neighborhood has become integrated, he has watched his sister grow increasingly intolerant. As his father's job has grown more precarious, he has witnessed his father becoming more and more conservative and religious, turning to "pyramid schemes, Amway things" in a last-ditch effort to achieve the American Dream. His parents have started fighting— "My mom actually told me today, earlier today, like, my father, like, she asked him if he could marry all over again would he, and he said no"—and Wally obsessively searches his memories for signs that his parents have been unhappy all along. Disillusioned by marriage, he avoids committed relationships, unsure of how to find the "right" person and make a relationship last. He cannot imagine taking care of anyone but himself.

Wally is currently living "on people's couches" because he cannot afford to pay first, last, and security deposit on his own place. Like many other respondents, he says he "had no idea what the future was going to actually be like." Over the past four years, he has worked at a bakery, a butcher shop, and a small grocery store, where he currently stocks the frozen food section. His hours were recently cut to thirty-four a week, but he considers himself lucky to be earning $11.75 an hour when most employees only make $9. Like many respondents, he took a few community college classes to improve his labor market position, but quickly dropped out because: "I didn't really know what I wanted to do with it." Right now, he is focused on paying the credit card debt he built up over the last few years while trying to make ends meet.

In one very important way, however, Wally is vastly different from the other working-class people in my sample: he describes himself as a "revolutionary." When Wally was a teenager, his love of art and music led him to join a series of experimental music collectives in Richmond, Virginia.

He became inspired by the political aspect of "noise," an avant-garde musical genre that is "freeform by nature. It doesn't sound pretty all the time. What does sound pretty? Maybe some noise artist doesn't sound pretty to everyone. It's like anti-pop. It's also kind of, I consider it like the working-class sound. Anyone can make it. You don't need expensive instruments to do it." Wally's musical community has led him to teach himself about activism—he is currently reading *War on Labor and the Left*, despite the fact that he is a "slow reader" and gets easily distracted—and attempt to translate his politics into action. He described: "I do believe there needs to be like a major reform in the economic system, how we manage the US politically. I don't think there's going to be a revolution tomorrow. If there was one it would be beneficial to us. We would see like major reeducation and inspiration to people, like, to take things back." Some of his political projects include strengthening Virginia's labor laws, rallying his coworkers to form a union at the grocery store, protesting neighborhood gentrification, organizing sit-ins and protests on May Day, and fighting for universal health care:

> Like, I think it would be great, like, for people, like, mentally to not have to worry about having a job that has a health care program. They would probably be more, even more vocal about the injustices that if they find in a job, they wouldn't have to worry about losing their job. It's one thing like, yeah, OK I can get another job or I might get fired and there might not be any jobs to get but . . . National health care would definitely strengthen working people immensely. But yeah, that's one thing I worry about, like, if I do quit my job and if I need health care like . . . I would need another job though. I would have to settle down somewhere.

Wally also understands sexism and racism as structural problems, and could effortlessly list incidents where he witnessed female coworkers being paid less than males at his job, or black men being targeted disproportionately by the police during marches or protests. He added: "Growing up, I lived in a neighborhood that was mostly white. I remember growing up with my grandparents, both grandparents kind of talking down to either, like, the Hispanic people living in their complex or the black people that took over in my grandparents' neighborhood growing up, you know. Really sad. I didn't challenge it then, but later on I did. Just learning more and more about how everything actually went down." Unlike respondents who felt threatened by African Americans moving into their neighborhoods, Wally feels linked to other racial groups in his quest for social justice.

Being a political activist has proven taxing and frustrating. Recalling one organization he helped to run, he explained, "The collective aspect of it started to, like, just fall apart and it was just one other person doing everything with me and, like, there was a big falling out in 2006. I don't know, maybe it was my fault. Because I was getting angry about doing everything myself. So, like, after people started dropping out, I just decided it's no longer collective with just one person so . . ." Aside from difficulties in motivating people to stay involved, Wally lacks both the time and financial resources necessary for sustaining a political collective. Yet, Wally has not given up; he continued: "I sort of separated myself from everything that I hated and then sitting back and being really patient and realizing that getting angry about something or totally giving up wasn't an option. And I'm forcing myself to be more involved with, like, community groups and I'm trying to, like, figure out where I want to go with it. I'm still learning a lot about things I don't know, and just being involved with it. It's how I think I've always learned about things, just, like, sort of get myself into it and, like, telling people that they can rely on me so I will be reliable." Even in the face of disappointment and failure, Wally remains committed to his political goals of equal opportunity, risk-pooling, and social protection from the market. For him, a sense of "we" actually does exist.

While risk itself may be a constant of human experience, it is not inevitable that risks be shouldered by individuals alone. Hacker (2006b: 1) writes:

> Risk can bring people together, creating communities of shared fate. Yet risk can also split people apart. Societies have dealt with risk in many ways, and not all of these responses involve public solutions or broad insurance protections. Personal misfortune can be blamed on improvidence and irresponsibility. It can be chalked up to the workings of mystical forces beyond human control. It can be dealt with through private market institutions or through communal frameworks, through localized government action or through the immense powers of the nation state, or through some combination of all these. And, of course, risk does not have to be "dealt with" at all. It can simply be left to individuals and families to cope with, as best they can, on their own.

The last half century has witnessed a massive effort to roll back social protections from the market; deregulate (or fail to regulate) emerging financial institutions; privatize risks such as illness, disability, retirement, and unemployment; and support private profit over public institutions (Calhoun 2010). The consequences of such efforts crystallized in the economic crisis of 2008; the ensuing poverty, inequality, and unemployment that followed in the Great Recession serve as a continual reminder of the dangers of privatized risk (Krugman 2009).

As the coming of age stories of working-class young people reveal, the strain of risk-bearing has split individuals, families, and communities apart, leaving them with only the deep and unyielding belief that personal responsibility is the key to meaning, security, and freedom. In an era defined by neoliberal ideology and policy, collective solutions to risk run counter to common sense. Young working-class men and women understand personal choice and self-control as the very basis for who they are, and blame themselves, rather than large-scale economic precariousness and risk privatization, for lacking the tools they need to navigate their futures.

Yet, Wally's lone hope represents a tiny force of resistance against the rising tide of risk. At the heart of his vision of the future lies a firm belief in equal opportunity, social solidarity, and risk-pooling. He also offers the possibility of a concept of self-worth and personhood that is founded on collective well-being rather than individual suffering. Across the United States and around the world, glimmers of opposition to privatization and deregulation can be found in newspapers, political debates, and policy initiatives.

The Obama administration, for example, has attempted to reverse the privatization of risk and increase social protections from the market through credit card reform (The Credit Card Accountability Responsibility and Disclosure (CARD) Act of 2009), which protects young consumers from generating massive debt and regulates interest rates, penalties, and fees; the American Recovery and Reinvestment Act of 2009 (the "stimulus package"), which is intended to create jobs and promote investment and consumer spending; and the defunding of private, for-profit colleges that leave students with heavy student loans and no prospects in the labor market. The landmark but contentious Affordable Care Act, passed by Congress and signed into law in March 2010, is founded on the belief that everyone should have basic security—and protection from the market—when it comes to their health. Called "the most expansive social legislation enacted in decades" (*New York Times*, March 23, 2010), the law promises to protect Americans from the private health insurance industry (see Cohn 2007) and offer the uninsured the opportunity to obtain affordable health care plans.

The years following the economic crisis also saw thousands of ordinary people around the world joining in solidarity against rising income inequality, deregulation, public funding cuts, and global finance. In 2010, British students took to the streets, held rallies, and occupied government and university buildings to protest the proposed increase in tuition caps in public universities. In 2011, tens of thousands protested the Wisconsin Budget Repair Bill, the passing of which has severely limited collective bargaining rights and vastly reduced benefits like pensions and health insurance. They were followed a few months later by protests of the Spanish *indignados* against political corruption and the banking industry and the Greek fight against austerity measures that continues today. The Occupy Wall Street movement, which began in New York in the summer of 2011 and spread across the globe, has raised awareness of economic inequality, greed, corruption, and the influence of corporations on government. The Occupy slogan, *We are the 99%*, put into simple words the vision of a collective "we."

Yet these initiatives to make risk social have been met with extreme hostility and debate, as evidenced by the "Tea Party Movement," which demands lower taxes, "fiscal responsibility," a "constitutionally limited government," and the repeal of public health care "Contract from America," 2010). As unemployment and poverty reach unprecedented levels in the Great Recession, politicians demand lower taxes, more deregulation, the weakening of unions, and draconian cuts in public spending. And protestors are met with scorn and derision, accused of everything from violence to anarchy to drug use.[1]

Risk has thus become the new center around which heated political debates revolve: "The new centre is becoming the precarious centre" (Beck 2000: 70). At stake are cultural definitions of self-worth, freedom, and the possibility of a secure and meaningful life. In writing this book, I have attempted to call into question the viability of deeply held cultural notions of privatization, individualism, and personal responsibility. It is clear that the working-class men and women in this study are trapped by economic and social uncertainty and insecurity: lonely and betrayed, they cannot face their futures, form meaningful relationships, or achieve a sense of emotional well-being and self-respect.

Yet, their coming of age stories are still unfolding, their futures not yet written. In order to tell a different kind of coming of age story—one that promises hope, dignity, and connection—they must begin their journeys to adulthood with a living wage, a basic floor of social protection, and the skills and knowledge to confront the future. They must abandon the divisions of race for the solidarity of class—a solidarity that stems not from older models of the white, masculine working class but that allows for flexible identities and multiple voices. As they search for intimacy, they need cultural models that do not force them to sacrifice egalitarian gender ideals for the promise of lasting commitment or self-fulfillment for trust and certainty. Finally, young working-class men and women need new definitions of dignity and progress that do not reduce their coming of age stories to a quest to manage their emotions and will themselves to be content with insecurity and loss. The health and vibrancy of all our communities depend on the creation and nurturance of notions of dignity that foster connection and interdependence rather than hardened selves.

APPENDIX | Research Methods

INTERVIEWED 100 WORKING-CLASS YOUNG MEN and women from October 2008 to February 2010. Lowell, Massachusetts, and Richmond, Virginia, served as my primary research sites, but I would often travel outside these cities to meet informants. I centered on Lowell and Richmond because they each embody the economic forces responsible for increasing economic insecurity: the decline of industry, diminishing public funding, and the growth of low-paying service sector jobs.

The second planned industrial city in the United States, Lowell was the center of the textile industry for most of the nineteenth century. Even when production in the mills declined in the decades following the Depression, Lowell retained a concentration of employment in manufacturing of 50 percent above the national average (Gittell and Flynn 1995). In the 1970s and 80s, Lowell's economy experienced an economic boom that doubled employment, particularly in manufacturing; by 1989, over one-third of the local labor market's employment was in manufacturing, with industrial machinery accounting for over one-half of the manufacturing jobs. In the early 1990s, however, Lowell's economy shrank enormously, largely due to factories shutting down: from 1989 to 1994, total employment declined by nearly 9 percent and manufacturing employment by 28 percent (Gittell and Flynn 1995: 3). At the same time, a banking and real estate crisis led commercial property values to plummet and credit to dissolve. Today, the economy has recovered to some degree, but the manufacturing jobs for which the city of Lowell has been historically known have all but vanished. Recent economic growth has occurred mainly in service industries such as education, health, leisure, and hospitality.

Like Lowell, Richmond was built on a strong manufacturing and shipping base, emerging from the Civil War as the industrial powerhouse of the South. However, by the end of the twentieth century, Richmond had experienced massive capital flight from its city center and rising unemployment and racial divides (Sargent 2010). While Lowell has a large public sector workforce with strong unions, active collective bargaining, and benefits (despite the fact that the city cut overtime pay and raises at the peak of the recession), Richmond is located in a right-to-work state with weak labor laws and thereby less institutionalized protection from the market. It is not surprising that the men in my sample who took traditional pathways to adulthood were disproportionately from Lowell, where, for example, a police officer with one year on the job earns nearly $63,000 a year, versus $38,000 in Richmond.[1]

My informants were between the ages of twenty-four and thirty-four, with an average age of twenty-seven. Although most coming of age studies target high school age youth (MacLeod 1987; Walkerdine et al. 2001; Weis 1990), I was particularly interested in what happens when young people leave the structured setting of high school and attempt to navigate the labor market, the field of higher education, and romantic relationships on their own. My older age range also allowed me to explore the experiences of young people for whom traditional markers of adulthood have been delayed or postponed. While this age range may seem very broad, I did not find significant differences between those on the higher and lower ends of the spectrum; my sample includes thirty-four-year-olds who have not yet found lasting jobs or partners, and twenty-four-year-olds who are steadily employed and married with children. Access to stable employment, rather than numerical age, was the biggest predictor of a normative transition to adulthood.

I defined "working class" as having fathers without college degrees.[2] By using parents' rather than respondents' level of education to select respondents, I was able to understand how the children of the working class of a generation ago are re-creating what it means, objectively and subjectively, to be working class. Because of my interest in how expressions of class and selfhood among the American working class have changed across generations, all my informants and their parents were born in the United States. The sample is 60 percent white, 40 percent black, and divided evenly by gender. Comparing only blacks and whites allows me to situate my work against a backdrop of studies of the working class that focus only on whites (e.g., Johnson 2002; Rubin 1976; Weis 1990; Willis 1977) and within a body of comparative cultural sociology (e.g., Lamont 1992, 2000; Lareau 2003; McDermott 2006) which examines how blacks and whites compete against each other. Furthermore, while women have often remained invisible in social science literature constructing the working-class in masculine terms (see Bettie 2003 for a thorough discussion of the ways in which women have been historically invisible in class analysis), the centrality of women in the service economy and in single-parent families has made it impossible to ignore them as classed subjects. By varying both race and gender, I am able to speak not only to the ways in which the lives of black and white men and women diverge in patterned ways but also to whether they draw distinctions against each other (Lamont and Molnár 2002) in a neoliberal climate of competition and distrust.

I recruited informants through several approaches. I went to service sector workplaces, including gas stations, casual dining restaurants, coffee shops, fast food chains, retail chains, day care establishments, and temporary agencies. I also visited community, regional, and state colleges. Finally, I went to fire and police stations and military training sites. At these places, I approached young people and asked if they would like to participate in a study of "what it's like to grow up today."[3]

The men and women in my sample embody the disorderliness, reversibility, and delay of traditional markers of adulthood noted by previous researchers (Berlin, Furstenberg, and Waters 2010). Only fourteen respondents are employed, married, living with a spouse, and have children. Thirty-five live with a parent or older family member such as an aunt or grandmother. One respondent dropped out of high school; forty-five respondents have high school diplomas or GEDs; twenty-seven have some college but no degree;

three hold associate degrees; twenty have bachelor's degrees; and four hold master's degrees. The vast majority of respondents work in the service industry as bartenders and servers, medical billers, nannies, mechanics, security guards, salespersons, cashiers, customer service representatives, and janitors. Eight men work in civil service jobs, such as in fire or police departments, and six respondents hold professional jobs. Additionally, twenty respondents have military experience, whether in the armed forces or the National Guard. I ultimately decided to include such a high proportion of former or current soldiers because joining the military is often viewed as a vehicle for economic stability and success by socially disadvantaged youth, especially as job security in the civilian sphere declines. Indeed, it is not a coincidence that in 2008, a crisis year when the United States experienced staggering job losses, the military completed its best recruiting year since 1973, meeting and exceeding all recruitment goals (Gilmore 2009). More than half the respondents are single (56%) or dating (21%), eighteen are married, and five are divorced. Twenty-seven have children.

The purpose of my interview questions was to capture inductively how working-class young adults ascribe meaning and order to their lives, particularly their constructions of selfhood (see a sample of the interview questions at the end of the Appendix).[4] Establishing trust was crucial to this undertaking, and I carefully thought about how my own identity (as a twenty-seven-year-old white woman working toward a PhD at the time) shaped both my interactions with and analysis of my respondents (see Bettie 2003). Before I was even granted permission to conduct this research, the Institutional Review Board (IRB) at my university threw into relief the vast social distance between my respondents and me by expressing concern about my safety, urging me to take precautions when meeting with participants:

> The expedited reviewer has concerns about the safety of a researcher. This is not one of the concerns that the board asked to look at during the review of a protocol; however, the researcher is meeting with all types of people and in some instances might meet up with them at a later time. The board asks that precautions be taken so the researcher can protect herself.

I read "all types of people" as a euphemism for "dangerous," "lower class" and "black" men. I was surprised by such a response from an organization whose sole purpose is to protect the safety of powerless research *subjects*. This incident continues to serve as a powerful reminder of the institutionalized hostility, racism, and betrayal that characterizes working-class lives (see Hays 2003; Lareau 2003).

Over the course of my research, I was continually forced to think about the potential difficulties in forging connections across lines of power and identity—whether class, race, gender, or sexual orientation—though never in ways that the IRB envisioned. John, a twenty-seven-year-old black man who was studying for an accounting exam at a Richmond community college, stopped halfway through the interview to tell me point-blank: "You know, the average white woman won't even look me in the eye. They look away. I was so shocked when you sat down and talked to me and would even look me in the face . . . then I learned that you wanted something from me and it made sense." Yet another respondent scoffed at me when we met downtown one afternoon and I suggested we conduct the interview in a wine bar, the only place that was open during the post-lunch, pre-dinner afternoon hours: "I drink *beer*."

Being close in age to my respondents helped me to bridge the gap between our disparate social locations. In my typical graduate school uniform of jeans, a sweater, boots, and a ponytail, I could blend in at the community college or at Wal-Mart. When I laughed about my own prolonged transition to adulthood, talked about the fourteen-hour days my mom pulls as a small business owner, or recalled my experiences of apprehension as a first-generation college student, respondents would often visibly relax and respond with stories or even advice of their own.[5] Some, only partially jokingly, referred to the interview as "free therapy," seeming to savor the opportunity to communicate their difficult emotions to someone who would listen.

Others would ask to me to send them a copy of the book when it was finished, which I plan to do. About a third even "friended" me on Facebook—some before we met, as a sort of screening process, and others after the initial interview. Facebook proved to be an invaluable tool, as I was able to keep in touch with respondents, following their status updates and even sending personal messages if I needed to ask follow-up questions. Because my respondents' lives are generally unpredictable in terms of employment, housing, and relationships, Facebook allowed me to capture the ongoing sense of flux and dislocation that I would have missed in relying solely on a single panel interview methodology. Through sharing an interactive digital space with my respondents, I was at least somewhat able to avoid treating my subjects as "out there, far removed in time and space" from myself and my textual production (Bettie 2003: 26). Participants could and did "like" and respond to my status updates, view my pictures, chat casually with me online, and send me names of friends whom I could potentially interview. Candace, a twenty-four-year-old black woman, sent me a Facebook message following our meeting that read, "Your book is going to speak for so many people without voices." Yet another informant asked that I use his real name and thus make his story public. This hunger to find someone to bear witness to their experiences—to be *heard*—came to be central to my analysis of what it means to come of age in the risk society. It is my hope that this book delivers on its promise.

Interview Guide

The purpose of this project is to explore what it's like for young working-class people to make the transition to adulthood today. I will ask you a series of questions about your family background and relationships, your job, your education, your struggles, and your goals for the future. If at any time you feel uncomfortable or don't want to answer a question, just let me know and we will move on or stop the interview.

1. I'd like to start by getting a sense of your life history. Where are you from? What do your parents do? Have they had these jobs their whole life? Did they graduate from high school or college? Do they own their home? Are they married, divorced, separated, never married?
2. Can you remember times when your parents seemed to struggle economically? Was there a time when they couldn't pay the bills, or worried about money? How did they talk about this? What did they do about it?
3. Do you know if your parents got or get benefits from their jobs, like pensions and health care? Is this something they talk about? What would you do growing up if you were sick?

4. Do you have siblings? What do they do? How much education do they have?

5. Whom do you live with now? How long have you lived there? How did you make the choice to live in this place? Can you remember any times when you worried about where you would live, or how you would afford to pay rent?

6. Let's think back to when you graduated from high school. Did you like school? Walk me through the steps you went through when you were deciding what to do after graduation. What kinds of choices did you have? What did your family think you should do? Did you think about college? About a job? About joining the military? How much education did you ultimately end up getting?

7. What kind of work do you do now? How long have you had this job? How long have you been working? Tell me about how you found your job. What are your feelings about your current job?

8. Walk me through a typical day at work.

9. What are your relationships like with your coworkers? Boss? Customers? Are there times when it feel rewarding? When? How about challenging? Distressing?

10. How do you see your standing at work? Why?

11. Do you think there are opportunities for promotion? Do you get benefits, or could you?

12. Does your job pay you enough to pay your bills? What kinds of bills do you have to pay every month?

13. Are you in debt? Are you making payments on a credit card or student loans?

14. When you were younger, did you imagine yourself working here? Can you think back to a time when you thought about your future, or talked to your family about it? Where did you see yourself at your age? What kinds of things did you want out of life?

15. Are you married? Do you want to get married? Have children? Can you think of times when this seemed difficult to achieve? How? What stands in your way? What kind of partner would you want?

16. How do you plan to get ahead? How do you think you get ahead in America? Where did you get this idea?

17. What social class would you put yourself in? Can you walk me through a time when you felt like social class mattered in your life? How salient is class in your daily life?

18. Can you remember any times when your race made getting ahead, or achieving a goal, harder for you? When you experienced discrimination?

19. Can you remember a time when your gender made getting ahead, or achieving a goal, harder for you? When you experienced discrimination?

20. How do you see yourself in comparison to your parents? (Economically, socially, etc.). What were their lives like when they were your age?

21. Would you call yourself an adult? Walk me through a time when you felt grown up. What made you feel this way? What makes you not feel grown up?

22. How would you define adulthood? Why?

23. How would you define what it means to become a man or a woman? Are you able to meet these criteria?

24. What do you think is the hardest thing about growing up today? Was there ever a time when you felt like people misunderstood what it's like to be a young person today?

25. Walk me through a time when you felt like you just couldn't make it. What happened? What did you do?

26. Walk me through a time when you felt hopeful about your future.

27. What do you do for fun?

NOTES

Chapter 1

1. All names have been changed to protect the identities of respondents.

2. These are Brandon's words.

3. The SLM Corporation (commonly known as Sallie Mae) originated in 1972 as a government-sponsored enterprise managing federally backed student loans. In 2004, the government cut its ties to Sallie Mae, which is now a private corporation.

4. In making this point, Brandon calls to mind the sociological literature on the mass incarceration of young black men, especially those with low levels of education (Western 2006).

5. In the three years since our interview, Diana first moved to New York with her friends with $100 in her pocket and then moved back into her mother's home just a few weeks later. She recently started taking online classes at a for-profit college while working two part-time service jobs. She is still single.

6. See Booth et al. (1999: 254).

7. See, for example, Booth et al. 1999; Côté 2000; Goldstein and Kenney 2001; Osgood et al. 2005; Arnett 2006; Blatterer 2007; Kimmel 2008; Gerson 2009; Berlin, Furstenberg, and Waters 2010; Danziger and Ratner 2010; Brinton 2010; Waters et al. 2011.

8. See US Census, "Young Adults Living at Home: 1960 to Present."

9. See Copen et al. 2012.

10. The delay in marriage and childbearing can be partly explained by participation in higher education, which has increased significantly over the last few decades, especially for women. In 2010, 40 percent of young adults between eighteen and twenty-four were enrolled in higher education. (U.S. Department of Education, National Center for Education Statistics, 2012)

11. This trend has implications for greater inequality, as two incomes have become a necessity rather than a luxury for most American families (Warren 2006).

12. See Illouz (2007: 5) on emotional capitalism, "a culture in which emotional and economic discourses and practices mutually shape each other, thus producing what I view

as a broad, sweeping movement in which affect is made an essential part of economic behavior and in which emotional life—especially that of the middle classes—follows the logic of economic relations and exchange." This mutual constitution at the level of the self, I would argue, takes place within the mood economy.

13. This is not to romanticize the past: indeed, "stable," "predictable," and "gendered" in this historical moment meant limited freedom for women and African Americans, institutionalized racism and sexism that prevented women and minorities from accessing public benefits like Social Security, constrictive notions of gender and sexuality, and social exclusion (Coontz 2000; Katznelson 2005). Yet cultural understandings of security, solidarity, and social protection from the market as *worthwhile*—however exclusive and anemic it may have been in practice—were nonetheless a vibrant part of American culture (Sewell 2009). In fact, the sense of possibility, shared purpose, and reciprocity born of the postwar years would provide the impetus for the struggles for social justice—the civil rights movement, the Second Wave of feminism—that soon followed (Cowie 2010; Putnam 2000).

14. Paul later explained: "The freer the system, the better the health care." The entire debate can be viewed www.ronpaul.com/2011-09-07/gop-debate-tonight-8-pm-et-live-on-msnbc-cnbc-telemundo-politico-com-and-msnbc-com/.

15. To elaborate, workers spend a greater proportion of their paychecks on health insurance, yet also spend more on health costs than they did a generation ago (Cohn 2007). Employers contribute less to fixed income retirement plans, leaving workers bearing the risk of their own retirement saving through private retirement accounts (Mishel et al. 2007). In the neoliberal era, the worker is assumed to be knowledgeable, calculating, flexible, and self-aware; those who cannot adapt themselves to the rhythm of the ever-changing and ruthless labor market have no safety nets to rely on.

16. In terms of wealth, in 1962, the top 1 percent had 125 times the wealth of the median household; by 2009 the top 1 percent had 225 times the median household's wealth (Allegretto 2011).

17. The consequences of neoliberalism were thrown into relief by the economic crisis of 2008, in which the deregulation of the banking system, combined with the purposeful failure to regulate new financial instruments such as derivatives, made it increasingly difficult for homeowners and investors to defend themselves against Wall Street greed (Hacker and Pierson 2010; Krugman 2009; McLean and Nocera 2010). Although the youngest working-class men and women have yet to show up in studies of intergenerational mobility, it is predicted that this generation will be significantly less likely to be able to climb the social ladder than the previous one (Putnam et al. 2012).

18. As the historian Jefferson Cowie explains, working-class men have become the common enemy—"an 'other' dwelling outside of the New Politics built by and upon minorities, women, youth, and sexuality"—despised by the new Left for its backwardness and bigotry (2010: 240). The white working class, in response, has taken refuge in Ronald Reagan's politics of nostalgia, resentment toward affirmative action, God, and country (Cowie 2010; Stacey 1998).

19. To provide one sobering statistic, by 2009, the median white American had $98,000 in net worth while the median black American had just $2,200 (Owens 2012).

20. Beginning with Freud's Clark lectures in America, Eva Illouz (2007) traces how psychoanalytic discourse, combined with democratic ideals of self-help, have taken root

in American culture. In a variety of institutions—including psychiatry, psychology, media (e.g., talk shows and film), self-help literature, social welfare programs, corporate human resources, and even religion—the therapeutic ethos has become *the* language for talking about the self. In this way, a new form of popular theodicy has taken root, one that views all suffering as both purposeful and controllable: if we can only learn to manage our emotions, and thereby create a new relationship with our pasts, we can alleviate suffering and reach our true potential (Illouz 2008).

21. This book spent over 200 weeks on the *New York Times* best-seller list.

22. In this spirit, *Bitch Magazine* ran a story in August 2011 satirically entitled *Eat, Pray, Spend*; for Gilbert, happiness required a year of seeking from Italy to India to Indonesia.

23. I thank Ahrum Lee for his insight into this point.

24. This is not to say that the following stories of pain, suffering, and even transformation that I will recount in this book are not real; like culture, emotions are socially patterned and transcendent even while they are experienced as individual, irrational, and subjective (Hays 1994; see also Collins 2004; Hochschild 2003; Illouz 2007; Williams 1977).

Chapter 2

1. The International Association of Fire Fighters (IAFF) is the labor union that represents professional firefighters in the United States and Canada. While the union membership rate in the private sector has fallen to 6.9 percent, it is over five times that in the public sector (37%). Within the public sector, local government workers such as teachers, police officers, and firefighters have the highest membership rate—43.2 percent. Young adults are much less likely than older workers to be unionized: the union membership rate in 2011 was highest among workers fifty-five to sixty-four years old (15.7%) and lowest among those ages sixteen to twenty-four (4.4%). In 2011, among full-time wage and salary workers, union members had median usual weekly earnings of $938, while those who were not union members had median weekly earnings of $729 (see the US Bureau of Labor's "Union Members Summary," 2013 www.bls.gov/news.release/union2.nro.htm).

2. Despite gains in higher education, women still earn 80 cents for every dollar men earn. Women pay a motherhood penalty of 5 percent for one child and 12 percent for two children. For married African American men, however, fatherhood is associated with a 7 percent increase in wages and for married white and Latino men fatherhood is associated with a 9 percent increase in wages (see Cohen and Bianchi 1999; Waldfogel 1997). Coltrane (2000) found that although women have reduced and men have slightly increased their hourly contributions to routine household tasks, women still do at least twice as much housework as men do.

3. In 2011, I asked Sandy and Cody to update me on their lives. They responded with the following story: in order to make their monthly mortgage payment, they took in a boarder, who lived in the unfinished basement and paid them $400 a month. When Sandy and Cody took the children away during summer vacation to visit Sandy's mother for a long weekend, they came back to find their television gone and their son's piggy bank shattered, all the money gone. Their boarder had thrown a party in their absence, and his friends had stolen these items. Sandy and Cody want to evict him but fear defaulting on their mortgage and thus have allowed him to remain in the house. They did, they pointed out, have the locks changed.

4. In an experiment designed to test the persistence of discrimination in the low-wage labor market, Pager et al. (2009) found that black applicants were half as likely as equally qualified whites to receive a callback or job offer. Moreover, black and Latino applicants with clean backgrounds fared no better in the labor market than white applicants just released from prison.

5. Indeed, racial disparities persist within the housing market (Beveridge 2010; Massey and Denton 1993), employment (Pager et al. 2009; Wilson 1997), and lending (Bond and Williams 2007).

6. Using data from the 2008 National Household Survey of Credit Card Debt among Low-and Middle-Income Households, García and Draut (2009) found that the average credit card debt of low- and middle-income credit card indebted households in 2008 was $9,827, an increase from $9,536 in 2005. Just over one in four of these households had credit card debt over $10,000. Moreover, one in four households reported paying 20 percent interest or more on their card with the highest balance. Households of color are much more likely to be paying such high interest: nearly one-third of African American (32%) and Latino (30%) households paid interest rates higher than 20 percent, compared to less than one-quarter (22%) of white households. Three out of four low- to middle-income households reported using their credit cards as a plastic safety net, relying on credit cards to manage car repairs, home repairs, layoff or job loss, starting or running a business, or college expenses.

7. Subprime lending, or the practice of making loans to people who may have difficulty maintaining the repayment schedule, has been shown to disproportionately affect minority neighborhoods (Beveridge 2010). Importantly, as Alexandra's experience reveals, these loans are characterized by high interest rates, presumably to compensate for higher credit risk.

8. In 2001, young adults had the second highest rate of bankruptcy, just after those aged thirty-five to forty-four (Sullivan et al. 2001). However, since the recession of 2008, the eighteen to twenty-four and twenty-five to thirty-four age cohorts have seen a combined decrease in bankruptcy rates of 31 percent, perhaps because of dwindling access to credit, while older Americans (such as Craig's mother) have seen an increase of 19 percent. Over 70 percent of debtors did not graduate from college, and the majority of bankruptcy filers earn $40,000 a year or less ("2010 Annual Consumer Bankruptcy Demographics Report: A Five Year Perspective of the American Debtor").

9. In the early 1980s, credit card debt was virtually nonexistent, as credit cards were not widely available and were not marketed aggressively to college-aged students (Draut 2005). However, as the credit card industry was deregulated as part of the neoliberal policy paradigm (see in particular the landmark Supreme Court Case, *Marquette National Bank of Minneapolis v. First Omaha Service Corp.*), banks were permitted to charge unlimited interest rates and late fees and to target low-income borrowers with especially high rates. According to Federal Reserve Data, the median consumer debt (including student loans, credit card debt, and car loans) for borrowers under thirty-five has tripled from $3,989 in 1983 to $12,000 in 2000. On average, young adults in 2001 spent over a quarter of their income on debt repayment (not including mortgages), more than twice the amount that their Baby Boomer counterparts spent in 1989 (Draut 2005; Kamenetz 2006).

10. In the city of Lowell, for example, civil service exam scores are ranked, with disabled veterans, veterans, minorities, children of civil servants killed in the line of duty, and Lowell residents given hiring preference.

11. This is not to imply that racial minorities have equal access to these jobs or that affirmative action has resolved deeply embedded racial tensions. I will address this point directly in Chapter 4.

12. See "A National Report Card on Women in Firefighting," Institute for Women and Work, Cornell University.

13. A typical contract specifies eight years of military service.

14. In January 2012, Secretary of Defense Leon E. Panetta announced a plan for cutting the defense budget that proposed to limit pay raises for troops, increase health insurance (Tricare) costs for retired soldiers and their families, close selected military bases, and reduce the size of the US Army and Marines over the next five years (see www. defense.gov/speeches for full text of speech). Thus, the military, especially for enlisted soldiers, may become increasingly competitive and insecure, no longer an escape from the civilian labor market.

15. These criteria for adulthood are from Jay, a young black man who works at a coffee shop.

16. Only 40 percent of students who enter community colleges earn any kind of degree or certificate within five years. Only 25 percent achieve associate or bachelor's degrees, and 48 percent drop out within five years without achieving any credentials at all (Roksa 2006).

17. US Census Bureau data reveal that, on average, male and female workers with an associate degree make only $3,766 (13.8%) more than those with a high school diploma annually, while workers with a bachelor's degree earn over $20,000 (65%) more than those with an associate degree (US Census 2003).

18. As Dougherty (2001: 67) asserts in *The Contradictory College*: "The community college is indeed a central supplier of trained workers across a wide variety of 'middle-level' or 'semiprofessional' occupations. But its response to the labor market's call is much more clumsy than is acknowledged by both its defenders and critics. The community college often under- and overshoots the demands of the labor market: in many cases training far more people than the labor market can absorb and in other cases producing fewer workers than business would like. In short, the community college dances to the rhythms of the labor market, but it rarely keeps good time."

19. According to the Economic Mobility Project (2007), about one-third of men and women are upwardly mobile in the sense that they surpass their parents' family income and their parents' economic position (defined by quintiles). This mobility tends to occur in the middle of the income distribution, as sons and daughters born at the top end and the bottom end of the income distribution are likely to end up in the same position as their parents. Mobility is particularly low for girls born in the bottom of the income distribution: nearly half (47%) of low-income girls compared to 35 percent of low-income boys end up in the bottom fifth upon adulthood.

Chapter 3

1. From March 1975 to March 2000, the labor force participation rate of mothers with children under age eighteen rose from 47 percent to 73 percent. Women have also attained higher levels of education: among women aged twenty-five to sixty-four who are in the labor force, the proportion with a college degree roughly tripled from 1970 to 2008. Women's earnings as a proportion of men's earnings also have grown over time. In 1979, women working full-time earned 62 percent of what men did; in 2008, women's earnings were 80 percent of men's ("Women in the Labor Force: A Datebook, 2009 Edition").

2. The number of women in their forties who are childless is up from 8 percent in the 1970s to 18 percent in 2000.

3. Among women married in 1970 to 1974, 24.3 percent of college graduates experienced a marital dissolution within ten years, compared to 33.7 percent of women with less educational attainment. For women married in 1990 to 1994, only 16.7 percent of four-year college graduates experienced a marital dissolution within ten years, compared to a still high 35.7 percent of women with less educational attainment (Martin 2004).

4. These men represent "neo-traditional" gender attitudes (Gerson 2009). None of them were in stable jobs or in relationships with women whom they viewed as marriage-worthy, many fearing that they lacked the necessary time and resources to sustain a relationship, or worrying about finding a woman whom they could trust.

5. At the start of the Great Recession at the end of 2007, the black unemployment rate averaged 8.4 percent but the white unemployment rate stood at only 4 percent. While Americans across class, race, and gender lines experienced significant job loss during the Great Recession of 2007–2009, unemployment rates for many black groups continued to rise even after they started to drop for whites. Specifically, the black unemployment rate averaged 16.1 percent in the spring of 2011, compared to an average of 7.9 percent for whites in the same period. Broken down by gender, the unemployment rate among black women was 14.1 percent in the second quarter of 2011 compared to 7.4 percent among white women. The unemployment rate among black men was 18.3 percent while the unemployment rate among white men was 8.3 percent. Among young adults, the unemployment rate of black youth was an astronomical 41.3 percent in the second quarter of 2011 compared to 22.3 percent for white youth (Weller and Fields 2011).

6. Among nonreligious Americans, 76 percent of unions that began with cohabiting end within fifteen years (Cherlin 2009).

7. In *Talk of Love: How Culture Matters*, Ann Swidler (2001) argues that within contemporary American culture, two competing vocabularies for talking about love predominate: love as a voluntary choice (i.e., the pure or therapeutic relationship) or love as commitment. In the first model of love, "the question is whom one loves and why, and what one gives and receives in a relationship" (ibid. 26); if one is not satisfied, then the partnership can be terminated. In the second model of love, commitment to the relationship itself supersedes individual fulfillment: "It is unique, irreplaceable, and not fully rationalizable into a set of benefits given and received" (ibid. 26).

8. When I asked Kiana if her pregnancy was planned, she laughed: "No. Who plans for that?"

9. WIC (Women, Infants and Children) is a federally funded program that helps families by providing checks for buying foods from WIC-authorized vendors, nutrition education, and help finding health care and other community services. A system of collective rather than privatized protection from risk, WIC flies in the face of neoliberal ideology and represents a site of intense political conflict. The 2012 federal budget reduces WIC funding from $6.734 billion to $6.001 billion, a cut of $733 million. See www.fns.usda.gov/wic/aboutwic/wicataglance.htm.

10. Existing literature documents how child rearing leads parents to widen what we might call their "responsibility horizons," noting that the skills, responsibility, and maturity born of parenting can serve to benefit those who undertake it, including, for example, low-income unmarried women who might otherwise experience a sort of social unmooring. In their study of unmarried low-income caregivers, Edin and Kefalas (2005: 180)

reported that "over and over again, mothers tell us their children tamed or calmed their wild behavior, got them off the street, and helped put their lives back together." Caregiving held redemptive promise for young women whose lives before parenthood felt purposeless and chaotic. Other studies also establish connections among parenting, redemption, and personal growth. McMahon (1995) found that working-class women undergo a process of self-transformation upon becoming mothers in which the "redemptive powers" (169) of motherhood lead them to "settle down" (165), behave more responsibly and maturely, and put others before themselves. The middle-class women in her sample, on the other hand, were more likely to talk about their experiences of mothering in psychological terms of self-actualization and personal growth (166), perhaps because middle-class mothers understood maturity as a precondition to having children. Exploring young men's paths to fatherhood, Marsiglio and Hutchinson (2002: 122) find that fathering a child represents a milestone for many men, prompting them to abandon their partying lifestyles, take work and education more seriously, and embrace their roles as providers.

11. This is not to imply that parenting *practices* do not vary by social class. Using the concepts of "concerted cultivation" and "natural growth," Lareau (2003) argues that middle-class parents consciously cultivate the skills, knowledge, and sense of self necessary for navigating the middle-class milieu, while working-class parents rely on a model in which children's development occurs naturally without the requirement of ever-present adult intervention. Hays's (1996, 2003) analyses of mothers across a wide range of social locations, however, suggest that Lareau's emphasis on "natural growth" as a cultural *model* for working-class parents may be misplaced. Hays clearly demonstrates the widespread ideology of what she calls "intensive mothering" and the real commitment to such an ideology across lines of class and race. My data support this finding. It is perhaps more useful to think of Lareau's concept of "natural growth" as describing the *practices* of working-class parents.

Chapter 4

1. In 2008–2009, the US Treasury and the Federal Reserve System "bailed out" numerous large banks and insurance companies, General Motors, and Chrysler through the Troubled Asset Relief Program (TARP). The Obama administration estimates that this bailout will cost the government $117 billion (www.whitehouse.gov/the-press-office/president-obama-proposes-financial-crisis-responsibility-fee-recoup-every-last-penny).

2. The video clip of this controversy is available here: http://video.foxnews.com/v/3971448/markdowns-for-martin-luther-king-jr/.

3. However, as the sociologist Pierre Bourdieu (1998) argues, nostalgia for the glory days of neoliberalism is profoundly ahistorical, concealing massive economic, social, and political changes that have taken place both in the United States and worldwide.

4. Indeed, as Durkheim once observed, "Mourning is not a natural movement of private feelings wounded by cruel loss; it is a duty imposed by the group" (1995: 443).

5. Furthermore, it is *through* emotion that culture (systems of meanings and symbols) is "created, denigrated, or reinforced" in micro-encounters (Collins 2004: xii). Thus, emotion is one key to understanding why social reproduction occurs or fails to occur. That is, successful interaction rituals producing high levels of emotional energy can lead to the desire to repeat them (thus remaking existing social structures), while failed rituals can lead to low levels of emotional energy, and consequently avoiding the ritual in the future (thus leading to structural change).

6. Recent data on levels of generalized social trust—or whether people feel like "most people can be trusted"—reveal growing gaps between middle- and working-class twelfth graders. While the percentages of upper-middle class and working-class twelfth graders who report that most people can be trusted declined until the mid-1990s, it has since rebounded for the upper-middle-class youth but not for their working-class counterparts (Putnam et al. 2012).

7. ADHD, or attention deficit hyperactivity disorder, is a developmental disorder characterized primarily by "the co-existence of attentional problems and hyperactivity" in early childhood. The causes, diagnosis, and treatment of ADHD have been controversial since the 1970s (Biederman 1998).

8. With these criminal acts on their records, respondents faced difficulties when attempting to secure employment. As Western (2006: 5) notes, "although the normal life course is integrative, incarceration is disintegrative," making the achievement of adult markers such as full employment or financial stability more problematic.

9. The one exception is the Stafford loan, which is not need-based and must be paid back (see The Higher Education Opportunity Act of 2008).

10. See www.finaid.org/otheraid/parentsrefuse.phtml for a thorough description of financial aid policy.

11. *The American Heritage Dictionary of the English Language*, Fourth Edition.

12. The US government ostensibly provides Social Security Disability Insurance (SSDI) (a federally run benefits program that provides aid to people who are unable to achieve gainful employment due to a permanent disabling condition). But according to its own website, nearly 60 percent of applicants for SSDI are denied, and applicants are encouraged to seek legal counsel to improve their chances of approval (www.socialsecurity-disability.org/content/about-ssdi). In a sense, then—especially for those who cannot afford legal counsel—Allan correctly assesses the government's treatment of the disabled.

13. The study of symbolic boundaries seeks to articulate the relationship between symbolic boundaries—the conceptual distinctions social actors and groups make to categorize social reality—and social boundaries, particularly as they relate to patterns of exclusion, inequality, and class or racial segregation (Lamont and Molnár 2002). Scholars seek to capture the ways in which boundaries are socially and historically constructed within fields of power, with the implication that ostensible differences do not precede or cause inequality, but rather are produced, maintained, and naturalized through ongoing struggle (Bourdieu 1984). The process of legitimation is perpetually ongoing, changing according to the dynamics of a particular space, the kinds of resources to be won or lost, and the culturally available schemes of perception for categorizing difference (Bourdieu 1990).

14. As members of the dominant racial group in the United States, they see whiteness as the *absence of race*—as normal, and therefore nonracial (Bonilla-Silva 2003: 115). While some respondents acknowledge the persistence of racial discrimination and inequality in the abstract, they have rarely witnessed discrimination against people of color in their own lives and thus have very little to say about the subject of race. I believe that this lack of knowledge about race occurs because they live in predominantly white neighborhoods, go to white schools, and work and socialize mainly with other whites. Thus, social and spatial segregation (historically produced and institutionally sanctioned, to the benefit of whites) produces a sense of color blindness in these respondents, allowing them

to live out their lives in a universe of whiteness that makes them oblivious to race on a structural level. In this way, they can emphasize their lack of racism—"I have absolutely no problems with any race whatsoever"—in the abstract.

15. "Bonding capital" is "inward looking and tend[s] to reinforce exclusive identities and homogeneous groups," while "bridging capital" is "outward looking and encompass[es] people across diverse social cleavages" (Putnam 2000: 22).

16. Because these interviews took place before the repeal of Don't Ask, Don't Tell, no one I interviewed in the military identified as gay, which makes their homophobia all the more insidious.

17. This is on the website for the City of Lowell.

18. To reiterate, civil service exam scores are ranked, with disabled veterans, veterans, minorities, children of civil servants killed in the line of duty, and residents given hiring preference. Interestingly, test-takers can log onto a website to see the exam results, which document the name of the job candidate, his or her score, veteran status, city of residence, and whether his or her father was killed in the line of duty; yet minority status is *not* listed, leading to confusion, speculation, and racial tension (which I observed through conversations with respondents waiting to be hired, or with older white firefighters who want their children to be hired).

19. According to the US Census, there have been increases in the percentage of minorities in law enforcement and firefighting, due to years of affirmative action and employment discrimination litigation. However, the percentage of black firefighters remains at 8 percent, far below the 50 percent projected by Joseph (see Royster 2003).

20. 2010 statistics from the National Poverty Center at the University of Michigan show that 27.4 percent of blacks and 26.6 percent of Hispanics were poor, compared to 9.9 percent of whites and 12.1 percent of Asians. Yet whites disproportionately make up a third of welfare (TANF) recipients.

21. Williams explains: "At any time, forms of alternative or directly oppositional politics and culture exist as significant elements in the society . . . but to the extent that they are significant the dominant hegemonic function is to control or transform or even incorporate them. In this active process the hegemonic has to be seen as more than the simple transmission of an unchanging dominance" (113). That is, the existence of meanings that run contrary to the dominant culture is not enough to create change. In fact, he argues, alternate meanings always exist, but most of the time, they are incorporated *into* dominant understandings of reality.

Chapter 5

1. To reiterate, the therapeutic narrative unfolds as follows: first, it compels one to identify pathological thoughts and behaviors; second, to locate the hidden source of these pathologies within one's past; third, to give voice to one's story of suffering; and, finally, to triumph over one's past by reconstructing an emancipated and independent self (Illouz 2008). In conceiving of all suffering as purposeful—that is, the result of "mismanaged emotions" that can ultimately be repaired at the level of the *self*—the therapeutic narrative allows for a sense of control and meaning over the disruptions and uncertainties inherent in modern day life (Illouz 2008: 247).

2. I would like to thank Stephan Fuchs (via Ahrum Lee) for helping me to identify and develop the phenomenon of the mood economy.

3. Rates of mental illness and substance dependence are higher in my sample than in the US population (National Survey on Drug Use and Health, 2009). While it could be argued that my sample is skewed toward young people with particularly high rates of mental illness and addiction, I would argue that therapeutically oriented institutions in fact *foster* narratives of illness and addiction among the young people in my sample (see www.nimh.nih.gov/statistics/SMI_AASR.shtml).

4. According to the US National Library of Medicine, obsessive-compulsive disorder is "an anxiety disorder in which people have unwanted and repeated thoughts, feelings, ideas, sensations (obsessions), or behaviors that make them feel driven to do something (compulsions)."

5. To understand illness or addiction as socially constructed—or occurring within a particular set of historical and cultural conditions—is not to deny the very real pain and suffering that these men and women experience. See Bordo (2003) on the social construction of illness.

6. Rates of depression and anxiety among young adults have been increasing dramatically over the past fifty to seventy years, even when diagnostic criteria and measurement are held constant (Twenge et al. 2010).

7. Referring to a fifty-six-year-old African American janitor whom she interviewed, she writes: "This working-class man was left with the experience of a suffering all the more intolerable in that it remained meaningless, without an interpretive frame to account for it" (2008: 234).

8. To quote Marx (1959: 494): "Not only do the objective conditions change in the act of reproduction, e.g. the village becomes a town, the wilderness a cleared field etc., but the producers change, too, in that they bring out new qualities in themselves, develop themselves in production, transform themselves, develop new powers and ideas, new modes of intercourse, new needs and new language."

9. That is, informants who tell their coming of age stories through a therapeutic lens understand *severing* family ties to be vital to their own health and happiness. Rachel and Joseph, on the other hand, mend their broken relationships not by confronting their painful memories but simply by living and working with, and depending on, their parents.

10. See Silva and Pugh (2010) and Silva (2012) for a more thorough discussion of the different kinds of witnesses invoked by respondents.

11. As an interviewer, I also served as a potential witness to my interviewees. Indeed, some men and women openly admitted to agreeing to the interview in order to make public, and hopefully validate, their narratives of suffering and self-transformation. Eileen, who continues to be haunted by a harrowing childhood in which her father was imprisoned for assault and her mother committed suicide, began the interview: "I guess one of the reasons too why I wanted to talk with you because I felt, I'm still in therapy, going through things and everything. . . . And I feel like it would help for me to get my story out there a little bit better." Yet another informant gave me permission to record the interview—on the condition that I use his real name and thus make his story public.

12. Seemingly personal qualities such as laziness, anger, depression, attitude problems, or lack of "follow-through" appear most threatening to their life chances. Even those who acknowledged structural barriers such as unemployment or lack of health insurance as risks viewed themselves as ultimately responsible for finding a way to make their lives work out through personal qualities such as determination or will power.

As Steven, a restaurant manager who was forced to drop out of college because he could not get the loans he needed, explained, his biggest risks are financial instability and having no savings account. But he worries that he will not be able to *make myself stay on track.*" Additionally, young people who have struggled with mental illness and drug addiction see relapse as their greatest risk. As Michelle, a twenty-eight-year-old white woman who recently lost her job, reflected: "Alcohol abuse has lessened considerably, though I was mostly functional. I'm five weeks dry. What a funny little drug that is. I think people take for granted what an easy escape it is. I've blocked it, nailed shut that escape, and I'm left very angry about having to navigate my days sober."

13. For many young people, trying something new—a city, a job, a relationship—feels scary because they could lose what little they have. Kevin, a twenty-five-year-old customer service representative who is afraid to move out of his father's house, explained, "There are times when I want to just move out, you know, and I will think about it, but I would run the risk of not making it, and I would feel that I couldn't go back home because I would feel like a failure. . . . That is a risk I want to take but I don't." Kevin understands economic insecurity as well as his own tendency to "play it safe" as explanations for his delay in achieving traditional markers of adult success.

14. Particularly useful here is the work of Marxist philosopher Louis Althusser (1970) on the relationship between social institutions and selfhood. Althusser famously reshuffled the classical metaphor of determining base and determined superstructure by arguing that class domination can only be explained through an analysis of how these two concepts continually act on, with, and through each other. He developed the concept of *ideological state apparatuses*—including religion, education, the family, the legal system, among others—which function primarily through ideology to maintain the hegemony of the ruling class. While the state can repress people through violence to bring about class reproduction, ideological state apparatuses veil domination and inequality by providing an "imaginary relation of those individuals to the real relations in which they live" (165). In this way, Althusser explicitly rejected a conception of ideology as epiphenomenal, simply a reflection of the base, instead stressing its material existence in *everyday, routine* practice, whether a church service or a community gathering. Althusser argued that there is no sense of self that does not derive from cultural categories of personhood: "Thus ideology hails or interpellates individuals as subjects . . . which amounts to making it clear that individuals are always-already interpellated by ideology" (176). That is, ideology produces subjects who experience their subjugation as natural, inevitable, and freely chosen, and therefore reproduce existing relations of production "by themselves" (181).

Conclusion

1. See, for example, www.foxnews.com/on-air/oreilly/2011/11/17/bill-oreilly-failure-occupy-wall-street-movement.

Appendix

1. I attained this information by calling the police department in each city.

2. There is a great deal of ambiguity and disagreement surrounding the concept of social class within sociology (Lareau 2008). Class has been defined and operationalized with varying levels of theoretical and empirical precision (e.g., Sorensen 2000). I rely on father's attainment of a college degree as a marker of middle-class status both because

this matches the general population's understanding that a college degree indicates middle-class status (Hout 2008: 35) and because of the number of empirical studies linking parental education to income and occupational prestige (e.g., Blau and Duncan 1967; Warren et al. 2002) and to children's academic success (e.g., Dumais 2002; Lareau 2003).

3. I also relied on snowball sampling through multiple entry points. Snowballing took me out of Lowell and Richmond and into neighboring towns. I also conducted several interviews in Florida, following a family who moved from Massachusetts to Florida in search of lower tax rates. While most people were enthusiastic about participating, offering me their phone numbers or email, or even setting up a time to meet, it proved very difficult to entice these recruits—who often did not have their own means of transportation, a predictable work schedule, or reliable child care—to actually show up for the interview. Snowball sampling proved more effective because participants were more likely to appear if a friend or acquaintance recommended me. I also gained entry into certain fields—firefighting, police, EMTs, and the military—through my father, who is a firefighter and in the National Guard. With his introduction or simply by mentioning his job, I was treated as somewhat of an insider and allowed to wander around at National Guard drills and hang out at fire and police stations, recruiting, interviewing, and making observations. Toward the end of my eighteen months of data collection, during which I traveled back and forth from Massachusetts to Virginia, I conducted four interviews over the phone with respondents who had moved away.

4. Interviews were semi-structured and lasted approximately two hours. All but four interviews were conducted in person at a location chosen by the respondent. They were digitally recorded with the permission of the respondent and completely transcribed.

5. The most memorable example of this advice came from a twenty-seven-year-old white firefighter, who warned me that as my boyfriend of one year had failed to propose, this should be a "red flag."

REFERENCES

"2010 Annual Consumer Bankruptcy Demographics Report: A Five Year Perspective of the American Debtor." 2011. Institute for Financial Literacy, Inc. 2011. Retrieved on February 13, 2013. Available at http://www.financiallit.org/PDF/2010_Demographics_Report.pdf.

"An Act Providing Access to Affordable, Quality, Accountable Health Care." Chapter 58 of the Acts of 2006 of the Massachusetts General Court. Retrieved on July 9, 2010. Available at www.lawlib.state.ma.us/subject/about/healthinsurance.html.

Alexander, Jeffrey C. 2004. "Cultural Pragmatics: Social Performances between Ritual and Strategy." *Sociological Theory* 22: 527–573.

Allegretto, Sylvia A. 2011. "The State of Working America's Wealth, 2011: Through Volatility and Turmoil, the Gap Widens." Briefing paper #292, *Economic Policy Institute*, Washington DC.

Althusser, Louis. 2001 [1970]. *Lenin and Philosophy and Other Essays*. New York: Monthly Review Press.

Amenta, Edwin. 1998. *Bold Relief: Institutional Politics and the Origins of Modern American Social Policy*. Princeton, NJ: Princeton University Press.

Anderson, Elijah. 1999. *The Code of the Street: Decency, Violence, and the Moral Life of the Inner City*. New York: Norton.

Anderson, Kristen and Debra Umberson. 2001. "Gendering Violence: Masculinity and Power in Men's Accounts of Domestic Violence." *Gender and Society* 15: 358–380.

Arnett, Jeffrey Jensen. 1998. "Learning to Stand Alone: The Contemporary American Transition to Adulthood in Cultural and Historical Context." *Human Development* 41: 295–315.

Arnett, Jeffrey Jensen. 2004. *Emerging Adulthood: The Winding Road from the Late Teens Through the Twenties*. New York: Oxford University Press.

Barich, Rachel, and Denise Bielby. 1996. "Rethinking Marriage: Change and Stability in Expectations, 1967–1994." *Journal of Family Issues* 17: 139–169.

Beck, Ulrich. 2000. *The Brave New World of Work*. Cambridge, UK: Polity Press.

———. 1992. *Risk Society: Towards a New Modernity*. Thousand Oaks, CA: Sage.

Beck, Ulrich, and Elisabeth Beck-Gernsheim. 1995. *The Normal Chaos of Love.* Cambridge, UK: Polity Press.

Bellah, Robert N., Richard Madsen, William M. Sullivan, Ann Swidler, and Steven M. Tipton. 1985. *Habits of the Heart: Individualism and Commitment in American Life.* Berkeley: University of California Press.

Berlin, Gordon, Frank Furstenberg Jr., and Mary C. Waters, editors. 2010. *The Transition to Adulthood. Special Issue of The Future of Children* 20(1). Washington, DC: Brookings Institution.

Bettie, Julie. 2003. *Women without Class: Girls, Race, and Identity.* Berkeley: University of California Press.

Beveridge, Andrew. 2010. "Homeowners No More: A First Look at the Foreclosure Crisis's Effects on Neighborhoods and Communities across the United States." A paper presented at the Eastern Sociological Society Annual Meeting, Boston, MA.

Biederman, Joseph. 1998. "Attention-deficit/hyperactivity Disorder: A Life-span Perspective." *Journal of Clinical Psychiatry* 59: 4–16.

Black, Timothy. 2009. *When a Heart Turns Rock Solid: The Lives of Three Puerto Rican Brothers On and Off the Streets.* New York: Vintage Books.

Blatterer, Harry. 2007. *Coming of Age in Times of Uncertainty.* New York: Berghahn Books.

Blau, Peter M., and Otis Dudley Duncan. 1978. *American Occupational Structure.* New York: The Free Press.

Boardman, Jason D., Brian Karl Finch, Christopher G. Ellison, David R. Williams, and James S. Jackson. 2001. "Neighborhood Disadvantage, Stress, and Drug Use among Adults." *Journal of Health and Social Behavior.* 42: 151–165.

Bobo, Lawrence. 1991. "Social Responsibility, Individualism, and Redistributive Policies." *Sociological Forum* 6: 71–92.

Bond, Carolyn, and Richard Williams. 2007. "Residential Segregation and the Transformation of Home Mortgage Lending." *Social Forces* 86: 671–698.

Bonilla-Silva, Eduardo. 2003. *Racism without Racists: Color-Blind Racism and the Persistence of Racial Inequality in the United States.* Lanham, MD: Rowman and Littlefield.

Booth, Alan, Ann Crouter, and Michael J. Shanahan. 1999. *Transitions to Adulthood in a Changing Economy: No Work, No Family, No Future?* Santa Barbara, CA: Praeger.

Bordo, Susan. 2003. *Unbearable Weight.* Berkeley: University of California Press.

Bourdieu, Pierre. 1998. *Acts of Resistance against the New Myths of Our Time.* Cambridge, UK: Polity Press.

———. 1977. "Cultural Reproduction and Social Reproduction." Pp. 487–511 in *Power and Ideology in Education,* edited by J. Karabel and A. H. Halsey. Oxford: Oxford University Press.

———. 1984. *Distinction: A Social Critique of the Judgment of Taste.* Cambridge, MA: Harvard University Press.

———. 1990. *The Logic of Practice.* Palo Alto, CA: Stanford University Press.

Brinton, Mary C. 2010. *Lost in Transition: Youth, Work, and Instability in Postindustrial Japan.* New York: Cambridge University Press.

Calhoun, Craig. 2010. "The Privatization of Risk: Introduction." Retrieved on June 28, 2010. Available at http://privatizationofrisk.ssrc.org/.

Chauvel, Louis. 1998. *Le Destin des générations. Structure sociale et cohortes en France au XXe siècle*. Paris, France: Presses Universitaires de France.

Cherlin, Andrew J. 2009. *The Marriage Go-Round: The State of Marriage and the Family in America Today*. New York: Vintage Books.

Chodorow, Nancy. 1978. *The Reproduction of Mothering*. Berkeley: University of California Press.

Clausen, John S. 1991. "Adolescent Competence and the Shaping of the Life Course." *American Journal of Sociology* 96: 805–842.

Cohen, Philip N., and Suzanne M. Bianchi. 1999. "Marriage, Children, and Women's Employment: What Do We Know?" *Monthly Labor Review* 122:22–31.

Cohn, Jonathan. 2007. *Sick: The Untold Story of America's Health Care Crisis*. New York: HarperCollins.

Collins, Patricia Hill. 1994. "Shifting the Center: Race, Class, and Feminist Theorizing about Motherhood." Pp. 45–65 in *Mothering: Ideology, Experience, and Agency*, edited by Evelyn Nakano Glenn, Grace Chang, and Linda Rennie Forcey. New York: Routledge.

Collins, Randall. 2004. *Interaction Ritual Chains*. Princeton, NJ: Princeton University Press.

Coltrane, Scott. 2000. "Research on Household Labor: Modeling and Measuring the Social Embeddedness of Routine Family Work." *Journal of Marriage and Family* 62: 1208–1233.

"Contract from America." Retrieved on June 27, 2010. Available at www.thecontract.org/.

Coontz, Stephanie. 2000. *The Way We Never Were: American Families and the Nostalgia Trap*. New York: Basic Books.

Copen, Casey E., Kimberly Daniels, Jonathan Vespa, and William D. Mosher. 2012. "First Marriages in the United States: Data From the 2006–2010 National Survey of Family Growth." *National Health Statistics Report* 49: 1–22. Available at http://www.cdc.gov/nchs/data/nhsr/nhsr049.pdf.

Côté, James. 2000. *Arrested Adulthood: The Changing Nature of Maturity and Identity*. New York: New York University Press.

Côté, James, and S. Schwartz. 2002. "Comparing Psychological and Sociological Approaches to Identity: Identity Status, Identity Capital, and the Individualization Process." *Journal of Adolescence* 25: 571–586.

Cowie, Jefferson. 2010. *Stayin' Alive: The 1970s and the Last Days of the Working Class*. New York: New Press.

Cushman, Philip. 1996. *Constructing the Self, Constructing America: A Cultural History of Psychotherapy*. Reading, MA: Addison-Wesley.

Danziger, Sheldon, and David Ratner. 2010. "Labor Market Outcomes and the Transition to Adulthood." Pp. 133–158 in *Transition to Adulthood. Special Issue of the Future of Children* 20(1), edited by Gordon Berlin, Frank Furstenberg Jr., and Mary C. Waters.

Davis, Joseph. 2005. "Victim Narratives and Victim Selves: False Memory Syndrome and the Power of Accounts." *Social Problems* 52: 529–548.

Dear Colleague Letter GEN-03-07 and page AVG-28 of the Application Verification Guide. Retrieved on February 13, 2013. Available at: http://ifap.ed.gov/dpcletters/GEN0307.html.

Denzin, Norman K. 1993. *The Alcoholic Society: Addiction and Recovery of the Self*. New Brunswick, NJ: Transaction.

———. 1987. *The Recovering Alcoholic*. New York: Sage.

DiTomaso, Nancy. 2010. "Work with and without a Future." A paper presented at the Eastern Sociological Society Annual Meeting, Boston, MA.

Dougherty, Kevin. 2001. *The Contradictory College: The Conflicting Origins, Impacts, and Futures of the Community College*. Albany: State University of New York Press.

Draut, Tamara. 2005. *Strapped*. New York: Anchor Books.

Dumais, Susan A. 2002. "Cultural Capital, Gender, and School Success: The Role of Habitus." *Sociology of Education* 75: 44–68.

Durkheim, Emile. [1912] 1995. *The Elementary Forms of Religious Life*. Translated by Karen E. Fields. New York: Free Press.

"The Economic Mobility Project." 2007. An Initiative of the Pew Charitable Trusts. Philadelphia, PA, and Washington, DC.

Edin, Kathryn, and Maria Kefalas. 2005. *Promises I Can Keep: Why Poor Women Put Motherhood before Marriage*. Berkeley: University of California Press.

Elias, Norbert. 2000. *The Civilizing Process: Sociogenetic and Psychogenetic Investigations*. Malden, MA: Blackwell.

Ewick, Patricia, and Susan Silbey. 1995. "Subversive Stories and Hegemonic Tales: Toward a Sociology of Narrative." *Law and Society Review* 29: 197–226.

FinAid | Other Aid | "What If No Help from Parents?" Retrieved on July 9, 2010. Available at www.finaid.org/otheraid/parentsrefuse.phtml.

Foucault, Michel. 1979. *Discipline and Punish*. New York: Vintage Books.

Fraser, Nancy. 1995. "From Redistribution to Recognition? Dilemmas of Justice in a 'Post-Socialist' Age." *New Left Review* 212: 68–93.

Friedman, Milton. 1962. *Capitalism and Freedom*. Chicago, IL: University of Chicago Press.

Fry, Richard. 2009. "College Enrollment Hits All-Time High, Fueled by Community College Surge-Pew Social & Demographic Trends." Retrieved on July 8, 2010. Available at http://pewsocialtrends.org/pubs/747/college-enrollment-hits-all-time-high-fueled-by-community-college-surge.

Furedi, Frank. 2004. *Therapy Culture: Cultivating Vulnerability in an Uncertain Age*. London: Routledge.

Furstenberg, Frank F., Sheela Kennedy, Vonnie C. McLoyd, Rubén G. Rumbaut, and Richard A. Settersten Jr. 2004. "Growing Up Is Harder to Do." *Contexts* 3: 33–41.

García, José, and Tamara Draut. 2009. "The Plastic Safety Net: How Households Are Coping in a Fragile Economy." *Demos*. Available at www.demos.org/sites/default/files/publications/PlasticSafetyNet_Demos.pdf.

Gerson, Kathleen. 2009. *The Unfinished Revolution: How a New Generation Is Reshaping Family, Work, and Gender in America*. New York: Oxford University Press.

Giddens, Anthony. 1991. *Modernity and Self-Identity: Self and Society in the Late Modern Age*. Oxford, UK: Polity Press.

———. 1992. *The Transformation of Intimacy: Sexuality, Love and Eroticism in Modern Societies*. Palo Alto, CA: Stanford University Press.

Gilbert, Elizabeth. 2006. *Eat, Pray, Love: One Woman's Search for Everything across Italy, India and Indonesia*. London: Bloomsbury.

Gilmore, Gerry J. 2009. "All Services Meet or Exceed October Recruiting Goals." *American Forces Press Service*, November 13. Retrieved on February 13, 2013. Available at http://www.defense.gov/News/NewsArticle.aspx?ID=56685.

Gittell, Ross J., and Patricia M. Flynn. 1995. "The Lowell High-tech Success Story: What Went Wrong?" *New England Economic Review* 57–70.

Goffman, Erving. 1959. *The Presentation of Self in Everyday Life*. Garden City, NY: Doubleday.

Goldstein, Joshua, and Catherine T. Kenney. 2001. "Marriage Delayed or Marriages Foregone? New Cohort Forecasts of First Marriages for US Women." *American Sociological Review* 66: 506–519.

Gowan, Teresa. 2010. *Hobos, Hustlers, and Backsliders: Homeless in San Francisco.* Minneapolis: University of Minnesota Press.

Hacker, Jacob. 2006a. "The Privatization of Risk and the Growing Economic Insecurity of Americans." Retrieved on July 9, 2010. Available at http://privatizationofrisk. ssrc.org.

———. 2006b. *The Great Risk Shift: The Assault on American Jobs, Families, Health Care, and Retirement and How You Can Fight Back.* New York: Oxford University Press.

———. 2007. "Suffering, Selfish Slackers? Myths and Reality about Emerging Adults." *Journal of Youth and Adolescence* 36: 23–29.

Hacker, Jacob, and Paul Pierson. 2010. *Winner-Take-All Politics: How Washington Made the Rich Richer—And Turned Its Back on the Middle Class.* New York: Simon and Schuster.

Hagenbaugh, Barbara. 2002. "U.S. Manufacturing Jobs Fading Away Fast." Available at http://www.usatoday.com/money/economy/2002-12-12-manufacture_x.htm.

Hall, Peter A., and Michèle Lamont. 2009. "Introduction." Pp. 1-22 in *Successful Societies: How Institutions and Culture Affect Health*, edited by Peter A. Hall and Michèle Lamont. New York: Cambridge University Press.

———. 2013. "Introduction." In *Social Resilience in the Neoliberal Era*, edited by Peter A. Hall and Michèle Lamont. Cambridge: Cambridge University Press.

Halle, David. 1984. *America's Working Man Work, Home, and Politics among Blue Collar Property Owners.* Chicago, IL: University of Chicago Press.

Harvey, David. 2005. *A Brief History of Neoliberalism.* New York: Oxford University Press.

Hays, Sharon. 1996. *The Cultural Contradictions of Motherhood.* New Haven, CT: Yale University Press.

———. 2003. *Flat Broke with Children.* New York: Oxford University Press.

———. 1994. "Structure and Agency and the Sticky Problem of Culture." *Sociological Theory* 12: 57–72.

Higher Education Opportunity Act-2008. Retrieved on July 8, 2010. Available at www2. ed.gov/policy/highered/leg/hea08/index.html.

Hill, Shirley. 2005. *Black Intimacies: A Gender Perspective on Families and Relationships.* Walnut Creek, CA: Altamira Press.

Hochschild, Arlie. 1995. "The Culture of Politics: Traditional, Postmodern, Cold-modern, and Warm-modern Ideals of Care." *Social Politics* 2: 331–346.

———. 2003 [1983]. *The Managed Heart: Commercialization of Human Feeling, Twentieth Anniversary Edition, with a New Afterword.* 2nd ed. Berkeley: University of California Press.

Hoff Somers, Christina, and Sally Satel. 2005. *One Nation under Therapy: How the Helping Culture Is Eroding Self-Reliance.* New York: St. Martin's Press.

hooks, bell. 1989. *Talking Back: Thinking Feminist, Thinking Black*. Boston, MA: South End Press.

Hout, Michael. 2008. "How Class Works: Objective and Subjective Analyses of Class since the 1970s." Pp. 25–64 in *Social Class: How Does It Work?*, edited by Annette Lareau and Dalton Conley. New York: Russell Sage Foundation.

Illouz, Eva. 2007. *Cold Intimacies: The Making of Emotional Capitalism*. Cambridge, UK: Polity Press.

———. 1997. *Consuming the Romantic Utopia: Love and the Cultural Contradictions of Capitalism*. Berkeley: University of California Press.

———. 2003. *Oprah Winfrey and the Glamour of Misery*. New York: Columbia University Press.

———. 2008. *Saving the Modern Soul: Therapy, Emotions, and the Culture of Self-Help*. Berkeley: University of California Press.

Imber, Jonathan B., editor. 2004. *Therapeutic Culture: Triumph and Defeat*. Piscataway, NJ: Transaction.

Johnson, Jennifer. 2002. *Getting By on the Minimum: The Lives of Working-Class Women*. New York: Routledge.

Kalleberg, Arle L. 2009. "Precarious Work, Insecure Workers." *American Sociological Review* 74: 1–22.

Kamenetz, Anya. 2006. *Generation Debt: How Our Future Was Sold Out for Student Loans, Bad Jobs, No Benefits, and Tax Cuts for Rich Geezers—And How to Fight Back*. New York: Riverhead Books.

Katznelson, Ira. 2005. *When Affirmative Action Was White: An Untold History of Racial Inequality in Twentieth-Century America*. New York: Norton.

Kimmel, Michael. 2008. *Guyland: The Perilous World Where Boys Become Men*. New York: HarperCollins.

Kleycamp, Meredith. 2006. "College, Jobs or the Military? Enlistment during a Time of War." *Social Science Quarterly* 87: 272–290.

Krugman, Paul. 2009. *The Return of Depression Economics and the Crisis of 2008*. New York: Norton.

Kurz, Demie. 1999. "Women, Welfare, and Domestic Violence." Pp. 132–151 in *Whose Welfare?*, edited by Gwendolyn Mink. Ithaca, NY: Cornell University Press.

Lamont, Michèle. 2000. *The Dignity of Working Men: Morality and the Boundaries of Race, Class, and Immigration*. Cambridge, MA: Harvard University Press.

———. 1992. *Money, Morals, and Manners*. Chicago, IL: University of Chicago Press.

———. Forthcoming. *Social Resilience in the Neoliberal Era*. Cambridge: Cambridge University Press.

Lamont, Michèle, and Virág Molnár. 2002. "The Study of Boundaries in the Social Sciences." *Annual Review of Sociology* 28: 167–195.

Lareau, Annette. 2003. *Unequal Childhoods: Class, Race, and Family Life*. Berkeley: University of California Press.

Lareau, Annette. 2008. "Taking Stock of Class." Pp. 3–24 in *Social Class: How Does It Work?*, edited by Annette Lareau and Dalton Conley. New York: Russell Sage Foundation.

Lasch, Christopher. 1979. *The Culture of Narcissism: American Life in an Age of Diminishing Expectations*. New York: Norton.

Lee, Nick. 2001. *Childhood and Society: Growing Up in an Age of Uncertainty.* Philadelphia, PA: Open University Press.

Leonhardt, David. 2005. "The College Dropout Boom." Pp. 87–104 in *Class Matters*, edited by Correspondents of the *New York Times*. New York: Henry Holt.

Lively, Kathryn J., and David R. Heise. 2004. "Sociological Realms of Emotional Experience." *American Journal of Sociology* 109: 1109–1136.

Livingston, Gretchen, and D'Vera Cohn. 2010. "More Women without Children." Pew Research Center. Available at http://pewresearch.org/pubs/1642/more-women-without-children.

MacLeod, Jay. 1987. *Ain't No Makin' It.* Boulder, CO: Westview Press.

Mannheim, Karl. 1952 [1932]. *Essays in the Sociology of Culture.* New York: Routledge and Kegan Paul.

Marsiglio, W., and S. Hutchinson. 2002. *Sex, Men, and Babies: Stories of Awareness and Responsibility.* New York: New York University Press.

Martin, Emily. 2007. *Bipolar Expeditions: Mania and Depression in American Culture.* Princeton, NJ: Princeton University Press.

Martin, Steven P. 2004. "Growing Evidence for a Divorce Divide? Education and Marital Dissolution Rates in the United States since the 1970's." *Russell Sage Foundation Working Papers: Series on Social Dimensions of Inequality.* New York: Russell Sage Foundation.

Marx, Karl. 1959 [1932]. *Economic and Philosophical Manuscripts of 1844.* Translated by Martin Mulligan. Delhi, India: Progress Publishers.

Marx, Karl, and Friedrich Engels. 2002. *The Communist Manifesto.* Introduction by Gareth Stedman Jones. New York: Penguin Classics.

Massachusetts General Court Chapter 58 of the Acts of 2006.

Massey, Douglas S., and Nancy A. Denton. 1993. *American Apartheid: Segregation and the Making of the Underclass.* Cambridge, MA: Harvard University Press.

Masten, Ann S., Jelena Obradović, and Keith B. Burt. 2006. "Resilience in Emerging Adulthood: Developmental Perspectives on Continuity and Transformation." Pp. 173–190 in *Emerging Adults in America: Coming of Age in the 21st Century*, edited by Jeffrey Arnett and Jennifer Lynn Tanner. Washington, DC: American Psychological Association.

McDermott, Monica. 2006. *Working-Class White: The Making and Unmaking of Race Relations.* Berkeley: University of California Press.

McLanahan, Sara, and Christine Percheski. 2008. "Family Structure and the Reproduction of Inequalities." *Annual Review of Sociology* 34: 257–276.

McLean, Bethany, and Joe Nocera. 2010. *All the Devils Are Here: The Hidden History of the Financial Crisis.* New York: Penguin Group.

McMahon, Martha. 1995. *Engendering Motherhood: Identity and Self-Transformation in Women's Lives.* New York: Guilford Press.

Milkman, Ruth. 1997. *Farewell to the Factory: Auto Workers in the Late Twentieth Century.* Berkeley: University of California Press.

Mishel, Lawrence, Jared Bernstein, and Sylvia Allegretto. 2007. *The State of Working America 2006/2007.* Ithaca, NY: Cornell University Press.

Moore, Michael. 1989. *Roger & Me.* Warner Bros.

Morrison, Matthew G. 2011. "Empowering the Severely Mentally Ill?: Autonomy, Dependency, and Authority." A paper presented at the American Sociological Association Annual Meeting, Las Vegas, NV.

Moskos, Charles C., and John S. Butler. 1996. *All That We Can Be: Black Leadership and Racial Integration the Army Way.* New York: Basic Books.

Moskowitz, Eva. 2001. *In Therapy We Trust: America's Obsession with Self-Fulfillment.* Baltimore, MD: Johns Hopkins University Press.

"A National Report Card on Women in Firefighting," Institute for Women and Work, Cornell University. Retrieved on July 9, 2010. Available at www.i-women.org/images/pdf-files/35827WSP.pdf.

National Survey on Drug Use and Health, 2009. Available at http://oas.samhsa.gov/nsduh/2k9nsduh/2k9resultsp.pdf.

Newman, Katherine. 1992. *Falling from Grace: Downward Mobility in the Age of Affluence.* Berkeley: University of California Press.

————. 1999. *No Shame in My Game: The Working Poor in the Inner City.* New York: Russell Sage Foundation.

"NIMH: The Numbers Count: Mental Disorders in America." National Institute of Mental Health. Retrieved on February 13, 2013. Available at http://www.nimh.nih.gov/health/publications/the-numbers-count-mental-disorders-in-america/index.shtml.

Nolan, James. 1998. *The Therapeutic State: Justifying Government at Century's End.* New York: New York University Press.

Osgood, D. Wayne, Gretchen Ruth, Jacquelynne Eccles, Janis Jacobs, and Bonnie Barber. 2005. "Six Paths to Adulthood: Fast Starters, Parents without Careers, Educated Partners, Educated Singles, Working Singles, and Slow Starters." Pp. 320–355 in *On the Frontier of Adulthood: Theory, Research, and Public Policy*, edited by R. A. Settersten, F. F. Furstenberg, and R. G. Rumbaut. Chicago, IL: University of Chicago Press.

Owens, Lindsay. 2012. "Wealth." *The Stanford Center on Poverty and Inequality.* Available at http://www.stanford.edu/group/scspi/slides/Wealth.pdf.

Pager, Devah, Bruce Western, and Bart Bonikowski. 2009. "Discrimination in a Low-Wage Labor Market: A Field Experiment." *American Sociological Review* 74: 777–799.

Pew Research Center for People & the Press. 2013. "Majority Says the Federal Government Threatens Their Personal Rights." Retrieved on February 13, 2013. Available at http://www.people-press.org/2013/01/31/majority-says-the-federal-government-threatens-their-personal-rights/.

Pew Research Social & Demographic Trends. 2010. "The Decline in Marriage and Rise of New Families." Retrieved on February 13, 2013. Available at http://www.pewsocialtrends.org/2010/11/18/the-decline-of-marriage-and-rise-of-new-families/.

Pilcher, Jane. 1995. *Age and Generation in Modern Britain.* New York: Oxford University Press.

Putnam, Robert. 2000. *Bowling Alone: The Collapse and Revival of American Community.* New York: Simon and Schuster.

Putnam, Robert, Carl Frederick, and Kaisa Snellman. 2012. "Growing Class Gaps in Social Connectedness among American Youth, 1970–2009." Available at www.hks.harvard.edu/saguaro/pdfs/SaguaroReport_DivergingSocialConnectedness.pdf.

Raley, Kelly, and Larry Bumpass. 2003. "The Topography of the Divorce Plateau." *Demographic Research* 8: 245–260.

Reynolds, John, and Chardie L. Baird. 2010. "Is There a Downside to Shooting for the Stars? Unrealized Educational Expectations and Symptoms of Depression." *American Sociological Review* 75: 151–172.

Rieff, Philip. 1987 [1966]. *The Triumph of the Therapeutic: Uses of Faith after Freud.* Chicago, IL: University of Chicago Press.

Robbins, Alexandra, and Abby Wilner. 2001. *Quarterlife Crisis: The Unique Challenges of Life in Your Twenties.* New York: Putnam.

Roksa, Josipa. 2006. "Does the Vocational Focus of Community Colleges Hinder Students' Educational Attainment?" *Review of Higher Education* 29: 499–526.

Rosenfeld, Michael. 2007. *The Age of Independence: Interracial Unions, Same-Sex Unions and the Changing American Family.* Cambridge, MA: Harvard University Press.

Royster, Deidre. 2003. *Race and the Invisible Hand: How White Networks Exclude Black Men from Blue-Collar Jobs.* Berkeley: University of California Press.

Rubin, Lillian B. 1992 [1976]. *Worlds of Pain: Life in the Working-Class Family.* New York: Basic Books.

Sargent, Carey L. 2010. "iMusic: Living and Working as Musicians in Digital Capitalism." Ph.D. dissertation, Department of Sociology, University of Virginia, Charlottesville, VA.

Sawhill, Isabel V. and John E. Morton. 2007. "Economic Mobility: Is the American Dream Alive and Well?" *The Brookings Institution.* Retrieved on February 13, 2013. Available at http://www.brookings.edu/research/papers/2007/05/useconomics-morton.

Schutz, Alfred. 1953. "Common-Sense and Scientific Interpretation of Human Action." *Philosophy and Phenomenological Research* 14(1): 1–38.

Scott, Joan W. 1988. "Deconstructing Equality-versus-Difference: Or, the Uses of Post-structuralist Theory for Feminism." *Feminist Studies* 14: 33–49.

Segal, David R. 1989. *Recruiting for Uncle Sam: Citizenship and Military Manpower Policy.* Lawrence: University Press of Kansas.

Sennett, Richard. 1998. *The Corrosion of Character: The Personal Consequences of Work in the New Capitalism.* New York: Norton.

Sennett, Richard, and Jonathan Cobb. 1973. *The Hidden Injuries of Class.* New York: Vintage Books.

Sewell, William Jr. 2009. "From State-Centrism to Neoliberalism: Macro-Historical Contexts of Population Health since World War II." Pp. 254–287 in *Successful Societies: Institutions, Cultural Repertories, and Health,* edited by Peter Hall and Michèle Lamont. Cambridge: Cambridge University Press.

Silva, Jennifer M. 2008. "'A New Generation of Women?' How Female ROTC Cadets Negotiate the Tension between Masculine Military Culture and Traditional Femininity." *Social Forces* 87: 937–960.

———. 2012. "Constructing Adulthood in an Age of Uncertainty." *American Sociological Review* 77: 505–522.

Silva, Jennifer M., and Sarah M. Corse. 2011. "Dreams Deferred or No Dreams at All?: Class, Gender, and Future Aspirations." A paper presented at the Eastern Sociological Society Annual Meeting, Philadelphia, PA.

Silva, Jennifer M., and Allison J. Pugh. 2010. "Beyond the Depleting Model of Parenting: Narratives of Childrearing and Change." *Sociological Inquiry* 80(4): 605–627.

Slater, Don. 1997. *Consumer Culture and Modernity.* Cambridge, UK: Polity Press.

Smith, Christian, with Kari Christoffersen, Patricia Snell Herzog, and Hilary Davidson. 2011. *Lost in Transition: The Dark Side of Emerging Adulthood.* New York: Oxford University Press.

Smith, Dorothy. 1990. *The Conceptual Practices of Power: A Feminist Sociology of Knowledge.* Boston: Northeastern University Press.

Smith, Sandra Susan. 2007. *Lone Pursuit: Distrust and Defensive Individualism among the Black Poor.* New York: Russell Sage Foundation.

Sorensen, Aage. 2000. "Toward a Sounder Basis for Class Analysis." *American Journal of Sociology* 105: 1523–1558.

Stacey, Judith. 1998. *Brave New Families: Stories of Domestic Upheaval in Late-Twentieth Century America.* Berkeley: University of California Press.

The Stanford Center on Poverty and Inequality. Retrieved on July 17, 2012. Available at http://www.stanford.edu/group/scspi/slides/Income.pdf.

Stein, Arlene. 2011. "Therapeutic Politics: An Oxymoron?" *Sociological Forum* 26: 187–193.

Sullivan, Teresa A., Deborah Thorne, and Elizabeth Warren. 2001. "Young, Old, and In Between: Who Files for Bankruptcy?" *Norton Bankruptcy Law Advisor* 9: 1–11.

Sullivan, Teresa, Elizabeth Warren, and Jay Lawrence Westbrook. 1999. *As We Forgive Our Debtors: Bankruptcy and Consumer Credit in America.* Frederick, MD: Beard Books.

Swidler, Ann. 1986. "Culture in Action: Symbols and Strategies." *American Sociological Review* 51: 273–286.

———. 2001. *Talk of Love: How Culture Matters.* Chicago, IL: University of Chicago Press.

Taylor, Charles. 1989. *Sources of the Self: The Making of Modern Identity.* Cambridge, MA: Harvard University Press.

Taylor-Gooby, Peter. 2004. *New Risks, New Welfare.* Oxford: Oxford University Press.

Twenge, Jean M., Brittany Gentile, C. Nathan DeWall, Debbie Ma, Katharine Lacefield, and David R. Schurtz. 2010. "Birth Cohort Increases in Psychopathology among Young Americans, 1938–2007: A Cross-temporal Meta-analysis of the MMPI." *Clinical Psychology Review* 30: 145–154.

"Union Members Summary." 2013. US Bureau of Labor Statistics. Retrieved on February 13, 2013. Available at http://www.bls.gov/news.release/union2.nro.htm.

US Census, Estimated Median Age at First Marriage, by Sex: 1890 to Present. Available at www.census.gov/population/socdemo/hh-fam/ms2.pdf.

US Census, Young Adults Living at Home: 1960 to Present. Available at www.census.gov/population/socdemo/hh-fam/tabAD-1.pdf.

US Department of Education, National Center for Education Statistics. 2012. *Digest of Education Statistics.* Available at http://nces.ed.gov/programs/digest/d11/ch_3.asp.

Waldfogel, Jane. 1997. "The Effect of Children on Women's Wages." *American Sociological Review* 62: 209–217.

Walkerdine, Valerie, Helen Lucey, and June Melody. 2001. *Growing Up Girl: Psychosocial Explorations of Gender and Class.* London: Palgrave.

Warren, Elizabeth. 2006. "Families, Money, and Risk." Retrieved on July 1, 2010. Available at http://privatizationofrisk.ssrc.org.

Warren, John Robert, Jennifer T. Sheridan, and Robert M. Hauser. 2002. "Occupational Stratification across the Life Course: Evidence from the Wisconsin Longitudinal Study." *American Sociological Review* 67: 432–455.

Waters, Mary, Patrick J. Carr, Maria J. Kefalas, and Jennifer Holdaway, editors. 2011. *The Transition to Adulthood in the Twenty-First Century*. Berkeley: University of California Press.

Wayne, Osgood, E. Michael Foster, Constance Flanagan, and Gretchen Ruth Osgood, editors. 2005. *On Your Own without a Net: The Transition to Adulthood for Vulnerable Populations*. Chicago, IL: University of Chicago Press.

Weis, Lois. 1990. *Working Class without Work: High School Students in a De-Industrializing Economy*. New York: Routledge.

———. 2004. *Class Reunion: The Remaking of the American White Working Class*. New York: Routledge.

Weller, Christian E., and Jaryn Fields. 2011. "The Black and White Labor Gap in America: Why African Americans Struggle to Find Jobs and Remain Employed Compared to Whites." *Center for American Progress*. Available at www.americanprogress.org/issues/2011/07/black_unemployment.html.

Western, Bruce. 1997. *Between Class and Market: Postwar Unionization in the Capitalist Democracies*. Princeton, NJ: Princeton University Press.

———. 2006. *Punishment and Inequality in America*. New York: Russell Sage Foundation.

Western, Bruce, and Jake Rosenfeld. 2011. "Unions, Norms, and the Rise in American Earnings Inequality." *American Sociological Review* 76: 513–537.

Williams, Raymond. 1977. *Marxism and Literature*. Oxford: Oxford University Press.

Willis, Paul. 1977. *Learning to Labr*. New York: Columbia University Press.

Wilson, William Julius. 1987. *The Truly Disadvantaged: The Inner City, the Underclass, and Public Policy*. Chicago, IL: University of Chicago Press.

———. 1997. *When Work Disappears*. New York: Vintage Books.

"Women in the Labor Force: A Databook (2009 Edition)." US Bureau of Labor Statistics. Retrieved on February 13, 2013. Available at http://www.bls.gov/cps/wlf-databook2009.htm.

Zerubavel, Eviatar. 2003. *Time Maps: Collective Memory and the Social Shape of the Past*. Chicago, IL: University of Chicago Press.

INDEX

therapeutic selfhood, 18–22
   and institutions, 128–129, 138,
      141–142, 174n3
   and relationships, 57, 65, 69–70,
      72–74, 79
   narratives, kinds of:
      addiction, 64, 113–114, 122–124
      emotional, mental, or cognitive,
         118–121, 137, 140
      pain or betrayal in past
         relationships, 116–118, 174n9
   and redemption, 23–24, 115–116,
      122–124, 133, 136
   and religion, 51, 129–131
   and self–help media, 7, 19–21, 25, 72,
      88, 110, 111, 119–121, 141, 151
   and suffering, 21, 115–116, 124–127,
      151–152

Williams, Raymond, 20, 83, 98, 110, 131,
   167n24, 173n21

work
   changes in, 12, 13–16, 30, 47–50,
      81–84, 144–157, 159–162, 170n5
   civil service, 26–28, 30–31, 41–45,
      105–106, 130, 167n1, 173n18
   and gender, 15–16, 32–33, 44–45,
      60–64, 69–71, 169n1, 170n4,
      170n5
   insecurity, 4–5, 15–16, 18, 30–31, 59,
      84–87, 95–96, 135, 144–157,
      175n13
   obstacles to, 3–4, 14–16, 22–33,
      69–71, 137, 172n8
   pathways to, 50–52
   perceptions of, 4–5, 13, 19–20, 47–50,
      60–71, 81–87, 97–98, 105–109,
      135, 137
   and race, 15–18, 33–35, 41, 61–64,
      101–102, 105–109, 168n4,
      169n11, 170n5, 173n18
   service economy, 3–4, 15, 81–87